Microfinance Investment Funds

Ingrid Matthäus-Maier
J. D. von Pischke
Editors

Microfinance Investment Funds

Leveraging Private Capital
for Economic Growth
and Poverty Reduction

With 12 Figures and 23 Tables

 Springer

Ingrid Matthäus-Maier
KfW
Palmengartenstraße 5–9
60325 Frankfurt
Germany
ingrid.matthaeus-maier@kfw.de

Dr. J.D. von Pischke
2529 Trophy Lane
Reston
VA 20191-2126
USA
vonpischke@frontierfinance.com

ISBN-10   3-540-28070-7 Springer Berlin Heidelberg New York
ISBN-13   978-3-540-28070-5 Springer Berlin Heidelberg New York

Cataloging-in-Publication Data
Library of Congress Control Number: 2005938930

Springer is a part of Springer Science+Business Media

springeronline.com

© Springer Berlin · Heidelberg 2006
Printed in Germany

Hardcover-Design: Erich Kirchner, Heidelberg

SPIN 11533757   43/3153-5 4 3 2 1 0 – Printed on acid-free paper

Introductory Remarks: The Purpose of Our Endeavour

Ingrid Matthäus-Maier

Member of the Board of Managing Directors, KfW Bankengruppe

The KfW Financial Sector Symposium series began in 2002 when KfW recognised the importance of establishing a unique international forum for leaders in financial sector development. Our objective was to establish key principles that would promote communication and innovation.

- First, we wanted to invite experienced, forward-thinking decision-makers who have been influential in shaping the new frontier of development finance.

- Second, we wanted the symposia to be highly interactive, centred on open and provocative discussion.

- Third, we wanted to communicate the wide-ranging expertise and professional diversity of our participants to a wider audience through publication of their insights in a variety of media.

- Fourth, we wanted the symposia to encourage new collaborative relationships by providing space for informal discussion and networking opportunities.

Our first symposium was regional in scope, consisting of an assessment of lessons in financial sector development in Southeast Europe. Our second was supra-regional, looking ahead to the region's accession to the EU and the creation of public private partnerships.

This symposium, our third, looked to the future of financial sector development. The 2004 Symposium was truly global, focusing on engagement with the private sector through the innovative application of an established financial instrument. It was the first-ever high-level meeting on microfinance investment funds. These funds have the potential to help realise the promise of microfinance by unlocking vast new sources of capital and financial know-how. These funds also lead us into an examination of mission-oriented investment and ways to engage commercial financiers in development finance.

Capital Initiatives

But why should KfW Bankengruppe, a financial institution, be interested in symposium discussions? The simple answer is because as a leader in the industry, KfW strives to stand at the frontier of innovation and product development, which of course also requires intellectual capital.

Innovation has been central to KfW's mission since it was founded as the German Bank for Reconstruction after World War II. Its structure is designed to promote financial innovation through its four divisions:

- KfW Mittelstandsbank promotes SMEs (small and medium enterprises), business start-ups, and self-employed professionals throughout Germany and Europe through classic promotional loans as well as innovative financing instruments.

- KfW Förderbank offers promotional programmes in housing and energy conservation, environmental protection, infrastructure, education and asset securitisation.

- KfW IPEX bank offers export and project financing focused on products such as airliners, ships and power plants.

- KfW Entwicklungsbank provides funds and expertise on behalf of the German federal government, whereas DEG, another part of KfW, directly promotes private investments. Within the framework of financial cooperation, both contribute to sustainable improvement in living conditions in many countries.

KfW Entwicklungsbank's task in financial sector development is to assist our partners in the design and creation of institutions and systems that contribute to the alleviation of poverty. Our efforts in this important adventure have been comprehensive because financial markets are sophisticated and complex.

We are convinced that microfinance plays a very key role in the alleviation of poverty. We insist on serving "the bottom end of financial markets," where transactions involve important target groups consisting of microentrepreneurs, small businesses, and households using deposit accounts to save and to receive or send money transfers.

Our commitment is to ensure that the development function of financial systems continues to unfold independently of continued donor support. Therefore, we work with an expanding array of partners to expand the commercial basis of the microfinance industry. With its partners, KfW has pioneered successful initiatives in microfinance around the world. For example:

- We were among the first to support the Grameen Bank in Bangladesh and its contribution to the feminist agenda.

- We were among the first to establish microfinance in Sub-Saharan Africa. Together with GTZ, we supported the emergence of village banks in Mali.

- In order to reach out to the poorest in war-torn countries, KfW worked with IFC, FMO, and Triodos to upgrade ACLEDA, a microfinance institution in Cambodia, from an NGO to a full-fledged microfinance institution.

- Our support of FEFAD in Albania helped to engage the international community in the creation of nineteen microfinance institutions worldwide, ten of them in Eastern Europe. This gave rise to IMI AG (now ProCredit Holding AG), which serves almost half a million microcredit clients.

- Recently, we were among the first to invest in microinsurance facilities with the SEWA Foundation of India.

- In close cooperation with IFC and FMO, we facilitated the founding of several microfinance investment funds such as the Global Microfinance Facility and ACCION Investments in Microfinance.

Beyond our financial investments, we also make an extraordinary investment in the creation and dissemination of knowledge. Most importantly, KfW specialises in empowering our local partners with this knowledge and know-how in the form of technical assistance. This emphasis has also benefitted women in partner countries by highlighting their important role and by opening new windows of opportunity.

While our symposia may have recurring themes, the Greek philosopher Heraclitus is credited with the observation that, "No man ever steps in the same river twice, for it's not the same river and he's not the same man." With microfinance and financial sector development, we are never returning to the same river. Conditions around us are constantly changing, improvements are underway and setbacks may occur.

Innovation is doing. It has two parents: necessity and imagination. Our humanity obligates us all to continue in the work that we do, which is very much about putting the creation of wealth to work for the poorest in our world. For this to occur, we must jump into the cold river of knowledge to which Heraclitus refers, sharing wisdom from our experience and with bold new ideas that will engage a wider public in the campaign to eliminate poverty.

Investment in Innovation

Our 2004 Berlin Symposium focused on product innovations that will advance our vision for microfinance. This theme continues our efforts and those of our partners to explore the frontiers of finance, and the small end of financial markets in general, especially their capacity to assist poor households and to create employment.

The expectations and the institutions that KfW and a growing number of like-minded organisations inspired have grown almost beyond recognition compared to the structures that were in place and the standards that were applied a decade ago.

But this change follows a logical path that may in fact be one of the greatest triumphs of development cooperation focused on the relatively poor. The combined efforts of these organizations assisted in empowering large numbers of people, households and firms.

What began as a variety of initiatives almost simultaneously in Asia and Latin America in the early 1980s was assisted by public sector and private funds. Continued efforts led to the creation of new institutional forms for the provision of microfinance, to the development of standards and best practice, and to an increasing number and variety of investment vehicles that promote retail microfinance institutions (MFIs). These trends spurred greater definition and coherence, in the sense that objectives and purpose became more precise while at the same time diversity created space for nuance. The variety of financial services offered has expanded greatly in response to competition in an increasingly professionalised environment, producing developmental impact.

The financial elements of microfinance are seamlessly permeating financial markets. What was once the preserve of charity and public sector donor funding has attracted venture capital. As this pace continues, it is quite probable that within the next decade the portfolios of individual retail investors will include microfinance investments, often by participation in microfinance investment funds (MFIFs). It is also possible that the retail arms of large financial groups will routinely include microfinance among their range of services.

Our Symposium was designed to assess progress and to explore possibilities in this exciting integration. Participants included private equity representatives, investment fund leaders, national and international development cooperation experts, representatives of microfinance institutions and funds, commercial bankers, scholars and others.

Acknowledgements

Finally, the efforts of those who have contributed to this book deserve acknowledgement. They include the authors, panelists, moderators and the many others who provided time and effort to gather and present data, to share experience and to offer their professional advice and criticism. Their efforts and commitment have made it possible to identify the principal mechanisms and that increasingly link microfinance to broader financial markets and to investors.

The 2004 Symposium was financed by four sources: ADA, BMZ, FEFAD and KfW. ADA – Appui de Développement Autonome – is a non-profit organisation based in Luxembourg that offers financial support and technical services to microfinance institutions in developing countries. BMZ is the Federal German Ministry for Economic Cooperation and Development. The FEFAD Foundation was established in the 1990s by the Albanian government and KfW to support micro, small and medium enterprise in Southeastern Europe. (The purpose, structure and activities of KfW were briefly summarised above.)

The editors are grateful to Wolfgang Kroh, Norbert Kloppenburg, Hanns-Peter Neuhoff, Doris Köhn and Klaus Glaubitt of KfW for their consistent support in promoting the commercialisation and the financing of microfinance. We also offer our thanks to Mark Schwiete, Haje Schütte, Roland Siller and Lauren Day for their efforts in planning the Symposium, developing its concepts and themes, engaging partners, enlisting authors and managing a large logistical challenge. Jana Aberle assisted in the compilation of this book. Tina Butterbach's outstanding organisational and managerial talents were invaluable throughout, from the planning of the Symposium through the development of the manuscript.

Table of Contents

CHAPTER 1

Microfinance Investment Funds: Where Wealth Creation Meets Poverty Reduction

Norbert Kloppenburg

Senior Vice President, KfW Entwicklungsbank

An unacceptably high proportion of the world's population lives in dreadful conditions that consign them to Malthusian lives that are "nasty, brutish and short." While relief and other donations surely help to alleviate poverty temporarily, poverty can be fought decisively only by the creation of wealth where wealth is most lacking, which is among the poor. Wealth creation in this context is broadly defined as improvements in human productivity.

Wealth Creation?

Accordingly, wealth creation is a concept that deserves scrutiny by everyone who seeks to reduce poverty. In fact, it is a more positive and buoyant concept than poverty reduction because it provides a historically productive solution to poverty that has universal application. It includes the poor in a process that empowers them based on the things they can do. This is important because microfinance has shown that the working poor can create significant benefits for themselves with quite small loans. Describing their achievement as wealth creation enhances their dignity in a subtle way that contrasts with poverty reduction, a tough job with a heavy burden that singles them out as poor, unfortunate "others" (even though they constitute the majority of the world's population). Wealth creation may also be a bit more focused than poverty reduction.

The condition of the poor is all the more unacceptable because societies that make up a relatively small proportion of the world's population have found ways, over very lengthy periods of time, that have permitted them to create great wealth, to prosper and enjoy opportunities that would have been unimaginable in earlier generations. This dichotomy – between rich societies and poor ones – is the largest economic and social issue of our time, and also the largest disgrace.

Addressing the possibility of creating wealth among the poor is difficult and slow. One reason for this halting progress is that the institutions that create wealth are only imperfectly understood. Even where wealth creation has worked relatively well, as measured by various common standards, *perceptions* of the manner in which wealth is created make it very difficult in the current era for the process to be widely admired. Regardless of whether such perceptions are valid, gulfs in levels of wealth remain also in rich societies, causing conflict and violence. Wealth creation is a contentious business. This is highly unfortunate in view of its potential.

Dimensions of wealth creation that are especially difficult for modern society to place in context include sustainability and distribution. Because wealth creation is slow and uncertain, especially in economies that remain stubbornly poor, it is often difficult to comprehend. A central feature of wealth creation is the trade-off between the present and the future, or welfare now versus welfare later, that lies at the heart of every investment and other human endeavour. This conundrum is compounded by concerns about concentration – how is it possible to expand the wealth-creation process to include as many households as possible as rapidly as possible, especially since wealth creation is inherently uneven because capacities to create wealth vary, as does the willingness to take risks?

In view of these concerns and challenges in societies where technology, institutions and location have made wealth creation a matter of routine, what can be said about stimulating wealth creation in poor societies? Here the problems are more complex. Transforming or transplanting into poor societies the institutions that have created wealth in rich ones is subject to even more uncertainty, doubt, and conflict. This is the short history of development cooperation worldwide.

Financial Markets and the Creation of Wealth

Financial markets are subtle institutions based on risk and trust. They are often popularly thought of as the embodiment of wealth, but this perception requires qualification. Wealth in financial form represents only a fraction of a society's wealth, which consists of infrastructure, institutions, and values, all of which determine ways of and scope for transacting. In fact, financial assets are not really wealth. They do nothing on their own; their usefulness lies only in their capacity to stimulate activity and manage risk in the "real" or nonfinancial sectors of an economy. However, financial markets integrate real markets through rates of interest or rates of return that provide a basis for separating good investment proposals, or prospective uses of finance, from poor ones. These rates also help to determine the trade-off between investment and consumption now, and investment and consumption in the future. This gives financial markets considerable power and social utility, and the ways in which financial markets operate have important consequences for the creation of wealth. Other things remaining equal, societies with reasonably efficient financial markets fare better than those without.

Since the 1970s, wealth creation has been made easier by the liberalisation of financial markets. Liberalisation reformed repressive state policy. Reform allowed interest rates to be determined in financial markets rather than in government bureaux, permitted deposit-taking institutions to lend a larger portion of their funds from deposits rather than passing them on to the central bank, reduced government allocation of credit in favour of market allocation, and opened financial markets to greater competition. The result has been creative and, as might be expected, a bit disorderly. Crises have occurred, which have led to new insights into risk management and financial market regulation.

More importantly, great gains, widely distributed, have materialised. The costs of offering and using financial services are lower, permitting more people to transact. The variety of financial instruments and services has exploded, also expanding participation and outreach. The feature of financial markets that makes gains possible is their relentless quest for information and their capacity to price risk. As a result, financial intermediation makes it possible to assemble large sums and to disburse or intermediate these funds to specific projects and purposes. These projects and purposes increasingly include the creation of wealth among the poor. Microfinance is a part of this process, a vehicle that can achieve this objective when certain wealth-creating conditions apply. These conditions are increasingly better and more broadly understood.

Creating Wealth Through Microfinance

Microfinance, as it is known today, began with small experiments around 1980 that attracted official development assistance or cooperation. Official donors adopted microfinance as an exciting and worthwhile means of helping poor people in their commercially productive activities. Tiny businesses can create wealth where none existed before. The German government has been a leader in supporting microfinance through development cooperation. An important motive has been to create jobs in economies in which socialist state enterprises collapsed under their own weight and that of competition, and in developing countries where the working poor can be assisted by well-structured relationships with microfinance institutions (MFIs) that provide credit and, increasingly, accept deposits and offer payment services.

German efforts have been broad and diffuse because financial markets are intricate and complex. Specific objectives in this important adventure include institution-building, "picking winners" through experimentation with different models, defining regulations that are productive, balanced and effective, and also providing business development services. Well-structured and efficiently operated financial institutions, which are systems that create information and incentives, have significant potential to create wealth, even where framework conditions are somewhat unfriendly. Institutions have been designed to create confidence among all parties concerned, based on consistently good behaviour and on meeting reasonable expectations in a dependable way. Incentives that promote these qualities are highly valued and essential in well-functioning financial markets, especially at the high end where large investments occur.

Since the mid-1990s, it has become increasingly possible to link directly the high end of financial markets with the bottom end, where transactions involve microentrepreneurs, small businesses, and households using deposit accounts to save and to receive or send money transfers. This has occurred with the formation of microfinance investment funds (MFIFs). Some MFIFs have been created by MFIs and networks of MFIs as vehicles for attracting investment from outside parties, often official donors. These "house" MFIFs are complemented by independent MFIFs that invest in MFIs or networks selected on the basis of criteria that include investment returns, and in many cases also development impact. Dual-objective investors concerned about development impact are very prominent. In all cases, private investors, both individual and corporate, are increasingly courted and viewed as the natural owners of MFIFs.

The arrival of MFIFs extends the funding chain that provides wealth creation opportunities among the poor and others of modest means. This chain may be roughly characterised as follows, with broad estimates of the numbers of participants that could be expected in 2015:

- millions of private investors and thousands of institutions hold shares,

- in hundreds of microfinance investment funds (many organised as mutual funds),

- that lend and provide equity capital to thousands of retail microfinance institutions,

- that lend to hundreds of millions of microentrepreneurs and small and medium scale firms,

- in almost 150 developing countries and transition economies.

This exciting scenario for 2015 is possible because of several fundamental facts. First, microentrepreneurs and SMEs (small and medium enterprises) are excellent clients for MFIs that structure relationships with these clients in a manner that is productive for both lender and borrower. In poor countries and transition economies, clients' loan repayment rates, for example, are near-perfect for many MFIs with commercial orientations – superior to those of the commercial banking segment of these financial markets. Second, regulatory structures have been modified to enable MFIs to operate in ways that seem unconventional. These include the lack of solid tangible collateral, because the poor have few suitable tangible assets, and the absence of water-tight secured transactions in most developing countries and many transition economies.

Public sector support has enabled some MFIs to become sufficiently seasoned to engage capital markets and the rigorous discipline that these markets impose in order to function efficiently. The relatively new focus on private investment indicates that public sector support for MFIs has been catalytic. Based on the power to tax, public sector initiatives may be launched with less concern about risk than private sector initiatives that by definition are based on voluntary action and higher levels of risk aversion. Public sector assistance is therefore useful for experimentation and for getting things started, which is certainly the history of microfinance. Public sector donors and investors tend to seek new fields of activity as their older efforts mature. Exit permits them to undertake new investments. The shift from public sector to private sector ownership is also a response to the fact that financial markets have enormous funding capacity while public funds are limited.

Perspectives

However, all of this is still in the early days. Only an extremely small proportion of MFIs around the world are oriented towards commercial sustainability, although their asset market share is disproportionate to their number. Most that are currently without a commercial orientation will resist changes in their strategies. In addition, microfinance remains an ugly duckling at the high end in capital markets – it has not yet matured into an asset class that can attract hordes of mainstream investors. However, progress is highly visible and wealth creation is increasingly apparent at the small end, where microentrepreneurs and SMEs go about their daily affairs.

Before going further, an explanation is required: why are SMEs grouped with microfinance? The answer is that SMEs commonly also lack access to finance for expansion and that financial structures can be created that give SMEs incentives to honour loan contracts. Another answer is that a few micro businesses grow into small businesses and a few small businesses grow to medium scale, which is good news for the financial institutions that serve them. Yet another is that these also create jobs and improve community welfare. Finally, in what respect does size really matter when enterprise in general is unable to attract credit on reasonable terms? Is not the more important objective to create more efficient financial markets that serve society more broadly and more efficiently?

Some observers fear abandonment of microenterprise finance in favour of larger clients because of economies of scale in lending and other transactions. Some also fear that consumer lending, which uses statistical methods to issue loans without attempting to determine the debt capacity of each borrower, will crowd out microfinance that is based on this determination and also lead to the over-indebtedness of poor households. But microfinance has established itself as a market, if not an asset class, and its continuation can be assumed with a high degree of confidence. The number of new micro clients engaged, not the intake of all new clients, should be the criterion for evaluating lenders' commitment to "microfinance."

This Book and Its Structure

This book has three subsequent parts. The first explores the market for investment in microfinance, which is rapidly growing but until recently not comprehensively documented. Microfinance investment funds (MFIFs) that invest in microfinance institutions (MFIs) are playing an increasingly important role. MFIFs have a variety of forms, objectives and modes of operation. Part I includes compilation of data on what might be termed the early days of a rapidly growing industry with a structure that is increasingly complex. MFIs stand up well in times of crisis, offering a positive feature for investors.

Part II examines risk and governance of investment in microfinance. An important focal point is microfinance as an asset class. The authors of the chapters of Part II agree that investment in microfinance could be greatly expanded if microfinance were better defined as an asset class. For microfinance to become an asset class, a number of fiduciary issues have to be addressed, along with the determination of benchmarks that can guide potential investors and fund managers in their strategies and expectations. The microfinance funds market is highly inefficient in an economic sense, as also explored in detail in Part II. Promotional investors such as KfW are making this market more efficient by structuring deals that will attract more private investors. Relatively small proportions of funds from mainstream finance would constitute large injections into microfinance. At the same time, finance from local sources, including depositors, will surely play an important role. An anomaly arising from the institutional structure of microfinance investment is large open positions in foreign exchange. Funding is largely in USD and EUR while transactions by MFIs are conducted largely in local currencies. More attention to this risk is inevitable.

Part III looks ahead. The development of microfinance institutions and markets for their equity and debt has an interesting and instructive history, which has been largely donor-driven. KfW has written some of the most creative parts of this history. The thrust is essentially to deepen and broaden microfinance investment so that it becomes part of mainstream finance, using its efficient structures. Private capital is being attracted, but still at a relatively modest pace. Dual-objective investors, seeking financial returns and development impact, are an important source with diverse intentions and motives.

Financial engineering is increasingly important in attracting new private funding though deals that include different levels of risk and return for various classes of investors. KfW's approach is well-suited for this purpose based on its capacity to innovate and take risks while engaging private investors on a consistent basis over the long term. At some point donor-investors will seek exit as the trickle of private capital becomes a torrent. Unresolved questions include the types of exit vehicles chosen and, of greater importance, their implication for continued service to target groups of microentrepreneurs, small businesses and others who do not have access to the leverage provided by formal financial services.

PART I:

The Market for Investment in Microfinance

Introduction to Part I

Chapter 2 by Patrick Goodman and Chapter 3 by Guatam Ivatury and Julie Abrams describe the state and extent of the new emerging microfinance industry. These researchers provide classifications of microfinance investment funds (MFIFs) based on a variety of factors and indications of their size and orientations. Goodman has assembled the first comprehensive compilation of the microfinance investment fund industry, creating relatively detailed and valuable points of reference. Ivatury and Abrams document various dimensions of the debt and equity flows to, and also guarantees for, microfinance investment funds and the implications of these flows. They identify areas of geographic and institutional concentration. As might be expected, international financial institutions have played a substantial role in the promotion of microfinance. Much of Ivatury and Abrams' work is based on their analysis of a large survey conducted in 2004.

Thierry Benoit Calderon uses Latin American data and experience in Chapter 4 to explore a very important feature of microfinance, which is its stability in times of crisis. This characteristic presents interesting opportunities for investors. It also provides insights into a dimension of poverty and its dynamics as expressed in financial or transactional terms: the everyday economy of the household and microenterprise is surprisingly robust.

Chapter 5 offers the perspectives of a commercial bank that has invested in a number of specialised banks that cater quite successfully to microentrepreneurs and small and medium businesses in Southeast Europe. The author is Peter Hennig, the bank is Commerzbank, and the Southeast European banks form part of ProCredit Holding AG (formerly IMI AG).

CHAPTER 2:

Microfinance Investment Funds: Objectives, Players, Potential

Patrick Goodman[1]

Consultant

Introduction

Microfinance investment funds (MFIFs) are increasingly seen as a core part of the funding of microfinance institutions (MFIs). MFIFs take various legal forms and structures set up by a variety of players. But all serve the same purpose, which is to channel increasing funding to micro-entrepreneurs via MFIs in developing countries and transition economies.

MFIFs are also a convenient tool to invest collectively in a wide and diversified range of MFIs. Suppliers of funds are able to reach a larger number of local institutions through such diversified vehicles. The latest developments demonstrate that whenever a microfinance investment fund is structured appropriately for its targeted investors, there is no lack of financial resources. Even private donors and development agencies that have been the traditional sources of funding for microfinance are increasingly keen to create such structures in order to attract additional providers of financial resources.

An interesting parallel can be seen in the development of MFIs and microfinance investment funds. The requirements of private donors, development agencies and microfinance investment funds encourage the most advanced MFIs to evolve into true commercial entities having a specific objective: providing financial services to the poor. MFIFs are following the same pattern but are slightly less advanced in their move towards commercialisation. Ironically, microfinance investment funds sometimes require evolutions and improvements from MFIs which

---

[1] In collaboration with ADA, Luxembourg. This publication was prepared by Patrick Goodman as an independent consultant. ADA has sponsored the preparation of this study with the support of the Luxembourg Development Cooperation, as a contribution to the debates between the development aspects of microfinance and its increasing commercialisation. The opinions expressed are those of the author and do not necessarily represent the views of any other party.

they are not ready or are not prepared to undertake themselves. In any case there is a sound evolution for both types of institutions.

The next section of this chapter analyses the parties engaged in MFIFs. KfW initiated comprehensive surveys to collect data from all the major investment structures in microfinance. These were conducted jointly by CGAP, The MIX and the author on behalf of ADA in Luxembourg between July and October 2004. The characteristics of the funds, their product mix, the origin and destination of their funding are analysed in this paper. A following section examines the forms microfinance is taking as it becomes increasingly commercial, the new structures being established, and how the traditional financial sector is gradually taking an interest in microfinance. The concluding section summarises the main benefits of microfinance investment funds.

Parallels Between the Development of Microfinance Institutions and the Development of Microfinance Investment Funds

This section explores the way in which investment funds follow a pattern that is similar to that of the MFIs as they gradually become more commercial. While a large number of MFIs and some investment funds will continue to focus on social aspects, institutions of both types which are ready for a more sustained growth should do so through a broader participation in the general financial markets.

Initial Social and Development Objectives

Microfinance institutions very often began as non-profit enterprises with essentially a social objective: helping the poorest through access to credit and to deposits. These institutions have made loans, often at modest interest rates, and those that took deposits did so at little or no interest (in some cases even at a cost) but their primary objective was social. Their activities were made possible mainly through grants and donations.

Similarly, the first financial structures put in place to lend to MFIs were established by private donors and development agencies, again with a development objective in mind. Even Profund, which could arguably be considered as the first microfinance investment fund established with the objective of obtaining a financial return, was initiated and essentially owned by development agencies. Many lessons were learnt from this early initiative that invested mainly in equity participations in MFIs. This was seen as quite risky when the fund was launched in 1995. Probably only a few of the original participants expected to see a decent return on their investment. With an internal rate of return expected to be at least between 7 and 8 % p. a. over the 10-year life of the fund, this is certainly quite an achievement.

Realisation That a Financial Return May Also Be Necessary

Gradually, with the search for additional resources, some MFIs started to generate their own resources through profits and realised that a sustainable operation provided a sound basis for a continued provision of services to the poor. The central notion of microfinance is to hand over to an individual entrepreneur the responsibility for her/his own development, assisted by a loan. The same applies to MFIs. The more independent an institution is from initial subsidies and the more capacity it has to create the basis for its own growth, the better equipped it is to fulfil its original development mission.

The requirement of a financial return for most MFIFs was also probably less apparent as the stakeholders did not create them for a financial return, but mainly for a social return. Later in this paper the various investment philosophies of microfinance investment funds will be explored, and it will be clear that commercially oriented investment funds can be very complementary to socially oriented funds. The MFIFs with a commercial orientation would target precisely the MFIs which are more sustainable while the MFIFs focusing on social returns would try to ensure that the MFIs that are primarily motivated by social concerns also become sustainable.

The first dual-objective investment fund seeking both a financial return and a social return which was not launched by private donors or development agencies is the Dexia Micro-Credit Fund. It was established in 1998 by Dexia–BIL in Luxembourg. This fund was created later than many donor or development agency sponsored funds, but it grew faster, especially after its microfinance portfolio started to be actively and professionally managed in 2000. Many funds with a less commercial orientation have grown more slowly. Bigger is not necessarily better, but providing US$ 34 million in loans to MFIs in 20 countries (as of 31st December 2003[2]), starting from less than US$ 1 million at the beginning of 2000, certainly goes a long way in contributing to micro-entrepreneurship in developing countries.

Institutionalisation and Professionalisation

Formal Structure

Microfinance has gradually become more formal with the transformation of NGOs into regulated MFIs, the creation of new MFIs and the transformation of MFIs into banks. There are several advantages to transformation. In many countries, only regulated financial institutions or banks can take deposits. Providing deposit-taking facilities expands the services offered. More generally transformation allows MFIs to reach more customers.

Transformation also usually enables institutions to attract more commercial funding in the form of loans or equity capital. This provides greater stability in the

---

[2] Dexia Micro-Credit Fund – Annual Report as of 31st December 2003.

long term. Setting up a more formal structure also has a positive impact on governance and management accountability. The profitability of the institution is improved, which opens the door to innovation, product diversification and more professional services for clients.

Another form of transformation is from a portfolio to a structured investment fund or the creation of an MFIF. Based on the surveys referred to above, there are 38 microfinance investment funds (with another 5 which were expected by the first quarter of 2005[3]) in addition to the development agencies and private donors. Most of these funds, and all of the most commercial ones, have been created since the mid to late 1990s. The creation of these structures has mobilised funding to MFIs which otherwise would not have been invested in this sector.

These structures also help private donors or development agencies to pool their assets and diversify their investments, rather than holding direct investments in MFIs. The participation of the most active private donors and development agencies has prompted others to join these initiatives.

Microfinance investment funds specifically targeted at private and institutional investors are just starting to emerge. Such potential investors willing to invest in microfinance may not be comfortable with the existing structures or alternatives being offered. We have seen that MFIs are transforming into more formal structures in order to appeal to potential investors in order to provide a solid basis for their continued growth. Similarly, transparent investment fund structures with clear development and financial objectives should continue to be launched by promoters to respond to this nascent demand from private and institutional investors.

Professional Managers

The development of MFIs and MFIFs has been accompanied by a professionalisation of those managing loans and portfolios. Loan officers and office managers are now an integral part of an MFI. They are being trained by MFIs that are doing their best to attract and retain good staff. An MFI manager requires skills different from those of a bank manager, but MFIs are in strong competition with local banks and local branches of foreign banks to fill middle and senior management positions.

Microfinance portfolios are increasingly being managed by professional fund managers who have worked in traditional financial markets. Independent fund management firms are being set up to manage microfinance portfolios, but there are still very few of them. There will certainly be a growing demand for such firms, established by a few individuals with development and financial backgrounds or set up by traditional investment management firms. These firms need to strike a delicate balance between the traditional financial competencies the microfinance sector needs in order to professionalise itself and the overall social and development objectives of microfinance.

---

[3] Most of these five funds have actually been launched in the course of 2005.

Better Governance, Greater Transparency, Accountability

Providers of funding for MFIs put significant emphasis on assessments, ratings, standardisation of financial ratios, reviews and comparisons. Even those MFIs that start from a low base but that have good governance, transparency and that are fully accountable for their performance are more likely to be supported than those MFIs lacking these characteristics. A number of initiatives are aimed at standardising reporting tools in order to contribute to greater transparency. This is a logical trend in efforts to obtain access to commercial funding, although private donors and development agencies often do not require as much transparency and standard reporting or indicators.

The third edition of one of the first guides to performance indicators was put together in July 2003 by MicroRate together with the Inter-American Development Bank (IDB)[4]. Another initiative led by the SEEP Network published its guidelines in 2005[5]. These financial indicators provide very useful guidance to MFIs in presenting their numbers, highlighting those that are most important to providers of funds.

A CGAP/IDB initiative, the Microfinance Rating and Assessment Fund, partially supports ratings and assessments of MFIs, which helps small but growing MFIs to learn more about their strengths and weaknesses. The reports are prepared by recognised microfinance agencies.

Few studies have been made on microfinance investment funds. An early one was published by ADA in 2003[6], followed shortly by another by CGAP[7]. Both helped to provide a better understanding of the players active in the increasing commercialisation of microfinance. But it is quite apparent that there is a lack of consistency in the way financial data, portfolios and ratios are presented. There was a need to harmonise ratios for MFIs. There would equally be a need for standardised definitions applicable to microfinance investment funds.

A striking example of the current disarray is the valuation of equity participations, which may be at book value, at purchase value or at market value. One institution published its equity holding in another institution at 130,000 (for sake of argument), while the second institution valued it at 100,000. The difference is most probably the premium which the first institution paid to participate in the capital of the second. Yet another institution that invested in the second showed its

---

[4] MicroRate & IDB: Technical Guide – Performance Indicators for Microfinance Institutions – July 2003.

[5] SEEP Network: Measuring Performance of Microfinance Institutions – A Framework for Reporting, Analysis, and Monitoring (2005).

[6] Goodman, Patrick: International Investment Funds – Mobilising Investors towards Microfinance – ADA Luxembourg – November 2003.

[7] CGAP Focus Note Nr 25 – Foreign Investment in Microfinance: Debt and Equity from quasi-commercial investors – January 2004.

participation for the same number of shares at 115,000, possibly reflecting an earlier purchase date and hence a smaller premium over book value. Neither the second nor the third institution re-valued their investments. Some microfinance investment funds have a policy, either by choice or by law, of stating the purchase value of their equity holdings in their annual accounts, which understates the true value if the investee company has generated profits and retained them. Others attempt to show the market value of their investment.

The capital of some of MFIFs and of most MFIs is highly illiquid. The market price is basically what an investor is prepared to pay. A greater consistency between microfinance investment funds will be necessary as they increase their equity investments and as more commercial investors buy into them.

In the traditional investment fund industry, for example, the total expense ratio (TER) is increasingly used to indicate the percentage of total expenses to total assets. This ratio is hardly used by MFIFs. Return indicators are also very diverse: some microfinance investment funds treat subsidies received as operating income. Here again, as more commercial investors are approached to fund microfinance, greater transparency as well as a greater consistency will be required. This will allow investors to make comparisons using all the information available, as is customary when selecting a traditional equity or bond investment fund.

Diminishing Requirement for Subsidies

Subsidies form an integral part of the microfinance sector in its early stages of development, either for an MFI or for an investment fund. As these institutions mature, subsidies are no longer necessary. Some MFIs refuse subsidised lending. For example, Padmaja Reddy, the director of Spandana, a fast-growing MFI in India, mentioned early in 2003 that she had started to gradually decrease the number and the amount of subsidised loans to ensure that the MFI and her staff would operate more efficiently.

Most MFIFs have been subsidised in one way or another. Some are managed by private donors that provide grants and subsidies to the same regions. Managing a portfolio as well as grants and subsidies, even to different entities, saves travel expenses and time.

Another subsidy that is seldom mentioned is the one provided by investors who receive a lower financial return mainly due to the size of the investment fund. In most cases, MFIFs are too small to achieve economies of scale and to be viable on their own in the long term. The start-up costs and the fixed costs of small funds represent a relatively high proportion of their assets. The investor is usually the one who suffers from excessive costs. As commercial funds grow to sustainable sizes, this form of subsidy will diminish. Private investors will be able to choose MFIFs with the most attractive cost structure, which is one of the components in the determination of the overall return.

Better Use of Subsidies

Subsidies are often available when development agencies encourage greater participation by the commercial sector. For example, subsidies can take the form of first loss tranches.

Technical assistance is also used by some investment funds, creating a clear conflict of interest. To what extent does the provision of technical assistance influence or even interfere with investment management decisions? Some funds provide technical assistance because it is indispensable for some MFIs and some regions. An example would be a venture capital fund investing in the capital of green-field or start-up MFIs. Some form of technical assistance, seen as an "intelligent" use of subsidies, may be required to assist the development of such MFIs. Other investment funds, in growing numbers, will take investment decisions based upon the intrinsic value of MFIs. These MFIFs will most likely be attractive to investors seeking reasonable financial returns in addition to a social return.

Balance Between Social Return and Financial Return

One of MFIs' main fears about formalisation and shifting from grants and donations to inviting other investors to participate in their capital and liability structure is that their social and development mission may be at risk. Commercial funding is seen by some as necessarily diminishing social objectives. While clearly an issue, most transformed MFIs have found that it is possible to combine social objectives with financial sustainability.

Consider the case of MFIs which charge interest rates of 25 % to 50 % or more in relatively low inflation countries: Is the social objective being maintained? Is the main reason for such seemingly high interest rates really the high costs of reaching clients? If this situation is due to a quasi-monopolistic situation, the market will probably develop automatically with the entrance of competitors, decreasing interest rates progressively. This is the nature of financial markets: if there is a price distortion, someone will fill the gap, lowering interest rates in this case.

MicroRate's study in 2004 of the 30 leading MFIs in Latin America[8] showed that microfinance services can be a profitable business, in many cases exceeding the return on equity (ROE) of Citigroup and of local banks.

What constitutes a reasonable ROE for an MFI is beyond the scope of this paper, but the debate about the balance between the financial and the social aspects is probably the one which divides the most the MFIF community. For some funds the social aspect is paramount, reflected for example in the legal form of a non-profit company or a cooperative, or in the dividend distribution policy. Others stress the need to provide more commercial funding at competitive interest rates for the most mature MFIs.

---

[8] MicroRate: The Finance of Microfinance – September 2004.

As with the MFIs, the ability to maintain a development objective within a commercial investment structure is questioned. Commitment to development objectives can be stated in the statutes of the company or in the prospectus or equivalent documents. The domicile of the investment fund, the applicable regulations and the supervisory authorities have a crucial role to play in an MFIF's effort to maintain development objectives, making the choice of jurisdiction or domicile very important.

The need of the microfinance sector worldwide is huge and growing. The net investments in microfinance of the 43 existing and scheduled investment funds surveyed for this paper, excluding investments in other investment funds, reach € 501 million with a combination of equity participations, loans and guarantees[9]. Development agencies and foundations surveyed provide an additional net amount of € 884 million of microfinance investments. There is definitely room for a wide diversity in investment funds, from those that are socially oriented to those with more commercial objectives.

Search for Funding and for Investors

Growth for MFIs and investment funds can be sustained only with additional capital or loans. This realisation has led a number of MFIs to transform into commercial institutions. But most MFIFs have not yet realised that in many cases their corporate structures and objectives cause them not to be an interesting investment target for investors having commercial as well as social objectives. Even private investors seeking some financial return in addition to a social return have a very limited choice of funds worldwide.

An example is Incofin, a small cooperative company in Belgium with microfinance assets of just over € 1.4 million. As a cooperative company it can attract private and institutional investors who mainly have a social objective, in line with the cooperative's mission. But the Belgian cooperative structure has limitations: dividends are capped and investors exiting receive only their initial investment at best. There is no participation in profits although there is a participation in losses. As its portfolio grew, Incofin realised that the cooperative structure was inappropriate for some investors. In response, it convinced partner institutions to set up an investment company which was expected to mobilise between € 5 and € 10 million.

Another even more striking case is the securitisation initiative put together during 2004 by BlueOrchard Finance S.A. (based in Geneva), Grameen Foundation USA and Developing World Markets, based in the USA. A Special Purpose Vehicle (SPV) was launched with the sole objective of making seven-year loans to nine MFIs. Notes were issued for an initial amount of US$ 40 million, with several tranches of subordination depending on risk and potential return. A US$ 30 million

---

[9] Please refer to the appendices to this paper.

tranche bearing the least risk carries a guarantee from the US government and was bought by institutional investors. In a second closing targeting a total size of US$ 75 million, the fund finally managed to raise US$ 87 million in total.

Distribution – access to the final investor – is a key determinate of success in the traditional investment fund market. It will also become so in microfinance as new investment vehicles are structured to appeal to commercial investors.

Analysis of Microfinance Investment Funds

Microfinance investment funds are vehicles or institutions that channel funds to the microfinance sector. The term covers a diversified range of vehicles with different missions, objectives and types of shareholders. MFIFs' sponsors range from NGOs or development agencies to commercial players. A useful definition is that microfinance investment funds are vehicles which have been specifically set up to invest in microfinance assets (in some cases with trade finance investments) in which social or commercial, private or institutional investors can invest. Foundations would not qualify as investment funds, but they would qualify as investors in microfinance and take stakes in microfinance investment funds.

The results of a survey of investment funds are summarised in this section, with additional details in appendices to this paper. The survey, as noted previously, was conducted jointly by CGAP, The MIX and the author, on behalf of ADA in Luxembourg, between July and October 2004. It also identified the most active development agencies and donor institutions investing in microfinance. Summaries were prepared for all the investment funds which responded to the survey, and validated by the respective investment managers. A list of these institutions is provided in Table 1. These survey results highlight key characteristics of each investment fund in a consistent format. The target audience, in addition to microfinance practitioners, are potential investors in microfinance and MFIs seeking descriptions of potential investors.

A Summary of Survey Findings

Of the 43 microfinance investment funds identified, 38 were existing entities and 5 were new structures to be established in 2005, most of which have been launched since the surveys were conducted. The purpose of this study was to identify investment fund assets invested specifically in microfinance. The overall asset size of an investment fund tells little about how much is actually invested in MFIs. There are funds which invest actively but which include trade finance or similar activities. Some funds invest only in microfinance but hold a relatively high portion of cash, liquid assets or committed amounts not yet disbursed.

The total assets of the 38 MFIFs amount to € 700 million, but their combined microfinance portfolio is € 338 million. A small portion of these assets consists of investments in other funds (e. g. the responsAbility Global Microfinance Fund

Table 1. Key Players: Microfinance Investment Funds Surveyed between July and October 2004

• Accion Gateway	• Gray Ghost Microfinance Fund
• Accion Investments in Microfinance (AIM)	• Hivos-Triodos Foundation
• ADA-Luxmint	• Incofin
• Africap	• Investisseur et Partenaire pour le Développement
• Alterfin	• Impulse (Incofin) (New)
• ASN-Novib Fund	• Kolibri Kapital ASA
• AXA World Funds – Development Debt	• La Fayette Participations
• BlueOrchard Microfinance Securities I, LLC	• La Fayette Investissements (New)
• Calvert Social Investment Foundation – Community Investment Notes	• Latin American Bridge Fund (Accion)
• CreSud	• Latin American Challenge Investment Fund
• Deutsche Bank Start-up Fund (New)	• MicroVest
• Deutsche Bank Microcredit Development Fund	• Oikocredit
• Développement Int'l Desjardins – Partnership Fund	• Opportunity International (OTI)
• Dvt Int'l Desjardins – Guaranty Fund	• Solidus (New)
• Dvt Int'l Desjardins – FONIDI Fund	• PlaNet Finance – Revolving Credit Fund
• Dexia Micro-Credit Fund – Blue Orchard Debt Sub-Fund	• ProCredit Holding (formerly IMI)
• Etimos	• ProFund
• Fonds International de Garantie (FIG)	• responsAbility Global Microfinance Fund
• Global Microfinance Facility	• Sarona Global Investment Fund
• Global Commercial Microfinance Consortium (Deutsche Bank) (New)	• ShoreCap International
	• SIDI
	• Triodos Fair Share Fund
	• Triodos-Doen Foundation

investment in ProCredit Holding). Eliminating these duplications, the estimated net investment in MFIs by these 38 funds is € 321 million. Some funds are actively seeking further investment opportunities. Together with the 5 new funds, their liquid resources waiting to be placed will boost investment funds' net investments in microfinance by € 180 million. In total, the 43 microfinance investment funds' net investments in microfinance equal € 501 million.

The most active development agencies, foundations and NGOs acting as investors in microfinance have also been surveyed to assess the overall level of investments in this sector. These institutions are listed in Table 2.

Table 2. Investors in Microfinance: Development Agencies, Foundations and NGOs

Development agencies:

- BIO (Belgian Investment Company for Developing Countries)
- Corporacion Andina de Fomento (CAF)
- European Bank for Reconstruction and Development (EBRD)
- FinnFund

- FMO
- International Finance Corporation (IFC)
- Kreditanstalt für Wiederaufbau (KfW) / DEG
- Multilateral Investment Fund of the Inter-American Development Bank
- USAID

Foundations and NGOs:

- Cordaid
- DOEN Foundation
- Inter Church Organization for Development Co-operation (ICCO)

- NOVIB
- Partners for the Common Good
- Rabobank Foundation
- Unitus

The 16 development investors listed in Table 2 have a total microfinance portfolio of € 1,010 million. Eliminating the investments these institutions have in microfinance investment funds (such as IFC's investment in the Global Microfinance Facility), direct investments in MFIs by these development agencies, foundations and NGOs reach € 884 million. This means that, based on figures collected during the surveys, the total net microfinance portfolio invested by all these parties (microfinance investment funds, development agencies, foundations and NGOs) amounted to € 1,385 million, as listed in Table 3.

Table 3. Net Investments in Microfinance: All Institutions

	Net amounts invested in MFIs
43 existing and new microfinance investment funds	€ 501 million
16 development agencies, foundations and NGOs acting as investors	€ 884 million
Total	€ 1,385 million

Types of Investors

The main types of investors in microfinance investment funds are illustrated in Figure 1 and described below:

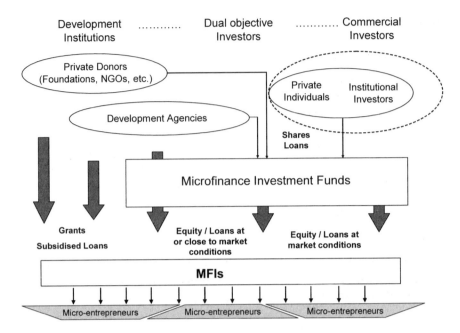

Figure 1. Evolution of the Funding of the Microfinance Sector

Private Donors

Private donors such as foundations and NGOs funded by corporations and private individuals have been paramount in the development of microfinance. They have been involved with microfinance for many years, directly supporting and creating MFIs in developing countries and transition economies through grants, donations, technical assistance and subsidies. They then gradually started to provide subsidised loans at little or no interest. Some private donors have advocated interest rates closer to market conditions for the most mature MFIs they finance.

Development Agencies

Bilateral and multilateral agencies include international financial institutions (IFIs) and development finance institutions (DFIs). Governments and supranational bodies created these development banks and other institutions to promote sustainable development in emerging countries. Development agencies have been instrumental in the promotion of MFIs, initially directly through grants, subsidised loans and equity participations.

As the microfinance sector matured, specific vehicles such as ProFund and LA-CIF were set up by development agencies and private donors to share experiences and to diversify their risks. The shareholders and lenders to these first generation MFIFs were exclusively these kinds of institutions.

Private Individuals

Before the mid to late 1990s there were very few avenues for investment in microfinance by private individuals. Incofin, established in 1992, and Alterfin, created in 1994, as Belgian cooperatives enlisted private investors as shareholders. In 1995 the Calvert Social Investment Foundation launched its Community Investment Notes that were available to private investors either directly or through broker-dealers. Another possibility was created by the Fonds International de Garantie (FIG) in Geneva, established in 1996.

The real breakthrough for private investors in microfinance was the Dexia Micro-Credit Fund launched in 1998 in Luxembourg and marketed actively since 2000. It offered all the advantages of a true investment fund similar to a traditional money market or bond fund but with a definite advantage: this fund combined a social return with a potential financial return.

Since then other dual objective investment funds have been set up, offering both a social and a financial return, targeting private individuals as investors:

- Although created in 1996, ASN-Novib, a Dutch investment fund, was opened to private shareholders in 2000.[10]

- Investisseur et Partenaire pour le Développement, a Mauritius investment company, was created in April 2002 by French entrepreneurs.

- Triodos Bank established the Triodos Fair Share Fund in the Netherlands in 2002 to build upon the expertise it gained in managing two microfinance investment funds, one for the DOEN Foundation and other one for the Hivos Foundation. The Triodos Fair Share Fund is targeted primarily at private individuals in the Netherlands.

- The responsAbility Global Microfinance Fund was founded in November 2003 by four Swiss banks and a social venture capital fund at the initiative of responsAbility Social Investment Services Ltd, Zurich. The promoter of this Luxembourg fund is Credit Suisse.

- Microvest I, LP was founded in 2003 by three non-profit organisations:[11] CARE, MEDA and SCDF, all based in the United States of America.

- Impulse, a Belgian fund, was recently launched at the initiative of Incofin.

---

[10] Information published on Novib's website: www.novib.nl.

[11] CARE – Cooperative for Assistance and Relief Everywhere; MEDA – Mennonite Economic Development Association; SCDF – Seed Capital Development Fund.

Institutional Investors

Institutional investors in MFIFs are certainly the most promising for the future of the sector. Institutional investors comprise pension funds, insurance companies, mutual and investment funds and other large-scale investors. A few pension funds are already investors, but institutional investors remain limited in microfinance, probably engaging only for image and visibility reasons or under the influence of a dual objective decision maker. Institutional investors are under extreme performance pressure and usually have limited understanding of microfinance. Bringing them on board is a slow process, but will accelerate as they understand the advantages of investments in microfinance.

There are two interesting examples of traditional investment funds that invest in microfinance either directly of through dedicated investment funds.

- The Calvert Social Investment Fund family invests between 1 % and 3 % of selected mutual fund assets in Community Investment Notes issued by the Calvert Social Investment Foundation. The proceeds from these notes are invested mainly in the United States but also in microfinance in developing markets. The total microfinance portfolio is US$ 16.7 million.

- The AXA World Funds – Development Debt is a sub-fund of AXA World Funds, a Luxembourg fund sponsored by AXA Investment Managers. This sub-fund participates in the sustainable development of emerging economies, mainly through the purchase of debt instruments from development financial institutions, but also by investing up to 10 % of the sub-fund in commercial paper issued by MFIs. As of mid-September 2004, € 1.22 million out of total assets of € 19 million were invested in certificates of deposit issued by Latin American MFIs. As this sub-fund grows, so will the microfinance portion.

These two examples show that traditional investment funds can invest some portion of their assets in microfinance, either directly or through dedicated investment funds. AXA has a small team of professionals specialised in microfinance investment. For other institutional investors that do not wish to develop their own microfinance expertise, microfinance investment funds are a convenient tool to make such investments by diversifying their risks

Summarising, a useful start has been made. The investment funds mentioned above are usually targeted at institutional investors, but progress is slow. The microfinance industry has to interact with traditional capital markets to understand fully the requirements and concerns of the market. Two recent structures using subordination tranches offer a pioneering example, as described in Table 4.

The senior noteholders of the Global Microfinance Facility are protected by the first and second loss tranches which must equal at least 50 % of the senior tranche. The BlueOrchard Microfinance Securities I deal protects OPIC, the issuer of the senior notes, by the subordinated tranches and share capital, which is approximately one-third the size of the senior tranche. The senior notes are guaranteed by the

Table 4. Pioneering Deals: Global Microfinance Facility and BlueOrchard

Structures	Global Microfinance Facility Ltd (established in 2004)	BlueOrchard Microfinance Securities I, LLC
Promoters	IFC Cyrano Management SA	BlueOrchard Finance SA Developing World Markets Microfinance Grameen Foundation USA
Type of structure	Cayman Islands investment company	SPV (special purpose vehicle) in the form of an LLC
Life	10 years	7 years
Size	$ 30.1 million	$ 40.1 million (first closing on 29 July 2004)
Funding structure in subordination order		
Equity	Charitable Trust: $ 1,000	Sponsors & investors close to MF*: $ 1.25 million: MFI Commitment Reserve: $ 95,000
1st loss tranche	Promoters: $ 2.1 million	Investors with MF experience: $ 3.555 million
2nd loss tranche	IFC, KfW: $ 8 million	Dual objective investors: $ 3.67 million
3rd loss tranche	NA	Institutional and private investors: $ 2.2 million
Senior Note Holders	BIO, Crédit Coopératif, other commercial investors: $ 20 million	An institutional investor and an investment fund: $ 29.3 million of Notes issued by OPIC with a US Government guarantee

* *MF = microfinance*

US government. Since the surveys were conducted a second issue was launched, bringing the total assets of the BlueOrchard Microfinance Securities I & II to $ 87 million.

These two examples represent a major evolution in structuring microfinance investment vehicles that appeal to commercial institutional investors. Their investments are safer than most of the other microfinance investment funds because of their subordination tranches. Their return is roughly in line or only just above investment-grade debt securities. These issues are well publicised, acquainting commercial investors with microfinance.

Commercial institutional investors are gradually turning their attention to microfinance. This type of investor should provide the bulk of the financing for micro-entrepreneurs worldwide as microfinance continues to innovate, to become known by traditional capital markets and to create structures that protect and maintain social goals.

Distribution of Microfinance Investment Funds Based on Their Objectives

The various types of MFIFs' are distinguished primarily by their objectives. The main factor is the balance between the financial objective and the social objective. What types of investors are attracted? What terms are offered to MFIs? Which MFIs are targeted?

Microfinance investment funds can be classified in three main categories:

- Commercial microfinance investment funds,

- Quasi-commercial microfinance investment funds,

- Microfinance development funds.

The commercial and quasi-commercial funds are usually set up as traditional investment funds or investment companies. Their aim is to provide a financial return to socially responsible and commercial private and institutional investors, while maintaining key social and development objectives. The main distinction between these first two categories is the nature of the investors targeted.

Commercial Microfinance Investment Funds

Commercial microfinance investment funds, listed in Table 5, would clearly target private and institutional investors. Development agencies and private donors would appear only as initial investors or as facilitators in structures with subordination tranches. These funds would be actively distributed by the original promoter as well as by external distributors.

The nature of the investors targeted by commercial investment suggests that these funds have clearer objectives than others. A commercial institutional investor will want to understand precisely the investment it is making, the financial return it can expect, and which MFIs are financed. The quality of the information provided in offering memoranda, prospectuses or annual reports very much depends on the targeted investors. For example, development agencies and private donors may not require such transparency and clarity in their official documentation.

Table 5. Commercial Microfinance Investment Funds

• ASN-Novib Fund	• Global Microfinance Facility
• AXA World Funds – Development Debt	• Gray Ghost Microfinance Facility
	• Impulse (Incofin)
• BlueOrchard Microfinance Securities I, LLC	• MicroVest
• Dexia Micro-Credit Fund – Blue Orchard Debt Sub-Fund	• responsAbility Global Microfinance Fund
	• Triodos Fair Share Fund

Very few microfinance investment funds, for example, provide adequate and sufficient information on their financial return, their cost structure, their total expense ratio and their loan loss provisions. This low degree of information makes it very difficult for traditional investors to compare such an investment with their mainstream investments. It also makes it difficult to compare microfinance investment funds. As commercial investors become more active in microfinance, the quality of the information provided will also improve.

Commercial funds mainly invest in loans. Funds investing in equity participations are held largely by development agencies and private donors. As the market matures, equity funds will also target institutional investors.

Quasi-Commercial Microfinance Investment Funds

Quasi-commercial microfinance investment funds (or "commercially-oriented" microfinance investment funds) also have clearly stated financial objectives but are currently targeting mainly private donors and development agencies. A fund such as ProCredit Holding (formerly IMI and which is really a financial holding company) will become a commercial MFIF as it solicits institutional investors, probably within the next two to three years.

The distinction between the two categories above does not give any indication of the profitability of each investment fund. Some quasi-commercial investment funds have actually fared significantly better than the commercial funds over the last few years, essentially due to their higher proportion of equity holdings.

Microfinance Development Funds

Microfinance development funds, such as those listed in Table 7, are commonly cooperatives or non-profit entities. Their aim is to make capital available to MFIs through sustainable mechanisms to support their development and their growth without necessarily seeking a financial return. The investors in these structures essentially seek a social return with the aim of maintaining the real inflation-adjusted

Table 6. Quasi-commercial Microfinance Investment Funds

• Accion Investments in Microfinance	• Investisseur et Partenaire pour le Développement
• Africap	
• Global Commercial Microfinance Consortium (Deutsche Bank)	• La Fayette Investissement
	• La Fayette Participations
• ProCredit Holding	• Latin-American Bridge Fund
• (formerly IMI AG)	• LA-CIF
	• ProFund
	• ShoreCap International
	• Solidus

Table 7. Microfinance Development Funds

• Accion Gateway Fund	• Etimos
• ADA-Luxmint	• Fonds International de Garantie (FIG)
• Alterfin	• Hivos-Triodos Foundation
• Calvert Social Investment Foundation – Community Investment Notes	• Incofin
	• Kolibri Kapital ASA
• CreSud	• Oikocredit
• Deutsche Bank Start-up Fund	• Opportunity Transformation Investments
• Deutsche Bank Microcredit Development Fund	
	• PlaNet Finance – Revolving Credit Fund
• Développement International Desjardins – Partnership Fund	• Sarona Global Investment Fund
• Dvt Int'l Desjardins – Guaranty Fund	• SIDI
• Dvt Int'l Desjardins – FONIDI Fund	• Triodos-Doen Foundation

value of their original capital if possible. This objective usually translates into favourable financial conditions to MFIs, usually subsidised or provided below market rates. Technical assistance may be provided by related institutions. The main investors would be private donors and development agencies as well as private individuals and corporations. These funds do not usually provide grants and donations to MFIs because doing so would deplete capital.

Due to the nature of their investor base and their social approach, microfinance development funds are very complementary to commercial and quasi-commercial microfinance investment funds. These funds should probably prepare MFIs for access to capital markets by focusing on those approaching sustainability, including greenfield institutions. As MFIs become sustainable, commercial investment funds should take over by providing larger resources on market terms. There would obviously be overlaps in this process but one can only question the necessity for a development fund to continue funding Banco Sol, for example, which clearly no longer needs below market funding. These resources could be usefully redeployed to MFIs which are at the stage that Banco Sol was at several years ago, rather than competing with funding that is increasingly commercial.

Categorising Funds by Overall Risk Profile

MFIFs can be classified according to two dimensions: the investment profile of the underlying investors, and the risk profile of the underlying investments.

All the MFIFs surveyed are shown on Figure 2 according to the type of their average investors and according to the funds' objectives. On the horizontal axis,

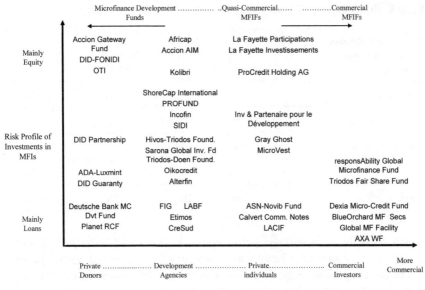

Figure 2. Risk Profile of Microfinance Investment Funds (MFIFs)

the most commercial investment funds are towards the right, the least commercial or most development oriented towards the left. These two elements, financial and social, are not opposed but place different emphasis on these two objectives.

The risk profile is determined by the proportion of equities, loans and guarantees in the investment funds' portfolios. The actual percentages can be found in the appendix.

The most commercial funds invest primarily in debt instruments or guarantees. For example, the responsAbility Global Microfinance Fund and the Triodos Fair Share Fund each have a small portion of equity investments. Considering their total size, the equity investment of all the commercial investment funds is negligible. This indicates that the commercialisation of microfinance is still in its very early days.

Categorisation of Microfinance Investment Funds by Size

Most microfinance investment funds are below the size required for sustainability, which is at least $/€ 20 million. Sponsors of traditional investment funds usually consider that the minimum sustainable size is at least $/€ 20 –30 million. As shown in Table 8, more than 76% of MFIFs are smaller than US$ 20 million. Of the 9 funds that are larger than US$ 20 million, 5 are commercial or quasi-commercial. The most commercial funds, together with ProCredit Holding have recently grown the fastest. Although ProCredit Holding's private institutional shareholders (other

Table 8. The 38 existing MFIFs by Asset Size – Market Share and Number

Size of Microfinance Investment Funds (Total Assets)	Value of MFIFs ($ million)	% of asset market share	Number of MFIFs	% of MFIFs
< US$ 5 million	15.1	1.7 %	10	26.3 %
US$ 5-10 million	39.1	4.5 %	6	15.8 %
US$ 10-20 million	178.5	20.5 %	13	34.2 %
> US$ 20 million	636.9	73.2 %	9	23.7 %
Total	869.6	100.0 %	38	100.0 %

than its founding members) represent a very small portion of its capital[12], this fund operates like a commercial institution, which contributes to its substantial growth.

The funds which have grown the most are those actively distributed. The key to success in the traditional investment fund market is distribution, which is the access to the final investor. This market is moving increasingly to an open architecture where promoters sell each other's funds, to the benefit of the largest and most profitable funds. Promoters of traditional investment funds are constantly examining their range of funds to determine whether it would be more profitable to close down small funds and sell similar funds from other providers.

The current volume of commercial microfinance investments funds is small, and at the same time there are many other investment funds which are not viable on their own and which require subsidies in one form or another. Consolidation may be helpful, but mergers may be difficult due to the nature of these funds. Instead investment funds which are structured to be attractive to commercial investors, both private and institutional, need to be more actively distributed. Such funds are building a necessary bridge between the microfinance sector and the commercial sector. Even if such an investment fund is small it "simply" needs to be actively distributed to the targeted investors. An example is the Triodos Fair Share Fund, launched in December 2002 and targeted essentially at Dutch private investors. Although it was still small in June 2004 (€ 4.9 million), its investment portfolio (microfinance and trade finance) grew by 376 % in one year and its total assets increased by 253 %. It more than doubled to € 12.2 million as of September 2005. It is certainly on the right track to become sustainable within the next year or two.

---

[12] www.procredit-holding.com – shareholder structure as of September 2005: 27.2 % held by founding members IPC and IPC Invest; 35.1 % held by a foundation, Doen Foundation, and an NGO, Fundasal; 35.9 % held by Development Finance Institutions; 1.8 % by two new commercial investors: responsability Global Microfinance Fund and Andromeda.

Increasing Commercialisation of the Microfinance Sector

Dual-Objective Investment and Financial Opportunities

The socially responsible investment (SRI) market has grown tremendously over the last few years. The Social Investment Forum[13] estimates that the SRI market in the US represents 11.4 % (or $ 2.16 trillion) of the $ 19.2 trillion in investment assets under professional management in the United States. According to the same study, "socially responsible investing is an investment process that considers the social and environmental consequences of investments, both positive and negative, within the context of rigorous financial analysis."

There is little doubt that investments in microfinance have their place in such socially responsible investments. Microfinance would be a new component of this universe, and institutional investors are likely to provide an increasingly greater proportion of microfinance investments. Institutional investors with a keen SRI focus could see advantages in microfinance: the International Monetary Fund has recently conducted hypothetical stress tests on Dutch pension funds.[14] The results show that their solvency ratios fall below 100 % (from 103.1 %) in nearly all the tests carried out. "Pension funds are more sensitive to market risks because they hold a greater proportion of equity and are more internationally exposed compared to insurance companies," the Washington-based body said. "In addition, results are more volatile because of longer duration fixed income assets that are marked to market."

Microfinance investments could balance such portfolios because they are more stable and uncorrelated with world markets. The default rates are also very low, especially when investments are made through investment funds. However, there seem to be very few funds which would appeal to pension fund investment managers. The Global Microfinance Facility and the BlueOrchard investment structure noted in Table 4, which immediately attracted interest from such institutional investors, are hopefully the beginning of a series of funds structured specifically for such investors. If appropriate structures appealing to institutional investors continue to be established, the potential for microfinance is significant. One percent of the US SRI market would exceed US$ 20 billion.

Current Situation: Growing Involvement in International and Local Capital Markets

The traditional financial sector has recently become more involved in microfinance, a development that may establish the foundations of the future landscape of microfinance.

---

[13] 2003 Report on Socially Responsible Investing Trends in the US – by the Social Investment Forum, December 2003.

[14] Reported on www.IPE.com – "Dutch pension funds fail IMF stress tests" – September 2004.

Traditional Banks Involved with Microfinance

A number of local banks are increasingly active in microfinance, providing loans and in some cases participating in the capital of MFIs. An example mentioned frequently by the MFIFs surveyed is Société Générale (France) which makes local currency loans in a number of African countries at competitive rates. In India, local regulations prompt local banks to lend to MFIs. ICICI, the country's largest private financial institution, has been active in securitisation deals.

Banks also distribute investment funds. Credit Suisse distributes the responsAbility Global Microfinance Fund, of which it is also the promoter. Some Swiss banks distribute the Dexia Micro-Credit Fund while some investment banks distribute Calvert Community Investment Notes. JP Morgan has ensured the placement of notes from the BlueOrchard Microfinance Securities deal. Such distributors are still few but there is little doubt that as the microfinance sector moves towards greater commercialisation, distributors will play an increasingly important role in placing investment funds with their private and institutional customers, which will contribute to the growth of microfinance.

Securitisation

The first two securitisation deals in microfinance were conducted in India by ICICI. The first involved Basix, India's oldest MFI, with the securitisation of US$ 1 million of crop loans. The second closed in early 2004, involving Share and the securitisation of US$ 4.3 million in microloans. Grameen Foundation USA provided US$ 325,000 in cash collateral, amounting to 93 % of the guarantee required by ICICI. The repackaged assets were bought in the form of interest-bearing notes by mutual funds and insurance companies, including the Life Insurance Corporation of India.[15]

The latest securitisation deal involved BlueOrchard Finance SA as the arranger together with Developing World Markets and the Grameen Foundation USA, as noted previously. The scale is much larger (US$ 87 million for the first two closings, in excess of the originally expected US$ 75 million) and broader, covering nine MFIs in seven countries for the first closing and fourteen MFIs for the second closing. The senior investors purchased notes guaranteed by OPIC, a US government agency, thereby giving it a AAA rating. OPIC is protected by subordinated investors willing to absorb the first potential losses.

Subordination and Senior Tranches

The BlueOrchard deal and the Global Microfinance Facility sponsored by the IFC involved senior tranches targeted at traditional institutional investors and subordinated tranches targeted at development agencies and other investors knowledgeable about microfinance. Due to the high protection enjoyed by the senior noteholders in both cases, the interest rate earned is very close to market rates. The subordinated

---

[15] High Commission of India website: http://hcilondon.net/.

investors have nevertheless enabled a much higher level of financing to be directed to MFIs than if the deals had been done without the commercial investors.

Traditional Investment Funds

Two examples of traditional investment funds making investments in microfinance are the AXA World Funds – Development Debt sub-fund and the Calvert Social Investment Fund. Other dual objective investment funds are likely to diversify their holdings in microfinance because of the social impact of microfinance and also because of the financial merits of an investment in microfinance.

Institutional Investors

Relatively few pension funds have invested in microfinance so far. Structures with senior tranches targeted at traditional institutional investors should help build confidence in this new investment class.

Funds of Funds

Although the responsAbility Global Microfinance Fund intended initially to make investments in other funds, it has made only a few investments of this type. There is nevertheless potentially a place for funds of funds, especially in terms of investment manager diversification, but there is still the question of overlapping costs. There can of course be retrocessions between funds to diminish overall costs but a fund of funds requires a certain size so that the advantage of diversification outweighs the disadvantage of the heavier cost structure.

There are many funds of funds in the hedge fund market. A fund of hedge funds may have up to forty or fifty positions in different hedge funds and may shift positions to achieve better results. This is clearly not yet possible in microfinance due to the small number of alternatives.

An interesting proposal to invest in local domestic microfinance investment funds was made initially by the Positive Fund. This project has been taken over recently by another promoter and should be launched soon. Although adding an extra layer of costs, such a fund would provide additionality. These domestic funds would make loans in local currencies, which is one of the requirements of many MFIs.

The new GrayGhost Microfinance Fund is probably the first true fund of microfinance funds. It is committing US$ 40 to 50 million over the next few years and should therefore be able to carry enough weight to negotiate reduced fees from the funds it invests in, reducing overlapping management costs.

Asset Managers

Asset managers, or investment managers, are gradually realising the interesting prospects of microfinance. So far only small investment management firms have specialised in microfinance. It would not be surprising if larger firms set up separate companies to manage microfinance investment funds or portfolios. AXA Investment Managers now has a small specialised team that manages the microfinance portion of its AXA World Funds – Development Debt sub-fund.

Investment managers willing to consider microfinance investments may do their own research to achieve the necessary specialisation in microfinance, or they appoint investment firms specialised in microfinance. A third alternative is to select and recommend existing microfinance investment funds to their customers.

Reaching Critical Size

Three aspects determine an investment fund's ability to reach a critical size, become sustainable in the long run, and attract a wider range of investors. These aspects consist of a) an appropriate structure based on targeted investors, b) distribution and c) a large initial investment or gradual growth.

The recent successes of some microfinance investment funds were due mainly to the clear targeting of specific investors and the establishment of an adequate structure consistent with their target market. These examples show that there is no lack of financial resources when the right structure is established. Once an adequate structure has been established, distribution is essential for the success of a new investment fund. Reaching a critical size is essential when targeting institutional investors. Considering the size of these investors and their minimum investment requirements, most of the current microfinance funds are simply too small for these institutions to consider such an investment. The rare institutional investors that have ventured in microfinance have done so through the larger vehicles available. These were established either with a critical size right from the beginning or gradually grew to a size attractive to large investors.

Main Benefits of Microfinance Investment Funds

Since the early to mid-1990s, microfinance investment funds have increasingly been used to channel funding to MFIs and to scale up the microfinance industry. Regardless of the different types of investment funds and of the players involved, there are a number of benefits from continuing to use and expand MFIFs:

- **Risk diversification**: investors and donors are able to diversify their risks through investment funds by allocating resources to a wider and more diversified group of MFIs.

- **Investor and donor coordination and harmonisation**: microfinance investment funds are an effective tool to promote coordination by their various participants. Harmonisation is difficult without a common structure.

- **Wide range of financial and social objectives**: investment funds can be tailored to a wide range of objectives. They can fund sustainable MFIs and be targeted to commercial investors, they can assist greenfield MFIs and be funded by development agencies or private donors, they can focus on loans or on providing capital, etc. The type of structure as well as the domicile of the investment fund will depend on such objectives and on the investors targeted.

- **Financial discipline**: investment funds can promote greater financial discipline by fostering competition in all aspects of microfinance. A more effective use of resources would result in reducing the overall costs of funding MFIs.

- **Flexible instruments**: Once set up, investment funds are more flexible than development or donor agencies. Decisions to fund MFIs are taken more efficiently because of lighter management structures and more flexible procedures. Development and donor agencies increasingly see MFIFs as efficient ways of funding MFIs.

- **Effective public-private partnership**: microfinance investment funds can leverage public funding by attracting private funds. Public institutions such as development agencies can provide the initial critical mass, the expertise, the track record and even guarantees or first-loss stakes which would encourage commercial investors to enter microfinance. Development agencies (or private donors) can contribute to the participation of the much larger commercial sector, thereby financing a greater number of MFIs around the world. MFIFs can be a bridge between this sector and traditional capital markets. The roles of the different parties should be clearly defined in order to minimise conflicts of interest and market disturbances.

References

CGAP Focus Note Nr 25 – Foreign Investment in Microfinance: Debt and Equity from quasi-commercial investors – January 2004.

Dexia Micro-Credit Fund – Annual Report as of 31st December 2003.

Goodman, Patrick: International Investment Funds: Mobilising Investors towards Microfinance – ADA Luxembourg – November 2003.

IPE: "Dutch pension funds fail IMF stress tests" – www.IPE.com – 30th September 2004.

MicroRate: The Finance of Microfinance – September 2004

MicroRate & IDB: Technical Guide – Performance Indicators for Microfinance Institutions – July 2003.

SEEP Network: Measuring Performance of Microfinance Institutions – A Framework for Reporting, Analysis, and Monitoring – 2005 – Edited by Alternative Credit Technologies and with the cooperation of experts from ACCION International, ACDI/VOCA, Bering Consulting, Chemonics International, CGAP, CPA, CRS, DAI, Freedom from Hunger, K-Rep Bank, MEDA, MFI Solutions, MicroRate, Planet Finance, Pro Mujer, The MIX, USAID and World Vision.

Social Investment Forum: Report on Socially Responsible Investing Trends in the United States – December 2003.

Annex

Table 1. Existing Microfinance Investment Funds

Name of the Fund	ACCION Gateway Fund	ACCION Investments in Microfinance (AIM)	ACCION Latin American Bridge Fund	ADA Luxmint
Sponsor	ACCION International	ACCION International	ACCION International	NA
Fund Manager	ACCION International	ACCION Investment Management Company	ACCION International	ADA Luxmint
Shareholders	ACCION International	Soc inst inv + priv ind; min $ 250,000	Soc inst inv + priv ind	NA
Where Incorporated	USA	Cayman Islands	USA	Luxembourg
Total Fund Assets USD / EUR	8.2 / 6.7 m	19.5 / 15.8 m	7.0 / 5.7 m	1.9 / 1.5 m
Microfinance Portfolio USD / EUR	7.8 / 6.4 m	2.8 / 2.3 m	1.5 / 1.2 m	1.8 / 1.4 m
Reference Date	30 Jun 04	30 Sep 04	31 May 04	31 Dec 03
Type of Fund / Structure	Microfinance Development Fund	Quasi-commercial Microfinance Investment Fund	Quasi-commercial Microfinance Investment Fund	Microfinance Development Fund
Financial Products *Equity*	100%	100%	0%	6%
Loans	0%	0%	0%	80%
Guarantees	0%	0%	100%	14%

Name of the Fund	Africap	ALTERFIN	ASN-Novib Fund	Axa World Funds - Development Debt Fund
Sponsor	Calmeadow	NA	ASN Bank + NOVIB	Axa Investment Managers
Fund Manager	AfriCap MicroVentures Ltd., Dakar	Alterfin	ASN Beleg. Beheer BV	Axa Investment Managers
Shareholders	Soc inst inv	Soc inst inv + priv ind	Soc inst inv + priv ind	Priv ind + inst inv
Where Incorporated	Mauritius	Belgium	The Netherlands	Luxembourg
Total Fund Assets USD / EUR	13.3 / 11.0 m	10.4 / 8.2 m	11.5 / 9.1 m	23.3 / 19.0 m
Microfinance Portfolio USD / EUR	3.2 / 2.7 m	2.7 / 2.1 m	7.0 / 5.5 m	1.5 / 1.2 m
Reference Date	31 Jul 04	31 Dec 03	31 Dec 03	15 Sep 04
Type of Fund / Structure	Quasi-commercial Microfinance Investment Fund	Microfinance Development Fund	Commercial Microfinance Investment Fund	Commercial Microfinance Investment Fund
Financial Products *Equity*	100%	14%	0%	0%
Loans	0%	86%	100%	100%
Guarantees	0%	0%	0%	0%

comm = commercial;   coops = cooperatives;   fin = financial;   ind = individual;   inst = institutional;   inv = investors;   NA = not available or not applicable;   org = organisation;   priv = private;   rel = related;   soc = social

Table 1 (continued)

Name of the Fund	BlueOrchard Microfinance Securities I, LLC	Calvert Social Investment Foundation - Community Investment Notes	CreSud	Deutsche Bank Microcredit Development Fund (DBMDF)
Sponsor	BlueOrchard Finance USA, Inc, Grameen Foundation USA, Developing World Mkts	Calvert Group	NA	Deutsche Bank
Fund Manager	BlueOrchard Finance USA, Inc	Calvert Social Investment Foundation	CreSud	Deutsche Bank New York
Shareholders	Soc + comm inst inv + priv ind	Soc inst inv + priv ind	Priv ind + fair trade coops	NA
Where Incorporated	USA	USA	Italy	USA
Total Fund Assets USD / EUR	40.1 / 33.3 m	55.0 / 45.2 m	2.5 / 2.0 m	2.4 / 1.9 m
Microfinance Portfolio USD / EUR	38.0 / 31.6 m	16.7 / 13.7 m	1.5 / 1.2 m	2.4 / 1.9 m
Reference Date	30 Jul 04	30 Jun 04	30 Sep 04	31 Dec 03
Type of Fund / Structure	Commercial Microfinance Investment Fund	Microfinance Development Fund	Microfinance Development Fund	Microfinance Development Fund
Financial Products *Equity*	0%	0%	0%	0%
Loans	100%	100%	100%	100%
Guarantees	0%	0%	0%	0%

Name of the Fund	Développement International Desjardins - FONIDI Fund	Développement International Desjardins - Guaranty Fund	Développement International Desjardins - Partnership Fund	Dexia Micro-Credit Fund: BlueOrchard Debt Sub-Fund
Sponsor	Développement International Desjardins	Développement International Desjardins	Développement International Desjardins	Dexia-BIL
Fund Manager	Gestion FONIDI Inc.	Développement International Desjardins	Développement International Desjardins	Dexia Asset Management, BlueOrchard Finance, S.A.
Shareholders	Four wholly-owned subs of the Desjardins-Group	NA	NA	Priv ind + some comm inv
Where Incorporated	Canada	Canada	Canada	Luxembourg
Total Fund Assets USD / EUR	0.4 / 0.3 m	0.6 / 0.5 m	5.7 / 4.7 m	47.8 / 38.8 m
Microfinance Portfolio USD / EUR	0.4 / 0.3 m	0.4 / 0.3 m	2.4 / 2.0 m	41.8 / 33.9 m
Reference Date	31 Mar 04	30 Jun 04	30 Jun 04	06 Oct 04
Type of Fund / Structure	Microfinance Development Fund	Microfinance Development Fund	Microfinance Development Fund	Commercial Microfinance Investment Fund
Financial Products *Equity*	100%	0%	46%	0%
Loans	0%	0%	54%	100%
Guarantees	0%	100%	0%	0%

comm = commercial;   coops = cooperatives;   fin = financial;   ind = individual;   inst = institutional;   inv = investors;   NA = not available or not applicable;   org = organisation;   priv = private;   rel = related;   soc = social

Table 1 (continued)

Name of the Fund	Etimos	Fonds International de Garantie (FIG)	Global Microfinance Facility	Gray Ghost Microfinance Fund LLC
Sponsor	NA	NA	IFC, Cyrano Management S.A.	Robert Patillo
Fund Manager	Etimos	Fonds International de Garantie	Cyrano Management S.A.	Gray Ghost
Shareholders	Soc inst inv	MFIs, soc inst inv + priv ind	Soc + comm inst inv	Priv soc inv
Where Incorporated	Italy	Switzerland	Cayman Islands	USA
Total Fund Assets USD / EUR	13.8 / 10.9 m	2.0 / 1.6 m	30.1 / 24.4 m	13.1 / 10.6 m
Microfinance Portfolio USD / EUR	3.7 / 2.9 m	1.7 / 1.3 m	7.6 / 6.2 m	4.0 / 3.2 m
Reference Date	31 Dec 03	31 Dec 03	30 Sep 04	15 Oct 04
Type of Fund / Structure	Microfinance Development Fund	Microfinance Development Fund	Commercial Microfinance Investment Fund	Commercial Microfinance Investment Fund
Financial Products				
Equity	0%	0%	0%	NA
Loans	100%	0%	100%	NA
Guarantees	0%	100%	0%	NA

Name of the Fund	Hivos-Triodos Foundation	Incofin	Investisseur et Partenaire pour le Développement	Kolibri Kapital ASA
Sponsor	Hivos Foundation + Triodos Bank	NA	NA	Korsvei
Fund Manager	Triodos International Fund Management B.V.	Incofin	I&P Etudes et Conseils	Kolibri Kapital ASA
Shareholders	NA	Soc + comm inst inv + priv ind	mainly priv ind + 1 listed company	priv ind + church-rel inst inv
Where Incorporated	The Netherlands	Belgium	Mauritius	Norway
Total Fund Assets USD / EUR	16.2 / 12.8 m	4.0 / 3.3 m	10.7 / 8.5 m	0.4 / 0.4 m
Microfinance Portfolio USD / EUR	13.5 / 10.7 m	1.7 / 1.4 m	1.5 / 1.2 m	0.4 / 0.3 m
Reference Date	31 Dec 03	30 Jun 04	30 Jun 04	30 Sep 04
Type of Fund / Structure	Microfinance Development Fund	Microfinance Development Fund	Quasi-commercial Microfinance Investment Fund	Microfinance Development Fund
Financial Products				
Equity	34%	53%	27%	100%
Loans	64%	47%	73%	0%
Guarantees	2%	0%	0%	0%

comm = commercial;   coops = cooperatives;   fin = financial;   ind = individual;   inst = institutional;   inv = investors;   NA = not available or not applicable;   org = organisation;   priv = private;   rel = related;   soc = social

Table 1 (continued)

Name of the Fund	La Fayette Participations	Latin American Challenge Investment Fund, S.A.	MicroVest	Oikocredit
Sponsor	Group Horus	Seed Capital Development Fund	MEDA, CARE, SEED	NA
Fund Manager	Horus Development Finance	Cyrano Management S.A., Panama	MicroVest Capital Management LLC	Oikocredit
Shareholders	Soc inst inv	Soc inst inv	Soc inst inv + priv ind	church-rel org incl. local parishes
Where Incorporated	France	Panama	USA	The Netherlands
Total Fund Assets USD / EUR	0.5 / 0.4 m	16.3 / 12.9 m	15.0 / 12.5 m	277.5 / 219.7 m
Microfinance Portfolio USD / EUR	0.5 / 0.4 m	15.8 / 12.5 m	2.6 / 2.2 m	66.7 / 54.9 m
Reference Date	30 Sep 04	31 Dec 03	31 Jul 04	30 Jun 04
Type of Fund / Structure	Quasi-commercial Microfinance Investment Fund	Quasi-commercial Microfinance Investment Fund	Commercial Microfinance Investment Fund	Microfinance Development Fund
Financial Products				
Equity	100%	0%	24%	16%
Loans	0%	100%	76%	83%
Guarantees	0%	0%	0%	1%

Name of the Fund	Opportunity Transformation Investments Inc. (OTI)	PlaNet Finance - Revolving Credit Fund	ProCredit Holding AG	PROFUND
Sponsor	Opportunity International	PlaNet Finance	Initiative of IPC	Calmeadow
Fund Manager	Opportunity International	PlaNet Finance	ProCredit Holding AG	Omtrix S.A., Costa Rica
Shareholders	Opportunity International	Donors	Soc + comm inst inv	mainly soc inst inv
Where Incorporated	USA	France	Germany	Panama
Total Fund Assets USD / EUR	13.5 / 11.1 m	0.4 / 0.4 m	110.1 / 89.3 m	12.6 / 10.3 m
Microfinance Portfolio USD / EUR	19.4 / 16.0 m	0.3 / 0.2 m	88.6 / 71.8 m	14.8 / 12.1 m
Reference Date	30 Jun 04	22 Jul 04	30 Sep 04	31 Mar 04
Type of Fund / Structure	Microfinance Development Fund	Microfinance Development Fund	Quasi-commercial Microfinance Investment Fund	Quasi-commercial Microfinance Investment Fund
Financial Products				
Equity	98%	0%	70%	90%
Loans	2%	100%	30%	10%
Guarantees	0%	0%	0%	0%

comm = commercial;   coops = cooperatives;   fin = financial;   ind = individual;   inst = institutional;   inv = investors;   NA = not available or not applicable;   org = organisation;   priv = private;   rel = related;   soc = social

Table 1 (continued)

Name of the Fund	responsAbility Global Microfinance Fund	Sarona Global Investment Fund Inc.	ShoreCap International	SIDI (Solidarité Internationale pour le Développement et l'Investissement)
Sponsor	Crédit Suisse	MEDA	Shorebank Corporation	Comité Catholique contre la Faim et pour le Développement
Fund Manager	Crédit Suisse Microfinance Fund Management Company (responsAbility Social Inv Ser. As Advisor)	MEDA Investments, Inc.	ShoreCap Management Ltd.	SIDI
Shareholders	Soc inst inv + priv ind	MEDA as shareholder, inst + priv ind as lenders	mainly soc inst inv + fin inst	soc inst inv + priv ind
Where Incorporated	Luxembourg	USA	Cayman Islands	France
Total Fund Assets USD / EUR	6.8 / 5.6 m	5.5 / 4.5 m	23.3 / 19.1 m	12.7 / 10.1 m
Microfinance Portfolio USD / EUR	6.3 / 5.2 m	2.2 / 1.7 m	1.5 / 1.2 m	4.9 / 3.8 m
Reference Date	30 Jun 04	30 Sep 04	31 Mar 04	31 Dec 03
Type of Fund / Structure	Commercial Microfinance Investment Fund	Microfinance Development Fund	Quasi-commercial Microfinance Investment Fund	Microfinance Development Fund
Financial Products				
Equity	20%	32%	100%	62%
Loans	80%	68%	0%	38%
Guarantees	0%	0%	0%	0%

Name of the Fund	Triodos Fair Share Fund	Triodos-DOEN Foundation
Sponsor	Triodos Bank	Triodos Bank + DOEN Foundation
Fund Manager	Triodos International Fund Management B.V.	Triodos International Fund Management B.V.
Shareholders	Soc inst inv + priv ind in the Netherlands	DOEN Foundation
Where Incorporated	The Netherlands	The Netherlands
Total Fund Assets USD / EUR	5.9 / 4.9 m	29.7 / 23.5 m
Microfinance Portfolio USD / EUR	3.4 / 2.8 m	22.4 / 17.8 m
Reference Date	30 Jun 04	31 Dec 03
Type of Fund / Structure	Commercial Microfinance Investment Fund	Microfinance Development Fund
Financial Products		
Equity	7%	29%
Loans	93%	69%
Guarantees	0%	2%

comm = commercial; coops = cooperatives; fin = financial; ind = individual; inst = institutional; inv = investors; NA = not available or not applicable; org = organisation; priv = private; rel = related; soc = social

Table 2. Additional microfinance portfolios from existing Microfinance Investment Funds and New Microfinance Investment Funds

Planned or projected new investments identified during surveys conducted between July and October 2004. Investments actually raised may be different from the numbers collected during these surveys.

Name of the Fund	ACCION Investments in Microfinance (AIM) (Invt of original commitments)	BlueOrchard Microfinance Securities II, LLC (launched in Q1 2005)	Deutsche Bank Start-up Fund (launched in early 2005)	Global Commercial Microfinance Consortium (launched in November 2005)
Sponsor	ACCION International	BlueOrchard Finance SA, Grameen Foundation USA, Developing World Mkts	Deutsche Bank NY	Deutsche Bank NY
Fund Manager	ACCION Investment Management Company	BlueOrchard Finance USA, Inc	Deutsche Bank NY	Deutsche Bank NY
Shareholders	Soc inst inv + priv ind; min $250,000	Soc + comm inst inv + priv ind	Deutsche Bank Foundation and soc inst inv	Soc + comm inst inv
Where Incorporated	Cayman Islands	USA	-	Cayman Islands
Total Fund Assets USD / EUR	19.5 / 15.8 m	75.1 / 60.9 m	0.5 / 0.4 m	50.0 / 40.5 m
Additional Microfinance Portfolio USD / EUR	16.7 / 13.5 m	33.2 / 26.9 m	0.5 / 0.4 m	50.0 / 40.5 m
Type of Fund / Structure	Quasi-commercial Microfinance Investment Fund	Commercial Microfinance Investment Fund	Microfinance Development Fund	Quasi-commercial Microfinance Investment Fund
Financial Products				
Equity	100%	0%	0%	0%
Loans	0%	100%	100%	100%
Guarantees	0%	0%	0%	0%

Name of the Fund	Global Microfinance Facility (Invt of original commitments)	Gray Ghost Microfinance Fund LLC (Invt of original commitments + new investments)	Impulse (launched in Q4 2004)	Investisseur et Partenaire pour le Développement (Invt of original commitments)
Sponsor	IFC, Cyrano Management S.A.	Robert Pattillo	Incofin	I&P Etudes et Conseils
Fund Manager	Cyrano Management S.A.	Gray Ghost	Incofin	Priv ind
Shareholders	Soc + comm inst inv	Priv soc inv	inst inv	
Where Incorporated	Cayman Islands	USA	Belgium	Mauritius
Total Fund Assets USD / EUR	30.1 / 24.4 m	40.0 / 32.4 m	6.2 / 5.0 m	10.5 / 8.5 m
Additional Microfinance Portfolio USD / EUR	22.5 / 18.2 m	36.0 / 29.2 m	6.2 / 5.0 m	9.0 / 7.3 m
Type of Fund / Structure	Commercial Microfinance Investment Fund	Commercial Microfinance Investment Fund	Commercial Microfinance Investment Fund	Quasi-commercial Microfinance Investment Fund
Financial Products				
Equity	0%	NA	NA	27%
Loans	100%	NA	NA	73%
Guarantees	0%	NA	NA	0%

comm = commercial; coops = cooperatives; fin = financial; ind = individual; inst = institutional; inv = investors; invt = investment; NA = not available or not applicable; org = organisation; priv = private; rel = related; soc = social

Table 2 (continued)

Name of the Fund	La Fayette Investissement	MicroVest	ShoreCap International	Solidus - Cyrano
	(launched in Q3, 2005)	(Invt of original commitments)	(Invt of original commitments)	(to be launched Q4 05)
Sponsor	Horus Development Finance	MEDA, CARE, SEED	Shorebank Corporation	Cyrano Management S.A.
Fund Manager	Horus Development Finance	MicroVest Capital Management LLC	ShoreCap Management Ltd	Cyrano Management S.A.
Shareholders	Soc inst inv	Soc inst inv + priv ind	mainly soc inst inv + 2 fin inst	Soc inst inv
Where Incorporated	Luxembourg	USA	Cayman Islands	Panama
Total Fund Assets USD / EUR	16.8 / 13.6 m	15.0 / 12.2 m	23.3 / 18.9 m	22.0 / 17.8 m
Additional Microfinance Portfolio USD / EUR	16.8 / 13.6 m	12.4 / 10.0 m	21.8 / 17.7 m	22.0 / 17.8 m
Type of Fund / Structure	Quasi-commercial Microfinance Investment Fund	Commercial Microfinance Investment Fund	Quasi-commercial Microfinance Investment Fund	Quasi-commercial Microfinance Investment Fund
Financial Products				
Equity	NA	24%	NA	0%
Loans	NA	76%	NA	100%
Guarantees	NA	0%	NA	0%

comm = commercial; coops = cooperatives; fin = financial; ind = individual; inst = institutional; inv = investors; invt = investment; NA = not available or not applicable; org = organisation; priv = private; rel = related; soc = social

Table 3. Development Agencies, Foundations and NGOs' Investments in Microfinance

Name of Investor	BIO	Cordaid	Corporation Andina de Fomento (CAF)	Doen Foundation
Sponsor				Dutch Post Code Lottery
Type/Structure	Development Finance Institution	Foundation	Development Finance Institution	Foundation
Legal Status	SA	Foundation	Multilateral Institution	Foundation
Shareholders	Directly and indirectly owned by the Belgian state	NA	Member countries, others	NA
Total Fund Assets USD / EUR	NM	275.6 / 218.2 m	NM	60.4 / 47.8 m
Microfinance Portfolio USD / EUR	19.8 / 16.3 m	38.5 / 30.5 m	42.2 / 33.0 m	54.5 / 43.1 m
Reference Date	30 Jun 04	31 Dec 03	30 Oct 04	31 Dec 03
Financial Products *Equity*	62%	2%	10%	97%
Loans	38%	97%	83%	3%
Guarantees	0%	1%	7%	0%

Name of Investor	European Bank for Reconstruction and Development (EBRD)	Finnfund	FMO	Inter Church Organisation for Development Co-operation (ICCO)
Sponsor				
Type/Structure	Development Finance Institution	Development Finance Institution	Development Finance Institution	Foundation
Legal Status		Limited liability company	Development Bank	Foundation
Shareholders	Member countries	Directly and indirectly owned by the Finnish state	Dutch state (51%), large Dutch banks (42%), other Dutch investors	NA
Total Fund Assets USD / EUR	NM	NM	NM	4.8 / 3.8 m
Microfinance Portfolio USD / EUR	201.5 / 159.5 m	8.0 / 6.5 m	28.5 / 22.6 m	3.1 / 2.5 m
Reference Date	31 Dec 03	30 Sep 04	31 Dec 03	31 Dec 03
Financial Products *Equity*	16%	62%	68%	7%
Loans	84%	38%	32%	26%
Guarantees	0%	0%	0%	68%

NA = not available or not applicable;   NM = not meaningful

Table 3 (continued)

Name of Investor	International Finance Corporation (IFC)	KfW / DEG	Multilateral Investment Fund (MIF/IADB)	NOVIB
Sponsor	Part of World Bank Group		Part of the Inter-American Development Bank	
Type/Structure	Development Finance Institution	Development Finance Institution	Development Agency	Foundation
Legal Status	Multilateral Institution	Development Bank - Corporation under Public Law	Multilateral Institution	Foundation
Shareholders	Member countries	Federal Republic of Germany & German Federal states	Member countries	NA
Total Fund Assets USD / EUR	NM	NM	NM	12.1 / 9.6 m
Microfinance Portfolio USD / EUR	225.0 / 182.5 m	477.3 / 388.4 m	63.0 / 49.8 m	12.1 / 9.6 m
Reference Date	30 Sep 04	05 Oct 04	31 Dec 03	31 Dec 03
Financial Products				
Equity	27%	8%	24%	2%
Loans	65%	92%	76%	77%
Guarantees	8%	0%	0%	21%

Name of Investor	Partners for the Common Good	Rabobank Foundation	Unitus	USAID
Sponsor		Rabobank		
Type/Structure	Non-profit organisation	Foundation	Non-profit organisation	Development Agency
Legal Status	Non-profit organisation	Foundation	Non-profit 501 (c) 3 corp	Govt agency
Shareholders	Social institutional investors	NA	NA	NA
Total Fund Assets USD / EUR	7.1 / 5.8 m	12.2 / 10.0 m	6.3 / 5.2 m	NM
Microfinance Portfolio USD / EUR	0.3 / 0.2 m	9.5 / 7.8 m	7.1 / 5.9 m	63.6 / 51.6 m
Reference Date	30 Sep 04	30 Jun 04	31 Aug 04	30 Sep 04
Financial Products				
Equity	0%	2%	5%	0%
Loans	100%	94%	92%	0%
Guarantees	0%	4%	3%	100%

NA = not available or not applicable;   NM = not meaningful

Table 4. Summary of Microfinance Investments Funds and Development Investors in Microfinance

	Total Fund Assets		Microfinance Portfolio	
	USD million	EUR million	USD million	EUR million
Table 1. Existing Microfinance Investment Funds				
Total for existing Microfinance Investment Funds	869.6	700.5	415.1	337.7
Total estimated duplications within existing MFIFs			20.0	16.2
Total net investments in microfinance by existing MFIFs			**395.1**	**321.5**
Table 2. Additional Microfinance Portfolios by existing MFIFs and by New Microfinance Investment Funds				
Total additional assets and microfinance portfolios	157.1	126.3	247.0	200.3
Total estimated duplications due to the additional assets			25.0	20.3
Total net current and expected investments in microfinance by existing and new MFIFs			**617.1**	**501.5**
Table 3. Development Agencies, Foundations and NGOs' Investments in Microfinance				
Total for Development Agencies, Foundations and NGOs			1,253.8	1,009.6
Total estimated duplications between development actors and MFIFs			155.0	125.7
Total net investments in microfinance by Development Agencies, Foundations and NGOs			**1,098.8**	**883.9**
Total net current and expected investments for Microfinance Investment Funds, Development Agencies, Foundations and NGOs in microfinance			**1,715.9**	**1,385.5**

CHAPTER 3:

The Market for Microfinance Foreign Investment: Opportunities and Challenges

Gautam Ivatury[1] and Julie Abrams[2]

[1] Microfinance Analyst, Consultative Group to Assist the Poor (CGAP)
[2] Consultant

Foreign investment for microfinance is on the rise. Socially-motivated foreign investors have placed US$ 1.2 billion in debt, equity and guarantees in about 500 specialised microfinance institutions (MFIs) and cooperatives.[1] These investments are provided by both privately-managed microfinance funds and public investors (the international financial institutions or IFIs). New and existing private investment funds have an estimated US$ 400 million on hand to invest in microfinance, and were expected to raise approximately US$ 255 million in additional capital in 2005. As the supply of foreign investment in microfinance continues to grow, it will be increasingly important to understand the appropriate role of foreign investors in helping to build strong institutions that provide financial services to poor people.

Specifically, CGAP (the Consultative Group to Assist the Poor) is interested in how foreign investment can help institutions grow and develop, realising their potential to become full-fledged domestic financial intermediaries for the poor. CGAP's interest stems from its belief that the future of microfinance lies with sustainable financial institutions that mobilise public deposits and tap domestic banks and capital markets to finance their expansion and serve poor people over the long term. Today, institutions that fit this description, such as state agricultural and development banks, postal savings banks and community banks, probably deliver financial services to more poor people in many countries than do specialised microfinance institutions, though they require improvements in service quality and efficiency. These institutions do not raise foreign debt or equity investment, which instead has been concentrated in dedicated regulated and unregulated institutions.

This paper analyses the supply of, and demand for, microfinance foreign investment. Its purpose is to provide insights into the behaviour of the market and

---

[1] The totals given here are primarily stocks (outstanding amounts) as of 2003 / 2004 as gathered from survey sources.

suggest opportunities and challenges ahead. It does not take into account the US$ 500 million to US$ 1 billion that donor agencies and private foundations contribute in subsidised or grant funding to microfinance each year. The paper builds on earlier work by CGAP and ADA[2] and new data generated by recent surveys of microfinance foreign investors and microfinance providers. This research has found that, unlike traditional foreign direct and institutional investment (FDI and FII), which are largely private and profit-oriented, microfinance foreign investment is dominated by socially-motivated public funding: at least 75 % of all foreign capital in microfinance is provided directly or indirectly by government agencies, particularly the IFIs. Having dedicated most of their funds to the start up and growth of nearly 170 regulated MFIs, many of which now attract private capital and deposits, the publicly-funded IFIs should now finance the growth and development of less mature institutions.

Despite the continued dominance of public funding in microfinance foreign investment, capital from other sources is growing. Today, the amount of capital invested in private microfinance funds by socially-motivated individuals and institutions is approximately three times as large as the amount these funders were estimated to have provided in 2003. In addition, regulated MFIs appear increasingly to finance their assets from commercially-oriented local sources through deposits, bank borrowings and capital market transactions. This is an encouraging sign that indicates that these institutions play a growing role as domestic financial intermediaries for the poor.

Survey Methodology

Between July and September 2004, CGAP, the Microfinance Information eXchange (MIX), and ADA (Appui au Développement Autonome) conducted a joint survey of the supply of foreign investment for microfinance.[3] The survey covered 54 foreign microfinance investors to ascertain their legal structures, investment focus, and financial performance. The detailed portfolio information gathered from this survey yielded data on investments in 505 MFIs and investments in 25 microfinance funds. All data were self-reported, and responses from some investors were corroborated or supplemented with information from annual reports.

To explore the demand for foreign investment, CGAP and the MIX issued an open invitation to MFIs and other financial institutions that serve the poor to complete a questionnaire on their capital structures and funding preferences. The ques-

---

[2] Ivatury, Gautam and Xavier Reille (2004). Consultative Group to Assist the Poor (CGAP) Focus Note No. 25. *Foreign Investment in Microfinance: Debt and Equity from Quasi-Commercial Investors.* Washington, D.C.: CGAP. Goodman, Patrick (2003), *International Investment Funds: Mobilising Investors towards Microfinance.* Luxembourg: Appui au Développement Autonome.

[3] The authors thank Isabelle Barrès of the MIX, and Patrick Goodman, consultant to ADA, for their collaboration in the survey of investment funds.

tionnaire was available online and in print format.[4] Two hundred sixteen institutions from 60 countries participated.[5] Where available, these responses were supplemented by balance sheet and financial performance data provided by major industry associations and service providers.[6] The analysis in this paper draws on results from both surveys.

The Supply of Foreign Debt, Equity Investment, and Guarantees

There are roughly 60 foreign investors in microfinance, of which 54 participated in the CGAP-MIX-ADA joint survey. These may be categorised as follows (see Appendix I):

- nine investment arms of bi- and multilateral development agencies (the international financial institutions or IFIs) financed with government funds or from capital markets at low rates due to the agencies' public status; such as the International Finance Corporation (IFC), Germany's Kreditanstalt für Wiederaufbau (KfW), and others.

- 45 privately-managed foreign investors and foundations ("private funds") financed predominantly by public, but also private sources of capital.

Private funds and IFIs generally take a commercial approach to investment analysis and monitoring. However, neither are fully commercial, taking greater risks and accepting lower returns than purely profit-maximising investors.[7]

Two types of retail institutions receive foreign investment from the publicly-funded IFIs and from private funds. One consists of regulated microfinance institutions such as microfinance banks and NBFIs (non-bank financial institutions) which are eligible to receive both debt and equity investment. The second comprises unregulated MFIs (such as NGOs and trusts) plus credit unions and cooperatives that are legally structured to receive debt but not equity invest-

---

[4] The assistance of the Microfinance Centre (MFC) in Poland, CAPAF in Senegal, and a number of microfinance foreign investors and MFI associations was invaluable in obtaining these responses.

[5] The English version of the survey is accessible at http://www.surveymonkey.com/s.asp?u=33938560773.

[6] The authors thank Glenn Westley of the Inter-American Development Bank (IDB), Damian von Stauffenberg and Todd Farrington of MicroRate, and Isabelle Barrès of the MIX for their assistance in gathering these data.

[7] The survey did not take into account international banks such as Société Générale, Citigroup and others that have made cross-border investments in financial institutions that serve the poor.

ment.[8] Of the 505 retail microfinance institutions that received foreign investment as identified by the investor survey, 166 were regulated MFIs and 196 were NGOs and credit unions or cooperatives. No information was available on the legal status of 143 of the recipients, although most, if not all, are likely to be unregulated MFIs. Regulated MFIs comprise about one-third of all retail microfinance providers identified, but attracted 87 % of all microfinance foreign investment.

Amount and Sources of Foreign Investment Funds

Table 1 indicates the amounts that IFIs and private funds have provided in the form of debt, equity and guarantee instruments. The IFIs have financed 56 % of the debt, equity and guarantees that were provided directly to retail microfinance institutions. These publicly-funded investors have also invested at least US$ 484 million in private microfinance investment funds. (These private funds then invest directly in retail-level institutions.) In addition to raising capital from the IFIs, privately-managed funds attract funding directly from socially-motivated investors and NGOs, as well as government lottery programmes and national development agencies. CGAP estimates that this non-IFI funding for microfinance amounts to about US$ 460 million, bringing the total foreign investment in microfinance to about US$ 1.6 billion.[9] When investments in microfinance by IFIs and government

Table 1. Foreign Investment in Microfinance (in US$ millions)

	Private Funds	IFIs	All Investors
Financing for retail microfinance providers (MFIs, cooperatives, etc.)	$ 511 44 %	$ 648 56 %	$ 1,159 100 %
Financing for other investment funds	$ 126 21 %	$ 484 79 %	$ 611 100 %
TOTAL	$ 637 36 %	$ 1,132 64 %	

Source: CGAP Analysis of Microfinance Foreign Investors (2004). The totals above include a combination of portfolio disbursements, committed and undisbursed funds, and portfolio outstanding, reflecting the variety of responses by the 54 investors surveyed.

---

[8] Foreign investors have made equity investments to assist the transformation of NGOs: the investor and the NGOs capitalise a new for-profit company to continue the NGO's microfinance operations, but as a regulated institution.

[9] As Table I shows, only about US$ 1.2 billion has been allocated to retail microfinance providers so far, leaving about US$ 400 million in uncommitted funding still available.

programmes are aggregated, the public sector directly or indirectly (e. g., through private funds) finances at least 75 % of all foreign capital investment for micro-finance.[10] As noted above, this does not include the approximately US$ 500 million to US$ 1 billion that bilateral and multilateral donors and private foundations provide in grants for microfinance each year.

In addition to the US$ 1.2 billion already invested in microfinance providers, public investors and private microfinance funds hold an estimated US$ 400 million in uncommitted funds and are expected to increase their capital by about US$ 104 million in the near term. Five new private funds were scheduled to become operational in 2005 with assets of about US$ 151 million, boosting total additional near term investment capital available for microfinance to US$ 655 million.

Survey results indicate clearly that there is considerable concentration in micro-finance foreign investment, in both the sources and uses of the funds. Four IFIs finance fully half of all foreign investment in debt, equity and guarantees for MFIs. Just six investors – four public and two private – fund two-thirds of all foreign investment in MFIs.

Patterns and High Concentration of Foreign Investment in Debt, Equity, and Guarantees

The bulk of foreign investment in microfinance debt, equity and guarantees is financed by a few large funds investing in a small number of relatively mature MFIs (Table 2). This investment is highly concentrated regionally in a small number of microfinance banks and NBFIs located in Latin America and Eastern Europe. Not surprisingly, the majority of the investments are in regulated institutions due to their typically larger size. Of the 505 recipients of foreign debt, equity or guarantees, 166 regulated MFIs have received 87 % of all foreign debt, equity and guarantees, and 96 % of all debt invested by public investors. Debt capital accounted for nearly 70 % of all foreign investment disbursed to MFIs and cooperatives.

Microfinance institutions in Latin America and Eastern Europe obtained 87 % of all investment in debt, equity and guarantees disbursed. Private funds have allocated the bulk of their support to Latin America, while the IFIs have primarily financed MFIs in Eastern Europe. Ten regulated MFIs in Eastern Europe (predominantly ProCredit banks) received over 50 % of the region's total foreign investment, and ten MFIs in Latin America obtained nearly one-third of all foreign investment in that region.

Most private funds and public sector investors seem to compete to finance a relatively small group of regulated MFIs. About one-third of all private funds have financed Banco Solidario in Ecuador and Confianza in Peru, while one-third of

---

[10] Private microfinance funds also invest in each other. Of the 45 private funds covered by the joint CGAP-MIX-ADA study, 19 reported having received funding from other private microfinance funds (US$ 71 million) as well as from IFIs (US$ 105 million).

Table 2. Foreign Investment Disbursed (in US$ millions and %) and Number of Recipient Institutions

	Private Funds			IFIs			All Investors	
	Debt	Equity	Guar-antees	Debt	Equity	Guar-antees	Total	Recipi-ents
Eastern Europe/ Central Asia (ECA)	$39 14%	$74 46%	$0 0%	$323 69%	$68 71%	$2 3%	$506 46%	89 18%
Latin America/ Caribbean (LAC)	$166 59%	$69 43%	$6 78%	$136 29%	$13 14%	$57 76%	$447 41%	193 38%
Sub-Saharan Africa (AFR)	$30 11%	$15 9%	$1 10%	$2 0%	$6 6%	$8 11%	$62 6%	104 21%
East Asia/ Pacific (EAP)	$23 8%	$2 1%	$1 9%	$6 1%	$4 4%	$0 0%	$36 3%	63 12%
South Asia (SA)	$23 8%	$1 1%	$0 3%	$0 0%	$5 5%	$1 1%	$30 3%	48 10%
Middle East/ North Africa (MENA)	$2 1%	$0 0%	$0 0%	$0 0%	$0 0%	$7 9%	$9 1%	8 2%
TOTAL	$283 100%	$161 100%	$8 100%	$467 100%	$96 100%	$75 100%	$1,090 100%	505 100%

Source: CGAP Analysis of Microfinance Foreign Investors (2004). Recipients are regulated and unregulated retail microfinance providers only. Total disbursement in Table 2 is US$ 69 million less than total foreign investment in microfinance from Table 1 (US$ 1,159 million) due to exclusion of this amount in uncommitted and undisbursed financing reported by the investors surveyed.

IFIs have invested debt or equity in a number of institutions in Eastern Europe that are part of the ProCredit network (formerly IMI) (Table 3). In several cases, public and private investors make overlapping investments in MFIs. One among several examples is BIO, an IFI funded by the government of Belgium. BIO owns approximately 15% of Banco Los Andes ProCredit, formerly Caja Los Andes, a Bolivian MFI, and also lends to the MFI. BIO also owns 8% of the equity of Pro-Credit Holding AG (a private fund), which in turn owns nearly 69% of Banco Los Andes. An additional chain of investments adds even more to BIO's exposure to Banco Los Andes: BIO owns equity in Alterfin (a private fund), which owns equity in SIDI (a private fund), which owns 2% of the equity in ProFund (a private

Table 3. Number of Foreign Investors in Selected Regulated MFIs (Debt, Equity, and Guarantee Investments in US$ millions)

Institution	Private Funds		IFIs		All Investors	
	Number (45)	Amount Invested	Number (9)	Amount Invested	Number (54)	Amount Invested
Banco Solidario (Ecuador)	17	$21.7	5	$19.1	22	$40.9
Confianza (Peru)	14	$5.8	1	$0.3	15	$6.1
Banco Los Andes ProCredit (Bolivia)	8	$9.5	6	$24.7	14	$34.2
FFP FIE (Bolivia)	7	$8.1	2	$14.0	9	$14.0
ProCredit Bank (Moldova)	3	$2.0	3	$6.4	6	$8.4
ProCredit Bank (Georgia)	1	$6.7	3	$32.8	4	$39.5
ProCredit Bank (Ukraine)	1	$9.4	3	$38.8	4	$48.2

Source: CGAP Analysis of Microfinance Foreign Investors (2004).

fund), which invests in Banco Los Andes. BIO has additional exposure to Banco Los Andes through SIDI's investment in LA-CIF (another private fund). BIO's direct and indirect ownership of the MFI is approximately 20 %.

BIO is not alone. Other IFIs, such as KfW and IFC, also have overlapping investments. The 14 investors in Caja Los Andes and the 22 investors in Banco Solidario (Table 3), for example, do not share risk according to the relative amounts of their direct investments. The IFC has direct exposure to both institutions, as well as indirect participation through two private funds, Acción Investments in Microfinance (AIM) and ProFund. Overlapping investments of this kind may mean that IFIs have far greater exposure to a given MFI than meets the eye. If the microfinance foreign investment industry follows the typical industry life cycle, it would not be surprising to find that consolidation will eventually occur, given the relatively small number of regulated MFIs that secure investment from foreign investors and the number of IFIs and private funds that make overlapping investments in them.

The IFIs and private funds have also concentrated debt and equity investment in the 18 ProCredit microfinance institutions, all regulated. These 18 MFIs have

Table 4. Foreign Debt, Equity and Guarantee Investment in ProCredit Institutions (in US$ millions and %)

	Private Funds		Public Investors		All Investors		
	Debt	Equity	Debt	Equity	Guarantees	Total	Number of Recipients
18 ProCredit Institutions	$7.3	$92.7	$210.9	$59.1	$4.8	**$374.7**	18
% of TOTAL	3%	58%	44%	61%	6%	**34%**	4%

Source: CGAP Analysis of Microfinance Foreign Investors (2004).
Note: ProCredit Holding AG is the successor to IMI (Internationale Micro Investitionen AG).

received nearly 60% of all equity invested by private funds, and 45% of all debt invested by public investors (Table 4).

The joint CGAP-MIX-ADA survey clearly demonstrates that foreign debt and equity are highly concentrated in a handful of MFIs, even within the set of 166 regulated institutions that have attracted 87% of all foreign debt, equity and guarantees. Since at least 75% of all foreign investment capital originates from public sources, the IFIs can be credited with having directly and indirectly financed what is today a set of mature, regulated MFIs in Latin America and Eastern Europe.

While most IFIs and private funds target their financing to the best-performing regulated MFIs, a handful of private funds have successfully focused on unregulated MFIs and cooperative institutions. Oikocredit, through a network of 11 regional offices, has financed 140 retail microfinance providers, virtually all of which are unregulated MFIs or cooperatives. Rabobank Foundation has made loans to 84 institutions at an average deal size of just over US$ 100,000, far below the average size (US$ 1.6 million) of all the loans that microfinance foreign investors reported making to microfinance providers. By making loans to small, unregulated MFIs, these privately-managed funds are accepting investment risks that most foreign investors, particularly public investors, are not.

Going forward, IFIs should seek to use their low-cost public money to take more risk. They should finance less mature, unregulated or transforming MFIs that can become the next generation of strong institutions. These investors should move beyond the same regulated MFIs they have financed during the past ten years.[11] Today, these commercialised MFIs can be more appropriately financed by foreign private commercial investors, and more importantly, by domestic banks, depositors and local financial markets.

---

[11] According to Jean-Philippe de Schrevel, a partner at BlueOrchard Finance, some public investors price their loans slightly lower and set tenors slightly longer than those of commercial, private funds such as the Dexia Microcredit Fund managed by BlueOrchard.

The Demand for Foreign Investment in Debt and Equity

Increasing Demand for Deposits as a Source of Funding

The results of the CGAP/MIX Survey of Funding Needs, plus other evidence, suggest that regulated MFIs are beginning to fund an increasing proportion of their balance sheet with local liabilities, with foreign debt and equity investment declining. (But the absolute amounts of foreign debt capital in MFIs will probably still increase.) These may be among the first signs that the leading group of 100 to 200 MFIs[12] that have obtained the most foreign debt and equity are turning to local sources of funding. Survey responses showed that regulated MFIs prefer to finance growth with deposits and retained earnings rather than from foreign debt and equity investment, underscoring the diminishing role of and rationale for public investors to allocate investment capital to these institutions.

Specifically, the 37 regulated MFIs that participated in the CGAP/MIX Survey of Funding Needs viewed as ideal a ratio of deposits to total liabilities that was 1.5 times higher than their actual levels.[13] But many MFIs that want to have deposits as the primary source of their liabilities will probably require technical assistance for product design and information system adaptation. Initially, they may find that deposits are more expensive than expected, because of the costs of adapting their operations, meeting central bank requirements, and operating the deposit mobilisation programme.

According to a recent rating report on ProCredit Holding AG (a private fund and sponsor of ProCredit greenfield microfinance banks in Eastern Europe), "retail deposits are regarded as the main source of future growth and it is hoped that the recent adoption of a unified ProCredit brand and group logo, and the confidence inspired by the 'foreign' elements of the ProCredit network (e. g. western managers, Frankfurt-based head office) will facilitate the attraction of retail deposits by the individual banks."[14] ProCredit's microfinance banks are also attempting to tap domestic capital markets where possible: in June 2004, ProCredit Bank Ukraine issued US$ 6.8 million in 3-year bonds, taking advantage of a liberalised domestic capital market and an opportunity to diversify its funding sources. Foreign investors are taking notice: six IFI investors and one private fund have invested roughly US$ 50 million in debt and equity in the bank since its inception. This amounts to roughly 10 % of all investment in Eastern Europe and Central Asia made by the 54 investors surveyed.

In Peru and other countries, the entry of profit-maximising deposit-taking institutions into the microfinance sector may encourage regulated MFIs to increase domestic financing of their liabilities. According to Fitch Ratings Peru, by June

---

[12] 148 MFIs receive US$ 1 million or more in foreign investment.

[13] 2004 CGAP Survey of Funding Needs.

[14] Fitch Ratings report on IMI AG (now ProCredit Holding AG), September 2004.

2004 seven commercial banks held 39 % of the microenterprise lending market. Banco de Crédito de Peru (BCP), the country's largest commercial bank, began a microenterprise lending programme (Financiera Solución) in 2001 that now has 14 % of the market in microenterprise lending. By 2004, BCP's Solución programme had a portfolio 73 % larger than that of Mibanco, the largest MFI.[15] Competition from domestic financial intermediaries such as BCP may be contributing to declining MFI portfolio yields and profit margins, encouraging MFIs to reduce costs by increasing deposits rather than debt to fund growth.[16] Between 1997 and 2003, portfolio yields for 11 Peruvian MFIs fell by 20 %, while deposits as a percent of total capital increased from 40 % to 62 %.[17]

A shift in the funding preferences of Peruvian MFIs towards domestic sources could mean that foreign investors would provide a smaller slice of the funding pie, even if it is growing: Peruvian MFIs have borrowed more capital from private microfinance funds than institutions in any other country, and Peru ranks fourth among all countries in the total volume of foreign investment in microfinance debt, equity and guarantees.

Still, both regulated and unregulated MFIs continue to seek foreign debt where local commercial borrowings are perceived as too expensive or require onerous forms of collateral, as can be seen in Table 5. Yet foreign lenders should not assume that such MFIs are a captive market: foreign lenders report that MFIs are increasingly "price-shopping" to obtain the lowest possible interest rates.

Foreign Debt and Currency Risk

The survey results indicate that regulated and unregulated institutions consider foreign debt to be less expensive than local commercial borrowing ("lower interest rate" emerged as the most important reason institutions seek foreign investment). But 92 % of foreign debt is in hard currency, creating a substantial foreign exchange mismatch for the majority of MFIs that use hard currency funding to make local currency loans. The results in Table 6 suggest that many recipients of foreign debt do not realise that the true cost of foreign currency borrowing must include the risk of foreign exchange rate movements. These MFIs may incorrectly perceive foreign debt as less expensive than local commercial borrowing. Of the 105 survey respondents that reported having foreign currency loans, only 25 fully hedged their foreign exchange rate risk. Spectacular exchange rate movements

---

[15] Chowdri, Siddhartha and Alex Silva, editor (2004). *Downscaling Institutions and Competitive Microfinance Markets: Reflections and Case Studies from Latin America.* Toronto: Calmeadow.

[16] Izquierdo, Johanna, Fitch Ratings Perú, Apoyo & Asociados (2004). *El Fondeo de las Instituciones de Microfinanzas: Oportunidades y Desafios.* Presentation at IADB Foro, Cartagena, Colombia, September 2004.

[17] Analysis of 1997–2003 MicroRate data.

Table 5. Why MFIs and Cooperative Institutions Seek Foreign Investment

Motivating Factor for Seeking Foreign Investment	% of Respondents Rating this Factor as "Extremely Important" or "Very Important"	
	36 Regulated MFIs	112 Unregulated MFIs and Cooperatives
Lower interest rate	86%	78%
Easier or lower amount of collateral	69%	72%
Investor's willingness to negotiate	69%	66%
Tenor (length of loan)	61%	66%
Speed of disbursement	56%	65%
Ability to attract other lenders and investors	56%	60%
Better choice of products	44%	56%
Technical assistance provided with foreign capital	32%	54%
Prestige	31%	40%

Source: CGAP/MIX Survey of Funding Needs (2004).

(such as the Dominican peso's 40% devaluation in 2003), and greater focus on and education about the issue by industry associations and investors will help to increase awareness. If more institutions understood that the true cost of foreign currency borrowings must take into account the risk of foreign exchange rate movements, more might seek local currency borrowings or attempt to cover the risk to the extent hedging products are available for the local currency and loan tenor.[18]

Uncertain Demand for Equity

Regulated MFIs will continue to seek more debt than equity from foreign sources despite a possible decline in the relative demand for foreign debt as a percentage of liabilities. These institutions' high levels of equity capital will lead them to increase their liabilities rather than raise new equity as they attempt to reduce their overall cost of funds. NBFIs reporting to *The MicroBanking Bulletin* have a 2.9x (2.9-to-1) average debt-to-equity ratio and specialised microfinance banks main-

---

[18] See Barrès, Chapter 8 in this volume for a discussion of the dynamics of currency risk and mismatches.

tain a 5.6x average ratio.[19] Financial regulators in most countries allow such institutions to maintain debt-to-equity ratios of between 5.0x to 8.0x.

A recent report of the Council of Microfinance Equity Funds (CMEF) revealed that of the thousands of MFIs in operation, only 115 would be candidates for foreign equity investment, given their legal status, profitability and size.[20] Many of these institutions are likely to have limited demand for such investment: the 26 MFIs with foreign equity that participated in the CGAP/MIX Survey of Funding Needs indicated that, on average, they would like foreign investors to hold 48% of their shares relative to the 45% these investors own now, only a small increase. The CMEF also interviewed eight general managers of leading regulated MFIs, seven of whom reported having no interest in obtaining additional equity capital over a three- to five-year period. These managers indicated a preference for using deposits or profits to finance growth.[21] Investors such as IFC that offer MFIs debt and equity confirm this preference.[22]

Unregulated MFIs are more numerous than regulated MFIs but considerably smaller in terms of assets. They are not structured to take equity investment and therefore are more likely to seek foreign debt than their regulated peers who can more easily obtain domestic borrowings. These NGOs are funded primarily through grants and are generally prohibited from taking public savings. Their legal structure does not include clear owners that banks can hold accountable in case of default. Hence, few domestic banks lend to these institutions beyond a 1.0x (or one-to-one) debt-to-equity ratio, and most require a mortgage on property as collateral for loans.[23] Foreign lenders will be attractive to these institutions if they are willing to lever these MFIs beyond a 1.0x debt-to-equity level and accept less burdensome collateral than required by local banks.

In general, unregulated MFIs and cooperative institutions may have a relatively greater interest in foreign debt investment than the 166 regulated MFIs that have received the bulk of foreign debt investment from IFIs and private funds to date. The results of CGAP's survey and other research suggest that these regulated MFIs are increasingly seeking domestic deposits to fund their liabilities, leaving only a limited role for foreign debt investment. Furthermore, as the risks of borrowing in foreign currency become more widely understood, more of these MFIs are likely to think carefully before using additional hard currency borrowings.

---

[19] *The MicroBanking Bulletin*, No. 9 (2003). Washington, D.C.: Microfinance Information eXchange (MIX).

[20] Kadderas, James and Elisabeth Rhyne (2004). *Characteristics of Equity Investment in Microfinance*. Council of Microfinance Equity Funds. Boston, MA: Acción International.

[21] Kadderas and Rhyne, p. 25.

[22] From interview with S. Aftab Ahmed, Senior Manager, Microfinance, International Finance Corporation.

[23] 2004 CGAP/MIX Survey of Funding Needs.

Conclusion: The Market for Foreign Investment in Microfinance

As noted in the beginning of this paper, CGAP believes that domestic financial intermediaries, including state-owned development, agricultural and universal banks, could play a dominant role in providing financial services to the poor. However, these institutions have much to learn from specialised MFIs that have matured during the past decade, supported largely by donors through grants and credit lines, and by foreign investors. By financing private microfinance funds through direct and indirect investment, IFIs in particular have used their commercially-oriented public capital to help bridge a critical financing gap between subsidised donor funding, in the form of grants and subsidised loans, and domestic financing for 166 regulated MFIs. They started up and supported a number of greenfield microfinance banks that now thrive. They also deployed debt and equity capital through dedicated private funds when domestic lenders and capital markets were not yet willing to finance MFIs. However, the regulated MFIs that have received the bulk of foreign debt now seem poised to finance a greater proportion of their liabilities from domestic sources. Results of the CGAP/MIX Survey of Funding Needs and research by the CMEF indicate little demand for foreign equity.

IFIs and private funds that continue to be market-responsive by offering competitively-priced debt that is in local currency or linked to local currency, or that hedge, or that provide longer-term financing than local banks offer, will continue to add value to these MFIs. To continue to serve the market effectively and help build the next generation of solid institutions that will become financial intermediaries, public money invested directly, or indirectly through private funds, should take more risk and innovate to meet demand more effectively. If IFIs continue to disburse low-risk credit primarily to mature microfinance banks and NBFIs in Eastern Europe and Latin America, a true opportunity will be missed. Worse, these publicly-funded investors risk displacing local capital, rather than complementing it.

Targeting smaller, emerging institutions will require public foreign investors to find inexpensive and more cost-effective ways to identify, appraise, and support promising NGOs and cooperatives. These institutions tend to be less transparent, and the average deal size will be significantly smaller.[24] Many lack high quality information systems and independently audited financial statements, and have not been rated by mainstream or microfinance rating agencies. Private funds that have been successful in investing in these smaller institutions have built partnerships with national and international microfinance networks to identify opportunities. In some cases they have even set up local offices to be close to the market.

---

[24] On average, NGOs and cooperative institutions have received loans of about US$ 617,177 from private funds, while regulated MFIs have received loans nearly 40% bigger (US$ 858,208) from the same set of investors. CGAP Analysis of Microfinance Foreign Investors (2004).

What is most encouraging is that the leading regulated MFIs are beginning to focus their financing strategies on domestic sources of funds, and have the potential to emerge as true domestic financial intermediaries. MFIs that have the capacity and opportunity to obtain local currency bank loans, issue bonds, and raise public deposits may improve their competitive position by reducing their cost of funds to levels below the cost of borrowing in hard currency. But for specialised microfinance providers to become true domestic financial intermediaries, further work is required on two fronts. Regulated MFIs will need training and support to raise large-scale deposits from the public more cost-effectively, and all MFIs will have to know how to quantify and mitigate the risk of borrowing in hard currency.

While IFIs and private funds clarify their roles in financing specialised MFIs so that they become viable domestic financial intermediaries, state-owned banks and private commercial banks should not be forgotten. With large pools of low-cost deposits and considerable branch and technology infrastructure, these big players have the potential to provide high quality financial services to vast numbers of the poor. The main constraint facing these types of institutions is technical, not financial. CGAP and others will continue to help these institutions understand the business potential for microfinance and the innovative ways in which they can profitably serve the poor.

Bibliography

Chowdri, Siddhartha and Alex Silva, editor (2004). Downscaling Institutions and Competitive Microfinance Markets: Reflections and Case Studies from Latin America. Toronto: Calmeadow.

Christen, Robert Peck, Richard Rosenberg and Veena Jayadeva (2004). Consultative Group to Assist the Poor (CGAP) Occasional Paper No. 8. Financial Institutions with a "Double Bottom Line": Implications for the Future of Microfinance. Washington, D.C.: CGAP.

Fernando, Nimal A. (2003). Mibanco, Peru: Profitable Microfinance Outreach with Lessons for Asia. Manila: Asian Development Bank.

Goodman, Patrick (2003). International Investment Funds: Mobilising Investors towards Microfinance. Luxembourg: Appui au Développement Autonome.

Ivatury, Gautam and Xavier Reille (2004). Consultative Group to Assist the Poor (CGAP) Focus Note No. 25. Foreign Investment in Microfinance: Debt and Equity from Quasi-Commercial Investors. Washington, D.C.: CGAP.

Izquierdo, Johanna, Fitch Ratings Perú and Apoyo & Asociados (2004). El Fondeo de las Instituciones de Microfinanzas: Oportunidades y Desafíos. Presentation at IADB Foro, Cartagena, Colombia, September 2004.

Jansson, Tor (2003). *Financing Microfinance: Exploring the Funding Side of Microfinance Institutions.* Sustainable Development Department Technical Paper Series. Washington, D.C.: Inter-American Development Bank.

Kadderas, James and Elisabeth Rhyne (2004). *Characteristics of Equity Investment in Microfinance.* Council of Microfinance Equity Funds. Boston, MA: Acción International.

The MicroBanking Bulletin, No. 9 (2003). Washington, D.C.: Microfinance Information eXchange (MIX).

Annex I:
Foreign Investors That Participated in the CGAP/MIX/ADA Survey

International Financial Institutions (IFIs)

Belgische Investeringsmaatschappij voor Ontwikkelingslanden (BIO)
Corporación Andina de Fomento (CAF)
European Bank for Reconstruction and Development (EBRD)
FinnFund
FMO Nederlandse Financierings-Maatchappij voor Ontwikkelingslanden NV (FMO)
International Finance Corporation (IFC)
Kreditanstalt für Wiederaufbau (KfW)
Multilateral Investment Fund (MIF) of the Inter-American Development Bank
    (IADB)
United States Agency for International Development (USAID),
Development Credit Authority (DCA)

Privately-Managed Microfinance Investment Funds

ACCIÓN AIM
ACCIÓN Gateway Fund
ACCIÓN Latin American Bridge Fund
AfriCap Microfinance Fund
Alterfin
ASN/Novib Fund (ANF)
AWF Development Debt
BlueOrchard Securities
Calvert Social Investment Foundation
Cordaid
CreSud
Deutsche Bank Microcredit Development Fund (DBMDF)
Développement International Desjardins (Fonidi Fund)
Développement International Desjardins (Guarantee Fund)
Développement International Desjardins (Partnership Fund)
Dexia Microcredit Fund
DOEN
Etimos
Fonds International de Garantie (FIG)
Global Microfinance Facility
GrayGhost
Hivos-Triodos Fund (HTF)
ICCO (Inter Church Organization for Development Co-Operation)
Incofin
Kolibri Kapital ASA
La Fayette Participations, Horus Banque et Finance (LFP)
La Fayette Investissement (LFI)

LA-CIF Latin American Challenge Investment Fund, S.A. (LA-CIF)
Luxmint – ADA
MicroVest (CARE/Sarona/MEDA)
NOVIB
Oikocredit
Opportunity International – Opportunity Microcredit Fund
Partners for the Common Good
PlaNet Finance Fund
ProCredit Holding AG (formerly Internationale Micro Investitionen Aktiengesell-
    schaft – IMI AG)
Profund
Rabobank Foundation
responsAbility Global Microfinance Fund
Sarona Global Investment Fund, Inc (SGIF)
ShoreCap International
Société d'Investissement et de Développement International (SIDI)
Triodos Fair Share Fund (TFSF)
Triodos-Doen Foundation
Unitus

Annex II:
Telephone Interviews Conducted by CGAP-MIX-ADA with Foreign Investors

Ahmed, S. Aftab, International Finance Corporation
Ben Ali, Bessam, PlantFinance Revolving Credit Facility
Crawford, Gil, MicroVest Capital Management
de Canniere, Loic, Incofin
de Groot, Michael, Rabobank Foundation
de Schrevel, Jean-Philippe, BlueOrchard Finance
de Ville, Axel, ADA
Groot, Emile, FMO
Harpe, Stefan, Africap
Lord, Stavely, United Stated Agency for Development, Development Credit Authority
Luppi, Daniela, Etimos
Pries, Gerhard, Sarona Global Investment Fund
Salcedo, Guillermo, Oikocredit
Silva, Alejandro, ProFund Internacional
van Doesburgh, Mark, ANF and NOVIB
van Golstein Brouwers, Marilou, Triodos Fair Share Fund, Hivos-Triodos Fund,
    Triodos-DOEN Foundation
Vyverman, Rik, BIO
Wattel, Cor, ICCO
Winter, Jacob, Cordaid

CHAPTER 4:

Micro-bubble or Macro-immunity?
Risk and Return in Microfinance:
Lessons from Recent Crises in Latin America

Thierry Benoit Calderón[1]

AXA Investment Managers & Sciences Po

At first glance, investing in microfinance institutions (MFIs) appears extremely risky. MFIs are small institutions in comparison to typical commercial banks, their clients generally cannot provide traditional guarantees, and they operate in risky country environments. In the last six years, the majority of Latin American countries with highly developed microfinance markets have suffered banking and/or financial crises: Bolivia, Peru, Ecuador, the Dominican Republic, Nicaragua and Colombia. The mystery is that commercially oriented investors are increasingly funding these MFIs, and often provide loans with comparable or lower interest rates than those they would be willing to accept from larger clients. A dilemma follows: either we are facing a "micro-bubble" based on irrational exuberance, or microfinance institutions are partially immune from macroeconomic or country risk factors. The issue of risk and return in microfinance is explored here, focusing on the quality of MFIs' assets, the riskiness of their liabilities and the threats posed by their integration into local banking systems.

Crises and Portfolio Quality

One of the most striking features of the recent development of regulated MFIs in Latin America is their capacity to maintain healthy portfolio quality in difficult times. I will briefly comment on the Bolivian, Peruvian and Dominican cases.

Bolivia

Bolivia has suffered a long period of economic stagnation and political turmoil that has taken its toll on commercial bank portfolios, which have considerably declined since 1995 (Figure 1). In comparison, the aggregate portfolio of regulated

---

[1] I would like to thank Fernando Lucano, Louise Schneider, Maria Otero, Camila Van Malle and Marc Flandreau for helpful conversations and comments.

MFIs[2] has rapidly grown; it equalled less than 2 % of the portfolio of commercial banks in 1995 and over 12 % in 2003 (Figure 2).

Furthermore, the banks' portfolio quality, measured by arrears over 30 days as a percentage of the loan portfolio, has heavily deteriorated. The arrears of MFIs have been lower than those of banks over the entire 1995 – 2004 period, except in 1999 (Figure 3). A more demanding measure of portfolio at risk (arrears plus re-programmed loans as a percentage of the loan portfolio) shows the extent of the difference between banks and MFIs (Figure 4).

Peru

The Peruvian case, shown in Figures 5 and 6, is less dramatic but reveals two similar patterns: MFIs[3] tend to have better portfolio quality than banks, and the spread between the arrears of banks and MFIs tends to be lower in times of prosperity (2002 – 2004) as might be expected.

The Dominican Republic

It is undoubtedly too early to draw definite conclusions from the recent banking and financial crisis faced by the Dominican Republic, even though anecdotal evidence tends to be consistent with the Bolivian and Peruvian examples. A large part of the banking system collapsed in 2003, at a cost of over 20 % of GDP. In contrast, MFIs such as ADOPEM suffered only a slight deterioration in portfolio quality. ADOPEM's arrears over 30 days peaked at only 3 % of its portfolio.

Other Cases

Data from other countries suggests that these are not isolated cases. Evidence includes the resistance of Ecuadorian MFIs and cooperatives to the financial and banking crisis of 1999. While two-thirds of the banking system collapsed, MFIs and cooperatives grew at a fast pace and maintained high levels of portfolio quality. More scattered evidence exists on the resistance of MFIs to the 1997 – 1998 Asian financial crisis (see references).

---

[2] We refer to the five regulated MFIs that are authorised to take deposits (BancoSol, Caja Los Andes, ECOFUTURO, FIE and PRODEM). Data are from the Superintendencia de Bancos y Entidades Financieras de Bolivia.

[3] The MFIs represented here consist of all regulated MFIs allowed to take deposits (Mibanco and the 13 Cajas Municipales). All data is from the Superintendencia de Banca y Seguros del Peru.

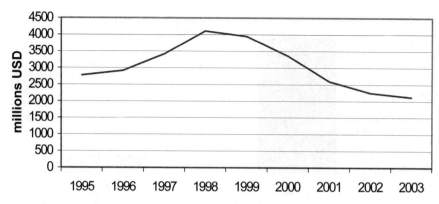

Figure 1. Aggregate Portfolio of Bolivian Banks[4]

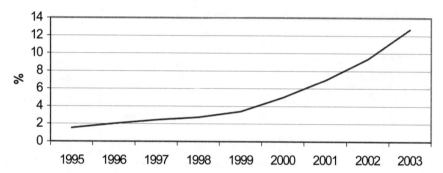

Figure 2. Portfolio of Regulated MFIs/Portfolio of Banks, Bolivia[5]

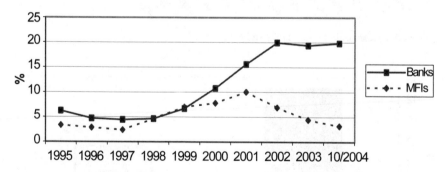

Figure 3. Arrears of Bolivian Banks and MFIs

---

[4] Figure 1 does not include BancoSol.

[5] Figure 2 includes BancoSol as an MFI and not as a bank.

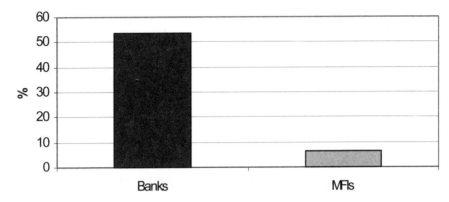

Figure 4. Portfolio at Risk of Bolivian Banks and MFIs, 31 July 2004

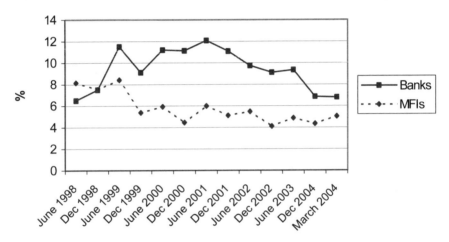

Figure 5. Arrears of Peruvian Banks and MFIs

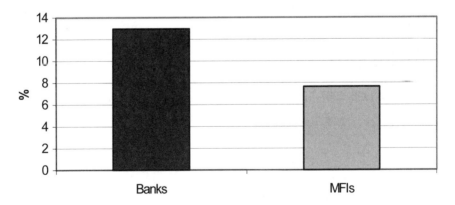

Figure 6. Portfolio at Risk of Peruvian Banks and MFIs, 31 July 2004

The Liability Risk

Although the portfolios of MFIs have proved resilient to various types of crises, important vulnerabilities remain, arising from the composition of their liabilities. Areas of concern include currency mismatches, liquidity and the concentration of investments in a handful of large MFIs.

Currency Mismatches

Massive currency devaluations often accompany macroeconomic crises, as illustrated in Ecuador, Argentina and the Dominican Republic. Institutions that rely heavily on unhedged hard currency funding to finance their portfolio growth are unlikely to survive a major devaluation even if they maintain healthy portfolio quality. Argentina's nascent microfinance sector was hit very hard by the 2001 crisis, in part because MFI managers were convinced of the credibility of the currency board. Fortunately, most large Latin American MFIs have diversified sources of funding based on client savings, local borrowing, and external borrowing which is increasingly being hedged. The development of forward markets in Latin America is encouraging, although they are limited to a few countries and short maturities. Bolivian and Peruvian MFIs can lower their risk of mismatching more easily because clients borrow and save in dollars as well as in local currency.

Liquidity Crunches

The second threat faced by MFIs is the impossibility of obtaining funding in times of crisis: local banks become unable to lend to MFIs and international investors wait for the situation to stabilise before providing new loans (or demand extremely high risk premiums). This threat is particularly serious for MFIs because most of their loans are not backed by guarantees. Clients repay in large part because they expect their MFIs to offer them new, often larger, loans at the end of their current loan cycle. If the clients anticipate that their MFI will not be able to issue new loans and the institution does not have credible means of enforcing repayment by threatening to liquidate guarantees, MFIs may face serious repayment problems. (A generalised liquidity crunch makes the threat of being excluded from loans from other institutions via credit bureaus irrelevant.)

MFIs should theoretically have an advantage over commercial banks because part of their funding is provided by international financial institutions (IFIs). These institutions should be more willing than private investors to lend to MFIs facing liquidity problems arising from external shocks. Maria Otero from ACCION described the difficulty MFIs face in obtaining access to funding from IFIs in such situations: due to internal procedures, IFIs typically take between 6 and 12 months to issue an "emergency" loan. The recent creation of an "Emergency Liquidity Facility" by the Multilateral Investment Fund (MIF) and its parent, the Inter-American Development Bank, is a first step in resolving this issue. It is especially encouraging that the Facility seeks to address moral hazard by applying strict criteria to MFIs seeking to qualify for these short-term loans.

Crowding Out?

The rapid development of microfinance funds coupled with the continuing lending by IFIs to large, financially self-sufficient MFIs, has caused a controversy over the crowding out of private investors. This issue is a valid concern that underlines the merits of having IFIs concentrate on the second-tier of smaller, less mature MFIs and on innovations such as the Emergency Liquidity Facility. However, this concern does not address what may be one of the largest looming risks in microfinance. The regulatory constraints faced by many funds lead them to favour loans to large, regulated MFIs that also receive funding from IFIs. More than crowding out, the biggest danger is that of a heavy concentration of funds invested in a few well-known MFIs, such as, say, Banco Solidario. The combination of growing funds already committed to microfinance, regulatory constraints and public funding may well lead to higher leveraging and lower risk-sensitivity. These are the ingredients of a "micro-bubble" in the industry. However, this risk is still limited, given the rapid development of MFIs in Latin America, and the still modest leveraging of the majority of institutions.

Microfinance and the Banking Sector

Having argued that the assets of regulated Latin American MFIs have proved more resilient to crises than those of commercial banks, it is disquieting to hear voices defending the transformation of microfinance institutions into typical banks, placing microfinance as one of a range of products offered by commercial banks. This (minority) view was defended at the 2004 KfW symposium as were the benefits of "virtual banking" for the development of microfinance. The following arguments discuss this issue and defend some distinctive features that have made microfinance a success.

- The success of individual microcredit mainly rests on the intensive selection and monitoring of clients by credit officers that are responsible for the entire relationship with their clients (excluding accounting and the collection of long overdue loans). The portfolio at risk of institutions that have heavily relied on credit scoring and standard banking procedures have rapidly ballooned (the Bolivian *FFPs de consumo* being the best example). Developing microfinance based on credit scoring and virtual banking is illusory.

- Latin American MFIs have carefully developed appropriate incentives for their credit officers. These incentives balance the advantages of low arrears, portfolio growth and growth in the number of clients. Changing these incentives or adopting those used in commercial banks could seriously damage the quality of microfinance assets.

- Finally, prudence is important in managing equity investments in MFIs. Latin American banks owned by local conglomerates have suffered from the transfer of assets to other companies. Assets have been stripped from banks and transferred to parent companies through false accounting and non-repayment of connected loans. Ecuador (Filanbanco, Banco del Progreso) and the Dominican Republic (Baninter, Mercantil, Bancrédito) offer recent illustrations. It is in the best interest of microentrepreneurs to have MFIs owned by long-term shareholders that do not face such conflicts of interest and that have a deep understanding of microfinance.

Conclusion

Returning to our initial question, the quality of MFIs' assets tends to reinforce the view that there is no "micro-bubble" in the sector. The capacity of Latin American MFIs to maintain good portfolio quality in times of crisis should reassure investors seeking confidence in the risk-return profile of microfinance investments. The main risk, as shown by the Argentinean case, is liability management. Currency mismatches and liquidity issues are progressively being addressed and should remain at the centre of our attention. The heavy concentration of investments in a few MFIs is becoming a risk that will probably continue to grow and that requires further public-private coordination. The best way to move forward is to adopt innovations such as currency hedging, emergency liquidity funding and credit bureaus without undermining the distinct methodologies and structures MFIs have created, which contrast to those of typical commercial banks.

References

Akerlof, George and Romer, Paul (1993) "Looting: the Economic Underworld of Bankruptcy for Profit", *Brookings Papers on Economic Activity*, 2: pp. 1 – 73.

Armendáriz de Aghion, Beatriz, and Morduch, Jonathan (2000), "Microfinance beyond group lending", *Economics of Transition,* 8: pp. 401 – 420.

Arriola Bonjour, Pedro (2003), "Las Microfinanzas en Bolivia: Historia y situación actual", ASOFIN.

Arriola Bonjour, Pedro "Microfinance in Bolivia in Times of Crisis", http://www.iadb.org/sds/doc/Mic-PArriolaE.pdf n.d.

Bouchet, Michel, Clark, Ephraim and Groslambert, Bertrand (2003), *Country Risk Assessment: A Guide to Global Investment Strategy*, Wiley.

Evans, Anna Cora (2001), "Strengthening WOCCU's Partners in a Time of Crisis Using PEARLS Financial Monitoring: The Case Of Ecuador", *The Microbanking Bulletin, Focus on Transparency,* issue 7.

Finrural (Bolivia), *Coyuntura Microfinanciera,* issues 3 – 27.

Jácome, Luis (2004), *The late 1990s Financial Crisis in Ecuador: Institutional Weaknesses, Fiscal Rigidities and Financial Dollarization at Work,* IMF Working Paper.

Jansson, Tor (2001), *Microfinance: From Village to Wall Street,* Inter-American Development Bank, Washington D.C.

McGuire, Paul (1998) "The Asian Financial Crisis – Implications for Microfinance", *BWTP Newsletter,* issue 11.

Matthäus-Maier, Ingrid and von Pischke, J.D. eds. (2004), *The Development of the Financial Sector in Southeast Europe,* Berlin/Heidelberg/New York: Springer.

Morduch, Jonathan (1999), "The Microfinance Promise", *Journal of Economic Literature,* Vol. XXXVII, pp 1569 – 1614.

Rhyne, Elisabeth (2001), "Crisis in Bolivian Microfinance", *Monday Developments.*

Steege, Jean (1998), *The Rise and Fall of Corposol: Lessons Learned from the Challenges of Managing Growth,* Microenterprise Best Practices.

ProCredit Banks in Southeast Europe: Successful Public-Private Partnership in Microfinance

Peter Hennig

Global Head of Financial Institutions, Commerzbank AG, Frankfurt am Main

It became increasingly clear at the beginning of the 1990s that the small and medium-sized business clients of Commerzbank were strongly and sustainably developing their activities in Central and Eastern Europe. This prompted Commerzbank to offer services locally for corporate clients in Prague, Budapest, Warsaw and Moscow. Commerzbank's early entry into the market enabled it to develop strong positions in these cities. It recently opened a branch in Bratislava as well.

This successful strategy, however, was not transferable to Southeast Europe, especially Bulgaria, Romania and the countries of the former Yugoslavia: foreign direct industrial investment grew only slowly. It was not until the end of the 1990s that a more energetic approach to the reform process was adopted across the full economic and political spectrum. The economies in the region were simply weak, the civil war in Yugoslavia being a major factor. Because of its traditionally very strong correspondent banking activity, Commerzbank entered into a business relationship with the newly established Micro Enterprise Bank in Sarajevo immediately after the Dayton Agreement. As a correspondent bank it became acquainted with the new bank's shareholders and their representatives.

A Pioneering Investment

Good business relations, attractive and serious shareholders, the German government's offer to support banking in Southeast Europe, and signs of increased efforts in Bulgaria and Romania to join the EU led Commerzbank to accept an invitation to become an investor in microfinance banks in the region. Commerzbank is the only private German commercial financial institution to have become a shareholder in microfinance banks.

The Micro Enterprise Bank in Kosovo was the first microfinance bank in which Commerzbank became an owner. That was in January 2000. Subsequently, Commerzbank has taken stakes of between 15 % and 20 % in microfinance banks in Serbia, Bulgaria, Albania, Bosnia and Herzegovina and Romania. Other shareholders with similar stakes include KfW/DEG, the European Bank for Reconstruction and Development (EBRD) in London, the IFC (a World Bank subsidiary) in Washington, what is now ProCredit Holding (formerly Internationale Micro Investitionen AG or IMI) in Frankfurt, and in some cases the Dutch state development institution FMO. There are no local shareholders. The banks are operated by the Frankfurt-based consulting firm IPC, which has an international reputation for this activity and provides management. Recently, the banks have adopted ProCredit Bank as their common name and with a common logo.

The shareholders view this public-private partnership as an effective vehicle for the commercialisation of development aid in the financial sector. These banks are profit-oriented, seeking a target after-tax rate of return (RoE) of 15 %. The shareholders seek to balance social and economic goals, and measure success in terms of market penetration as well as the volume of business and profits.

Engaging the Target Group

The ProCredit banks lend to micro entrepreneurs and to small and medium-sized enterprises (SMEs) that otherwise would have virtually no access to outside capital from formal institutions. The shareholders' objective is that these clients should build their businesses with outside capital raised on market terms without subsidies. The microfinance banks' approach is to provide services that respond precisely to their target group's capacity. In this way these banks build the SME sector, which is the backbone of economic (and also democratic) development. Hence, the business model that has been developed is valid, useful and important not only in Southeast Europe and in transition countries, but globally.

The ProCredit banks' average loan size is about € 6,000 in Southeast Europe, varying from country to country. The ProCredit banks provide constructive incentives to their clients, initially offering small, short-term loans that, when repaid in full and on time, qualify clients to obtain further loans that are usually bigger and with a longer term.

The loan default rate is low – less than 1 %. The main reason for this success is the credit technology that IPC has developed. The banks' structure of course complies with local legislation and generally corresponds to the normal corporate structure of banks on the continent of Europe: the low default rate reflects incentives provided to all parties, and in particular to the staff of these banks. While the managers of the ProCredit banks employed by IPC are predominantly from Western Europe, staff are recruited from the local workforce. They receive initial training by IPC, and continued training to serve customers on a day-to-day basis. Loan officers' incentive bonuses are based on the numbers of clients they serve and the size and quality of the portfolios they construct.

Rapid Growth and More Services

The banks have grown dynamically as indicated by the increase in staff numbers in Southeast Europe from below 100 to more than 750 in a few years. The banks have created a network of branches to serve SMEs over a wide area. Their clients often show similar growth. The banks keep pace with their customers as they develop and grow and have consequently expanded their range of services and clients. Initially, the microfinance banks concentrated on credit, deposits and international money transfers, but further products have since been added. Thus the lending authority of the ProCredit Bank in Bulgaria, which opened in 2001, is currently around € 600,000. A leasing subsidiary was launched in 2004.

Considering the size of the ProCredit banks in Southeast Europe, they can no longer be described as "micro" except in terms of their target group; in terms of their products, they have long been universal banks. All these ProCredit banks are members of SWIFT and have their own sites on the Internet. The shareholders of the ProCredit banks consider it extremely important to continue to serve micro clients and to retain the character of micro banks, even if expansion continues upmarket.

As a German bank with an extensive branch network that focuses particularly on small and medium-sized enterprises, Commerzbank finds that as these banks grow, its customers are also showing an increasing interest in the countries of Southeast Europe and in the ProCredit banks in the region. In addition, Commerzbank markets the ProCredit Banks internationally as well. One example: in 2004 it presented the ProCredit Bank concept in Tripoli, Libya, and required the participants to bank with these institutions.

Summing up, the activities of these banks contribute to the local economy and financial system. They are also proof of a successful, tried and tested public-private partnership.

PART II:

Risk and Governance in Microfinance Investment

Introduction to Part II

Chapter 6 consists of Mark de Sousa-Shields' exploration of the asset allocation strategies of local and international investors. He finds that their behaviour is broadly similar, which implies that a global market for microfinance investment could be possible. But microfinance is not yet sufficiently well described, and its risk and return characteristics are not yet well-enough understood to attract large numbers of investors. However, numerous sources of funding are likely to become available. Given the massive size of global investment markets compared to investment in microfinance, even small allocations to microfinance could have a large impact.

In Chapter 7 Margarete Biallas and Mark Schwiete offer a strategic view of KfW's role as an investor in microfinance investment funds (MFIFs). They describe how risk considerations, along with concern for costs, impact and economies of scale, have shaped investment criteria. MFIF structures are determined in response to risk, which in turn determine the investment products offered. KfW's MFIF investment strategy responds to risk through its capacity to influence individual investments, by balancing its role in corporate governance, and by engaging different classes of private investors through mechanisms in which it has an advantage as a public institution with an appetite for risk.

Isabelle Barrès discusses foreign exchange risk in Chapter 8 – a risk identified by Ivatury and Abrams in Part I. This risk has grown as investment in microfinance has accelerated. She finds that significant exposures are present in many credit arrangements between microfinance institutions and their foreign supporters, that these exposures are dealt with in diverse ways, and that the prudential tools customarily used to manage this risk are not always diligently applied in microfinance – and sometimes lacking altogether. Her well-documented description of this exposure should surely spur efforts to diminish the risk it poses.

Robert Pouliot places microfinance investment in the context of capital markets, the wider investment universe. A starting point for his concern, explored at length in Chapter 9, is the problematic status of microfinance investment as an asset class. As such, the microfinance investment market is highly inefficient, at times possibly verging on the naïve. His focus is on fiduciary problems that have to be rectified to elevate microfinance investment to the point where microfinance would be present in a multitude of diversified portfolios worldwide. The protection of investors that is required for this to occur requires attention to governance and to the creation of institutions (as ways of doing things as well as specific organisations) that encourage investor confidence, which in turn increases the number and amplitude of competitive deals that lead to efficient markets. Pouliot also promotes a charter of microfinance investor rights and offers a comprehensive glossary of fiduciary terms and practices as they apply to the investment industry.

CHAPTER 6:

Commercial Investment in Microfinance: A Class by Itself?

Marc de Sousa-Shields[1]

Director of Project Development, Enterprise Solutions Global Consulting

Commercial investors are guided by asset allocation strategies. These strategies basically define the universe of possible investments and the proportion of each asset class they will buy for a given portfolio.[2] This means that even before the quality of a specific investment can be considered, the relative interest of an investor is more or less set.

For the most common types of investors, asset allocation strategies are so well defined that they result in fairly predictable investment patterns. Generally speaking, asset allocation principles of the most common types of investors transcend international boundaries. This means that the relative proportion of a given asset class in a Peruvian or South African pension fund will be roughly the same as those found in a US or British fund, with obvious differences influenced by local economic conditions and regulatory regimes.[3] Thus, the processes investors use to allocate funding to asset classes are of great interest to microfinance; they define the type of investor and the proportion of assets that an investor is likely to con-

---

[1] This chapter is based on Part 2 of "Financing Microfinance Institution: The Context for Transitions to Private Capital," by Marc de Sousa-Shields, Cheryl Frankiewicz and others, commissioned as microreport #8 by the Accelerated Microenterprise Advancement Project (AMAP) of USAID, December 2004. The contractor was Chemonics International, Washington DC. (www.microLINKS.org) The author is Research Director for the Transitions to Private Capital topic of AMAP.

[2] Asset allocation, the process of dividing a portfolio into major asset categories, such as bonds, stocks or cash, is used to manage risk and maximise profit through portfolio diversification.

[3] Asset allocation strategies, as used here, are defined at the broadest level. In practice, asset managers have distinct views on the economy and adjust their holdings strategically. This usually involves differential weighting of higher and lower risk investments within portfolios. The most common difference is variations of the proportions of equity versus income investments.

sider investing in MFIs. (MFI investment is used in this chapter to refer to direct investments in MFIs *and* indirect investment through private microfinance investment funds – MFIFs – that invest in MFIs.)

Unfortunately, the asset class or classes to which microfinance investments belong is not yet established, making it difficult to explain them to commercial investors. It also makes benchmarking, or comparing the performance of a given asset against a group of its peers, difficult if not impossible. This diminishes the attractiveness of microfinance investments because most commercial investors must prove to regulators and clients that they are making sound investment decisions.

Establishing MFI investments as an asset class is therefore important if commercial capital is to be forthcoming on any scale. It is also a necessary step towards identifying where MFI investments fit within investor asset allocation strategies, and towards defining the "universe" of potential investors.

MFIs as an Asset Class

The risk and return potential of a given investment is normally understood by comparing it to an established asset class benchmark. Benchmarks are useful tools that define the relative standards by which competing investments are judged. Most equity mutual funds in the United States, for example, use the Standard & Poor's (S&P) 500 as a benchmark. When assessing an investment, it is important to compare it against the appropriate benchmark. For example, comparing a bond fund to a small capital company stock index is not particularly meaningful because they have distinctly different risk levels. Categorising an asset class is therefore critical for understanding an investment's expected risk and return potential.

Because they are not a well-defined asset class, investments in MFIs do not fit into the framework governing commercial investor asset allocations. As a result, commercial investors considering an MFI investment have to judge MFIs on the basis of perceived risk rather than established asset class expectations. Perceptions vary greatly and are not particularly helpful in understanding the potential for commercial investment in microfinance.

When no particular benchmark is available, a fund manager would customarily compare the perceived risk associated with each MFI investment instrument to the *closest approximate* perceived asset class. This is technically confusing because asset classes are normally compared to benchmarks, not to one another (e. g., saying MFI debt is comparable to the risk of a small capital equity). Hence, comparisons are not intended to be technically correct, but rather to provide a general sense of how private investors may perceive asset class risk on their risk spectrum. This approach provides an idea of the potential of an MFI investment opportunity relative to the risk spectrum understood by conventional investors.

Francis Coleman[4] of Christian Brothers Investment Services used this approach to attempt to place mature and profitable investments in MFIs on an investment risk spectrum. (See Figures 1 and 2.) As imprecise an exercise as this may be, the results are instructive.

Coleman explains that among *developed country* investors, MFIs would be classed as an emerging market, small capital investment.[5] This implies that in addition to normal liquidity and business risk, microfinance involves country, currency, transfer and settlement risks. MFI debt would be viewed as less risky than equity, but still the equivalent of small capital company equity. MFI equity is at the extreme end of the risk spectrum, reflecting concerns about ownership, mission, corporate culture and simply a lack of familiarity between MFIs and capital markets. Investing in an MFI investment fund, such as MicroVest, BlueOrchard or LA-CIF, would be considered equivalent to intermediate bonds. An "AAA" S&P rating for a local currency MFI bond, such as that issued by Compartamos, may be considered the equivalent to an emerging market large capital equity. An unrated bond issue, or debt of an MFI would be classed as junk, and probably would not be considered by investors at all.

The typical range of investment choices available in developing countries makes the risk/reward profile of investments in MFIs more attractive than it would be for international investors. (See Figure 2.) Since domestic investors have more intimate knowledge of local economic environments and because none of the added risks of international transactions exist, MFI equity would probably be considered a risky small capital equity.[6] MFI debt would vary depending on the MFI, but a mature institution would probably be considered the equivalent of an intermediate bond.[7]

---

[4] Francis Coleman is Vice President of Christian Brothers Investment Services (CBIS). CBIS is a socially responsible asset management company that manages funds of US$ 4 billion for Catholic institutions. The analysis was given at a workshop on Socially Responsible Investment and MFIs held September 3, 2003 in Guatemala City. See Cheng, Julie and Marc de Sousa-Shields, "Microfinance and Socially Responsible Investment in Latin America," Workshop Report, Enterprising Solutions and the Inter-American Development Bank, Guatemala, September 2003, http://esglobal.com/resources.htm.

[5] The MFI asset classification is generalised and based on input from several social investment fund managers bound by regulatory and fiduciary compliance in the US and Europe.

[6] The size of a small capital company (measured by the amount of equity) varies by country. In a developing country, a small capital company may have less than US$ 10 million equity capital, whereas in the US it is often defined as a company having equity of less than US$ 500 million.

[7] MFIs may have considerable foreign currency exposure, which adds to the risk factors that investors would consider.

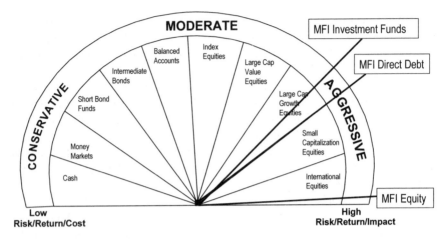

Figure 1. MFI Investment Perspective – Developed Country Investor

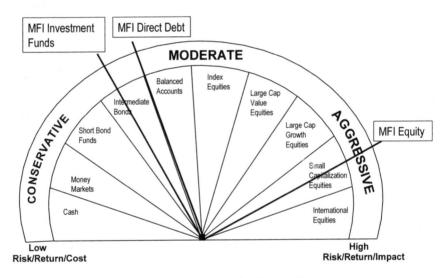

Figure 2. MFI Investment Perspective – Developing Country Investor

Asset Allocation and Commercial Investment

Commercial capital investment decision-making or asset allocation strategies follow fairly simple rules that balance return and income liquidity.[8] The relative importance of each is unique to every portfolio, but some generalisations apply.

---

[8] Liquidity is the ability to convert assets (in this case, MFI shares) into cash or cash equivalents.

In general, investors buy more lower-risk, higher-liquidity investments than higher-risk, lower-liquidity investments. As a result, the proportion of high-grade tradable securities in most large institutional portfolios is quite large, as it is in most individual portfolios. Fortunately for microfinance, asset allocations strategies are not about *reducing*, but rather *managing* risk. Each asset class has its appeal and a microfinance investment might find a place within any portfolio, large or small. Of course, asset allocations are different for each type of investor and they are also strongly affected by different economic conditions and regulatory and tax environments. Thus, the attractiveness of microfinance would vary by the type of investor.

An interesting feature of global investment is that, except for regulatory and macroeconomic studies of investment patterns, very little has been written about the investment decision-making patterns of developing country investors. Fortunately, basic asset allocation principles are not much different among countries. Thus, the probability that any of the common investor types listed below will consider or make investments in MFIs is much the same in a developing country as in a developed one. However, as noted, developing country investors are likely to consider investments in MFIs as being of less risk than international investors would, increasing their attractiveness locally.[9]

The following typology of commercial investors outlines typical asset allocation strategies and barriers that influence investments in MFIFs or directly in MFIs. Among the barriers, regulation and taxation issues strongly shape investment decisions.

Defined Liability and Institutional Funds

Defined liability and institutional funds include pension funds, insurance funds, trusts and other funds managed by or on behalf of a private institution. The pension fund assets of OECD countries exceed US$ 8 trillion. Insurance funds in the US control over US$ 3 trillion.[10] These funds invest in a wide variety of instruments, though regulation and fiduciary practice tend to limit most investment to high-grade, tradable securities.

Some very large funds buy higher risk assets, such as venture funds, private equity funds or emerging market investments. These purchases are used to offset risk posed by other assets in a portfolio and are typically part of well-defined risk diversification and decorrelation strategies. (Broadly, "decorrelation" refers to two conditions that investors believe exist: i) developing country markets and emerging markets are not correlated with the financial markets of developed countries;

---

[9] Lacking sufficient information on the investment patterns and habits of developing country investors, more investigation is required to build an effective case and strategy for encouraging more domestic investment in MFIs.

[10] For full statistics: see the Organization for Economic Co-operation and Development website: http://www.oecd.org/dataoecd/20/41/2768608.pdf.

ii) MFI performance suffers less or not at all from the economic environments that affect the fortunes of other financial institutions. Investing in emerging markets therefore offsets risk found in developed country investments.)

Only managers of very large portfolios would normally include a significant volume of high-risk investments. CalPERS, at US$ 146 billion the largest US pension fund, for example, invests around US$ 1.4 billion, or 1 percent of its portfolio in emerging markets.[11] Most are concentrated in South Korea, Taiwan, and other fairly well developed emerging markets. The combined total emerging market investment of 15 other large US pension funds, by contrast, is less than US$ 100 million. This reflects fiduciary practice that encourages defined liability funds to invest primarily in the market or currency of beneficiary liabilities. Transaction costs also limit higher-risk, specialty investments, such as investments in MFIs or MFI funds.[12] Larger funds also invest several millions of dollars in any single investment in order to reduce the relative costs of analysis and fiduciary compliance. Investments in MFIs are rarely this large.

Defined liability funds, including pension funds, are growing at a fast rate in developing country markets. They are subject to strict asset allocation regulations that often stipulate the exact quality and quantity of assets a fund may buy. Some countries restrict funds to purchasing government securities.[13] In many Latin American countries regulations are more liberal and most funds are able to buy a modest amount of high quality domestic tradable securities and smaller amounts of international securities.[14] This allowed Peruvian pension funds to buy MiBanco bonds that, with the help of guarantees from the International Finance Corporation (IFC) and the Corporación Andina de Fomento (CAF), were considered an acceptable, high-quality security. As in developed countries, however, defined liability funds will have a difficult time investing in MFIs without some form of guarantee until they become a defined asset class with an historical performance profile.

Publicly Available Funds

Publicly available funds must pass rigorous regulatory hurdles that permit them to sell to the general public. Mutual funds are the most common of this type.

---

[11] Data for 2003. See the CalPERS Annual Report at: https://www.calpers.ca.gov/mss-publication/pdf/xtCTINcuOVt0n_2003%20CAFR%20with%20art.pdf.

[12] Transaction costs include all expenses related to finding, assessing, managing and divesting or closing out an investment or loan.

[13] See Hanson, James A. (2003). Banking in Developing Countries in the 1990s, World Bank Policy Research Working Paper 3168, Washington, DC: World Bank.

[14] See Yermo, J., "Insurance and Private Pension Compendium for Emerging Economies, Book 2, Part 2:2a, Pension Funds in Latin America: Recent Trends and Regulatory Challenges." Organization for Economic Co-operation and Development, available at: http://www.oecd.org/document/28/0,2340,en_2649_201185_2742748_1_1_1_1,00.html.

They currently control over US$ 14.5 trillion in assets worldwide of which approximately US$ 6.5 trillion are held in the US. These funds primarily intermediate individual capital, but some is institutional capital. These funds invest in a wide variety of instruments, generally publicly traded securities. Asset allocation strategies are usually linked to a single asset class (for example, blue chip equities, bonds, small caps, etc.) geared to the market the strategy hopes to attract. The bulk of mutual funds invest in conservative bond or blue-chip equities. A much smaller number invest in higher-risk, small capital or specialty investments.

Mutual funds are bound by numerous rules regulating public offerings. In the US, for example, they must value at least 85 percent of their portfolio holdings daily. In theory, they can invest 15 percent in non-liquid investments, such as MFI opportunities. In practice, however, most funds want to value 100 percent of their holdings daily. There are exceptions: responsAbility, a new Luxembourg-registered, Swiss-based mutual fund dedicated to microfinance, has negotiated a special agreement with regulators to value their holdings monthly or quarterly. The US-based Calvert Foundation offers a "community investment note" that is publicly available. The notes are designed to pay a below-market rate of interest. Structured as promissory debt, these notes meet all federal and state registration requirements for public distribution.

The costs of launching and operating a publicly available MFI mutual fund is a second challenge, particularly for funds investing in businesses with limited market appeal. This is because a fund needs to amass US$ 50 million to US$ 75 million in assets within three years to be an attractive business proposition. Most fund managers do not believe they could achieve this size in microfinance due to the perceived risk level and difficulty of explaining a fairly complex investment.

As with managed money, public funds are also sensitive to transaction costs. In the mutual fund market, competition is so intense that most funds do not levy charges at the time of purchase. There are also tremendous pressures to charge the lowest possible management fees. As a result, complex investments in MFIs and related transactions are not affordable without great scale. Not surprisingly, responsAbility initially targets larger investments in other private funds investing in MFIs and potentially in very successful, large MFIs.

Public funds have a relatively short history in most developing country markets and tend to be available only where fairly large, upper middle class investor markets and relatively developed capital markets exist, as in Mexico, South Africa and Malaysia. Funds are typically conservative, favouring a mix of high-quality domestic and international tradable securities. Funds in these markets are subject to similar regulatory regimes and follow asset allocations similar to those found in developed markets. There are a small but growing number of social investment mutual funds in developing country markets. These funds, such as ABN AMRO's Fondo Ethical in Brazil, do not typically consider microfinance investments (even though, for example, ABN AMRO supports MFI activities).

Private Funds

Private funds are not approved by regulators for sale to the general public. Rather, they are sold privately to institutional investors such as pension, university and trust funds and persons with high net worth. These funds have a broad range of investments, often in medium- to high-risk instruments, such as private equity funds for strip malls and high-technology venture capital, or in specialised investment instruments such as hedge funds. Private funds are usually structured to fall within a single asset class and are bought by investors as part of their overall asset allocation strategies. Private funds are not heavily regulated and need only comply with their own prospectus and general business law.[15] Private funds often require minimum investments of several million dollars in order to maintain a low operating cost ratio.

Except for those private funds formed to invest in microfinance, few private funds would consider such an investment. Nonetheless, some small business emerging market venture funds and equity capital funds, including Avishkaar in India, have invested in MFIs. While a potentially interesting source of capital, local funds have not yet made significant investments in the microfinance sector.

There are also a handful of private MFIFs dedicated to investing in MFIs that operate in a manner consistent with private sector funds. They may be "house funds" linked to a specific network of MFIs, or they may have some of the characteristics of non-commercial funds. These are not discussed here because it is not yet clear, as a class, how commercial their operations really are.[16] Their owners include NGO support organisations, foundations, public sector banks and official agencies.

---

[15] A prospectus is a document disclosing specific financial information required by investment industry regulators (for example, the United States Securities and Exchange Commission). Companies issuing stocks or bonds, or selling mutual funds or other investment products to the public are required to provide a prospectus to investors prior to purchase. Regulations vary by instrument or investment (for example, the contents of a mutual fund prospectus is different from one for a bond issue or a new stock issue). The contents of a prospectus also vary by jurisdiction, though generally the same regulatory principles apply. For more information on this topic, see http://www.investorwords.com/cgi-bin/searchTerms.cgi?term= prospectus.

[16] Data on private funds are difficult to obtain because they are privately held and under no obligation to divulge business information to anyone other than their shareholders. Some organisations such as BlueOrchard, however, do provide regular information to the public.

Individual Investors

For convenience, individual investors can be divided into two types: i) those with modest portfolios; and ii) high net worth individuals (HNWI).[17] Individual investors place money in private and public funds, and invest directly in stocks and bonds through brokers. Asset allocation rules for both types of individual investors depend mostly on a person's age and portfolio size. Risk tolerance is generally negatively correlated with age and portfolio size. Thus, modest portfolios, or those under US$ 500,000, are reasonably conservative, consisting mostly of mutual funds, blue chip securities, high-yield bonds, and cash or cash equivalents. Due to the small size of most of their investments, owners of modest portfolios are usually risk averse and highly sensitive to transaction costs.

Asset allocations for HNWI are more sophisticated, and portfolio size allows for greater risk diversification into non-tradable investments such as MFIs. Investments of this sort vary widely and often reflect an investor's personal interests. They can include such things as luxury real estate, yachts, art collections, racehorses, or, in the case of social investors, organic farms, alternative energy holdings, and investments in MFIs. HNWI tend to be less sensitive to transaction costs, particularly when it comes to non-tradable hobby investments. However, given that HNWIs represent a small portion of the investor universe, and the large and diverse choice of investments competing for their funds, it is not surprising that there are not a large number of individuals investing in the microfinance sector.

In developing countries, HNWI place much of their investment portfolios in offshore, hard currency investments, making asset allocation decisions similar to those noted above. But both modest portfolio holders and HNWI also invest significantly in their own countries and often in small and medium-sized businesses. Typically, these businesses are owned by a family or by a small number of associates. Unfortunately, there is little information on the decision-making processes that result in these types of investments. As these are the investors with the greatest potential for investing in MFIs, research on how domestic investors decide which ventures merit equity investments could be of great benefit to microfinance.

---

[17] Accredited or sophisticated investors, including high net worth individuals (HWNI), institutional investors and certain other entities, are wealthy investors who have a net worth exceeding an amount specified by law. In the US, HNWI are those with over US$ 1 million in assets or over US$ 200,000 in income for more than two consecutive years. Definitions and regulations vary by jurisdiction, but HNWI are generally sufficiently knowledgeable about investments or can afford to pay for such information. Given their relative sophistication, institutional investors are free to suggest a much wider range of investment products and services than non-accredited investors. This means that any alternative investment, such as in MFIs or MFIFs, are potentially acceptable investment options for these investors.

Financial Institution Lenders

Banks and non-bank financial institutions make loans to businesses. Their main asset allocation considerations include loan portfolio management (such as diversification, pricing, terms, etc.), transaction costs, collateral and reserve requirements, and a host of other business and banking regulations. Banks regularly lend to businesses with risk-return profiles similar to those of MFIs, but normally do so only on the basis of long-established relationships and/or with full collateral coverage. Loan-loss reserve requirements increase as collateral coverage decreases, and this plays a large role in determining the attractiveness of the loan to the lender. As most MFIs cannot offer significant collateral and do not have long-standing relationships with banks, commercial bank loans are difficult to obtain. Even if an MFI can offer collateral, the lender may be frustrated by a typical MFI's inability to project cash flow. Most lenders are uninformed about the microfinance sector relative to the in-depth knowledge and data they have of other sectors.[18] Information barriers between commercial financial lenders and MFIs are indeed significant. A lack of supervision and rating of MFIs by "market approved" rating agencies, such as Fitch or Standard & Poor's, further compounds the market's lack of confidence in MFIs.

Depositors

Depositors' allocation decisions are distinctly different from those of other investors. There are five main elements influencing their decision on where to invest their savings: stability of the financial institution, yield (after inflation and fees), access, liquidity and the range of products offered by a deposit-taking institution. The relative importance of each depends on several factors, but the two most important are type of account and size of deposit.

Generally speaking, there are three types of savings accounts: passbook and demand, plus time deposits. Passbook and demand account holders typically favour liquidity over all other variables. Convenience, measured in the time and money needed to access an account, is also important. These considerations are exponentially important for low-income savers who comprise the bulk of MFI savers, while they are less important for higher-income passbook savers who want a range of complementary financial services that MFIs normally cannot provide (such as investment accounts and electronic banking). For time depositors, yield is typically the most important factor, followed by institutional stability. Liquidity, by definition, is less of a concern than convenience and ancillary services. The most important characteristic of time deposit savers is that they are highly rate sensitive and will switch institutions based on small interest rate differences.

---

[18] For a good overview see Schneider, Louise, "Strategies for Financial Integration: Access to Commercial Debt," Women's World Banking, Financial Products and Services Occasional Paper, Women's World Banking, New York, July 2004, p. 6.

Social Investors

Social investors seek both financial and social returns. Social investors are not a separate class. In fact, almost all (99.7 percent) of the US$ 2.8 trillion social investor funding worldwide is bound by the same fiduciary and securities laws that govern conventional investments. As a result, most funds specialising in socially responsible investing (SRI) are found in tradable securities, directed by asset allocation strategies remarkably similar to conventional investors. A comparison of the holdings of major SRI and non-SRI mutual fund companies, for example, could find the two sharing 80 percent of the same stocks.[19] This is because the great bulk of funds are held in screened portfolios that are managed to avoid only the worst companies doing what social investors consider offensive, such as selling tobacco or producing nuclear power.

Shareholder activists hold the next largest share of funds. They buy shares in companies they do not like with the explicit purpose of changing the business practices they regard as offensive. This is done through meetings with managers, via proxy resolutions at annual general meetings companies, or through publicity campaigns.

Social investors' unique strategies and those used by conventional investors determine involvement in MFI-like investments, limiting them to a narrow set of conditions: i) strong investor interest, creating great demand; ii) acceptable legal status of the investment; iii) attractive and achievable potential return; and iv) consistency with asset allocation strategies.

While these conditions are fairly restrictive, social investors have something their conventional counterparts do not: a natural predisposition to consider MFI-like investments. In fact, a survey of social investment professionals in 2002 indicated a strong interest in microfinance or equivalent investments in developing countries. While this appetite has yet to be tapped, similar impulses have led social investors to invest US$ 14 billion in MFI-like investments in developed countries. As much as an estimated US$ 120 million of social investment capital has been placed in MFIs.[20] In these cases, however, investors have received some form of tax incentive or have accepted below-market rates of return. It is important to note that asset allocation strategies of social investors in both developed and developing countries have permitted very few investments in MFIs. Part of the reason for this is that social investors' asset allocation strategies in developed countries largely exclude investments in developing countries. In fact, only about 0.1 percent of total SRI assets, or US$ 1.5 billion, has found its way to emerging markets. This limitation alone poses significant challenges to MFI funding by SRI.

---

[19] For a full treatment on social investment, see "Sustainable and Responsible Investment in Emerging Markets" by Enterprising Solutions, published by the International Finance Corporation (IFC) in 2003.

[20] Enterprising Solutions Global Consulting, "Social Investment, Microfinance & SMEs, The Potential for Social Investment in MFIs and SMEs in Developing Countries," Enterprising Solutions Brief No. 3, www.esglobal.com.

Social investors face many barriers to investments in MFIs. First, as noted, while demand appears to be significant, few social investment firms have the resources to develop a specialised instrument for microfinance. Second, even though there is demand, it is not clear to many social investment advisors that they could recommend an emerging market small business investment to any other than high net worth individuals. Third, few if any of the specialty funds available to social investors offer commercial terms, which are required by the great majority of social investors.

Summary – The Able and Willing

Asset allocation strategies and regulation combine to limit dramatically the universe of possible private sector investments in MFIs, *even before the quality of the asset is discussed*. The small amount that could legally be invested in MFI-like assets is further reduced by the absence of widely accepted benchmarks and/or ratings from credible rating agencies. Transaction costs and the difficulty of understanding an MFI investment also limit the availability of funding.

Investors in MFIs must be highly risk tolerant, particularly patient, able to absorb high transaction costs and free of regulatory concerns. Internationally, that would be high net worth individuals who are also socially responsible investors with an interest in both emerging market and community investments. Socially responsible institutional investors may also have an interest, but as with conventional investors, they fear unknown risks, high transaction costs and concerns about compliance with their fiduciary responsibilities.

The bottom line is that without simple, convenient investment offerings, few developed country investors will have the courage to invest in MFIs. Some sort of guarantee could attract institutional investors, social or otherwise, but only if transaction costs are tolerable compared to other competing investments. Otherwise, investments in MFIs are likely to come from social investor charitable fund allocations, from funds they can afford to lose entirely, from funding that will accept low rates of return, or when guarantees or subsidies are in place to offset risk or ensure a certain level of returns.

Developing country markets have good immediate and long-term potential to stimulate local investments. Local investors do not face the added risks inherent in international investment and have a clearer idea of local economic risks. MFIs may also offer a relatively more attractive risk-reward profile than competing local investment opportunities. Certainly, local high net worth investors should be interested if they are informed of appropriate opportunities. Some institutional investors could be attracted if guarantee programmes are in place for widely available instruments having low transaction costs, such as bond issues. A number of commercial banks have financed MFIs. They could do so increasingly with incentives such as tax and regulatory changes, and access to guarantee funds such as USAID's Development Credit Authority (DCA). For local interest to be cultivated and tapped, better information about microfinance is of great importance.[21] But even when investors are fully informed of the risk and return potential of MFI investing, local securities and banking regulations discourage domestic investors' interest.

References

CalPERS Annual Report: https://www.calpers.ca.gov/mss-publication/pdf/xtCTIN-cuOVt0n_2003%20CAFR%20with%20art.pdf

Cheng, Julie and Marc de Sousa-Shields, "Microfinance and Socially Responsible Investment in Latin America," Workshop Report, Enterprising Solutions and the Inter-American Development Bank, Guatemala, September 2003, http://esglobal.com/resources.htm

Enterprising Solutions, "Sustainable and Responsible Investment in Emerging Markets," Washington DC: International Finance Corporation (IFC), 2003.

Enterprising Solutions Global Consulting, "Social Investment, Microfinance & SMEs, The Potential for Social Investment in MFIs and SMEs in Developing Countries," Enterprising Solutions Brief No. 3, www.esglobal.com

Hanson, James A., "Banking in Developing Countries in the 1990s," World Bank Policy Research Working Paper 3168, Washington, DC: World Bank, 2003.

Investor Words.com, http://www.investorwords.com/cgi-bin/searchTerms.cgi?term=prospectus

Organization for Economic Co-operation and Development, http://www.oecd.org/dataoecd/20/41/2768608.pdf

Schneider, Louise, "Strategies for Financial Integration: Access to Commercial Debt," Women's World Banking, Financial Products and Services Occasional Paper, Women's World Banking, New York, July 2004.

Sousa-Shields, Marc de and Cheryl Frankiewicz and others, "Financing Microfinance Institution: The Context for Transitions to Private Capital," microreport #8, Accelerated Microenterprise Advancement Project (AMAP) of USAID. Washington DC: December 2004, www.microLINKS.org

Yermo, Juan, "Insurance and Private Pension Compendium for Emerging Economies," Book 2, Part 2:2a, Pension Funds in Latin America: Recent Trends and Regulatory Challenges. Paris: Organization for Economic Co-operation and Development. c. 2000.

---

[21] While still nascent, social investment is growing in many developing countries. In South Africa, for example, there is over US$ 1.2 billion in domestic SRI assets, much of which is held in community development investments, including financial service companies. SRI movements are also growing rapidly in Asia and, to a lesser extent, in Latin America and other parts of Africa.

CHAPTER 7

Investing in Microfinance Investment Funds – Risk Perspectives of a Development Finance Institution

Margarete Biallas[1] and Mark Schwiete[2]

[1] Senior Risk Manager, Risk Management, KfW Bankengruppe
[2] Principal Sector Economist, KfW Entwicklungsbank

Why Funds?

KfW Entwicklungsbank has a long history of supporting microfinance through funding and technical assistance. Apart from KfW funds, Financial Cooperation funding supplied by the German Federal Ministry for Economic Cooperation and Development (BMZ) is invested directly in MFIs. These BMZ funds are concessional or grant funds. Funding, usually in the form of debt, was initially made available through existing financial institutions that were willing to make smaller loans (downscaling). In a second phase KfW began to support specialised institutions, using two different methods. The first was upgrading, that is, transforming nonbank microfinance lending organisations into full-fledged financial service providers. The second approach was to establish new specialised financial institutions (greenfielding).[1] In a third, subsequent phase, KfW has provided further support for the development of microfinance by investing in microfinance investment funds (MFIFs).

In down-scaling projects, debt is made available to micro, small and medium-sized enterprises (MSMEs) through financial institutions with a well-established track record and the capacity to service the loans made by KfW. Initially, funding was provided exclusively against a sovereign guarantee of the recipient country, which was generally the common and sole hard structural element of these facilities. With the introduction of new debt instruments, funding became more flexible. Sovereign guarantees are of lesser importance and in some instances are no longer required, while risk considerations have become much more important.

---

[1] For a more detailed description of KfW's approaches s. Glaubitt/Hagen/Schütte in this volume.

The credit risk of down-scaled institutions has generally been mitigated through a high degree of portfolio diversification. In addition, the portfolio has been used to collateralise the loan. This has proven to be a very effective form of collateral. Even if the institution itself has failed, the portfolio pledged to KfW usually continues to perform if repossessed quickly enough. Other comforts include guarantees, additional collateral and/or pari passu clauses with other present or future investors. While the risks of down-scaling are controllable for an investor, returns are limited. Also, some countries lack financial institutions with sufficient down-scaling potential.

Specialised financial institutions have a larger developmental impact than conventional institutions, but a similar risk-return profile. As noted, such specialised institutions usually have a track record and receive debt or equity funding to increase portfolio build-up or for transformation into a formal, regulated financial institution. While investments in specialised institutions are associated with much the same risks as in the down-scaling approach, their magnitude is generally more pronounced because funding tends to represent a significant share of their overall liabilities. In addition further risks may emerge from rapid portfolio growth and the management challenges that result.

Most risks of investments in individual microfinance institutions (MFIs) lie in inadequate management information systems or mismanagement, such as failure to realise collateral, lack of monitoring or fraud. These risks are mainly contained through corporate governance. Defaults by any single retail borrower do not constitute a risk to the viability of the potential investee because investments are focused on MFIs with well-diversified, high quality portfolios.

Risks in equity funding centre on exit and on return on investment because potential buyers are hard to identify and returns are often not continuous due to irregular dividend payments. Institutional risks are also higher and, as noted, have to be addressed through strong involvement in corporate governance. The main instruments of risk mitigation are documentation, ensuring significant influence by the individual investor in the investee company, and special shareholder rights for development finance institutions (DFIs). Equity investments are generally required when creating specialised financial institutions. In addition to the risks of similar investments in existing institutions, risks and costs of investments in these institutions include the ability to find and train sufficient staff, to build institutional capacities and to ensure market penetration and acceptance. Few of these risks can be mitigated through commercial structuring, and once again require strong involvement in corporate governance, which ties up substantial resources and subjects the DFI to reputational risk.

In this context, provision of technical assistance (TA) to the investee portfolio company is a risk mitigation instrument. As agents funding the TA, the DFI has control over the TA provider, and thus can develop in-depth insight into the performance of the MFI. Also, some non-commercial risks such as market penetration, product design, and human resource development may be addressed through TA, which is within the framework of German Financial Cooperation provided by BMZ through KfW.

Relatively low investment volumes and comparatively high costs in upgrading and greenfielding diminish the risk-return of the investment profile. All of the above considerations have led to a greater focus on funds and wholesale vehicles such as AIM, GMF, LACIF, LFI, and ProCredit Holding AG, all described in Table 1 below. By supporting these funds, KfW Entwicklungsbank:

- promotes the MFI sector, helping it to mature by reaching even smaller institutions,

- increases the development impact by extending its outreach,

- realises economies of scale that result in a more favourable risk-return investment profile.

In addition, investments in MFIFs can create successful public-private partnerships (Köhn/Jainzik 2005; Glaubitt/Hagen/Schütte in this volume).

Investment Considerations

KfW Entwicklungsbank's investment strategy includes diversification of its exposure and limitation of its risk. Decisions to invest in MFIFs are based on a number of criteria, such as:

- target group orientation and target markets,

- quality of fund management,

- products offered by the fund,

- ability to leverage capital,

- sustainability, and

- additionality.

While the first three of these factors directly influence the risk profile of the fund, the latter three permit an assessment of development impact. Based on these considerations KfW has invested in the six MFIFs listed in Table 1.

In KfW's experience, the structure of a fund largely depends on the types of investment products it offers. Typical structures include managed accounts, special purpose vehicles (SPVs) and wholesale institutions or holding companies. The products offered in turn influence KfW's investment decision and the selection of the investment instrument. Clearly, equity funds will require mainly equity capital, while debt funds may largely be debt funded. Yet both debt funds and equity funds invest mostly in countries that are far below an investment grade rating. Accordingly, they cannot be financed wholly by straight debt, but will require more sophisticated financial structures that include loss cushions and possibly mezzanine

Table 1. Features of microfinance investment funds supported by KfW

Fund Name	Sponsor	Instruments Offered by Fund	Target Market	Clients
AIFH	Wendy P. Abt	Privatisation*	Sub-Saharan Africa	State banks
AIM	ACCION	Debt Equity	Latin America Sub-Saharan Africa	MFIs Commercial banks Greenfield MFIs
GMF	Cyrano	Debt	Worldwide	MFIs Commercial banks
LA-CIF	Cyrano	Debt	Latin America	MFIs Commercial banks
LFI	Horus	Debt Equity	Sub-Saharan Africa Asia	Greenfield MFIs
ProCredit Holding AG	IPC	Equity	Eastern Europe Latin America Sub-Saharan Africa	Banks of ProCredit Network

* AIFH is a fund that bids for state banks that are offered for privatisation in Sub-Saharan Africa with the objective of turning the banks around to become profitable and utilising their deposit base and network to introduce micro lending and other services for rural communities. 70% of KfW's equity investment is contributed by BMZ through Financial Cooperation funds. AIFH = African International Financial Holding; AIM = ACCION Investments in microfinance; GMF = Global Microfinance Facility; LA-CIF = Latin American Challenge Investment Fund; LFI = La Fayette Investissement.

tranches. Compared to loan products, equity and quasi-equity instruments require greater structuring to offset their greater risk. Similar arguments hold for newer funds as the trend is towards providing a mix of funding instruments to portfolio companies, such as:

- equity,
- subordinated debt,
- loans,
- term deposits,
- subscriptions to bond issues,
- guarantees and
- syndicated loans.

This in turn makes it possible for DFIs to employ a mix of investment products. This combination also leads to a more favourable risk-return profile for the investor.

Investors' Risks and Issues in the Structuring of Funds

Investors in funds face multiple risks with varying degrees of mitigation. Among the commercial risks are: liquidity, loan portfolio and asset quality, profitability, market penetration and investors' return. These may be addressed through structuring elements such as investment limits, incentive structures for the fund management, down-side floors and waterfalls or up-side participations, all of which are explored below.

Operational and qualitative risks include: quality and transparency of financial information, audit and internal control processes, management quality, strategic direction, market position as well as support. They can be addressed through good corporate governance as discussed later in this chapter.

The Concept of Limits

While an individual MFI's business model may enable it to create an extremely diversified portfolio, a limit system is required to ensure that an MFIF has at least a minimum degree of portfolio diversification. Limits are expressed as a percentage of total capital and include the maximum investment allowed in any single MFI, in a single country, and also in a single region in order to reduce spill-over risks from neighbouring countries. A fund is always less diversified than an MFI, but this disadvantage can be more than offset by spreading its investments globally or regionally, thus realising diversification possibilities not available to MFIs and mitigating portfolio risks while increasing development impact. Examples of such investment limits are:

- no more than 10 % of the portfolio may be invested in any single MFI,

- no more than 20 % of the portfolio may be invested in any single country,

- no more than 40 % of the portfolio may be invested in any specific region,

- no investment may be made in an MFI that exceeds 50 % of the net worth of the MFI.

For funds employing both debt and equity, additional limits, such as not more than 60 % of the portfolio invested in equity instruments, could make the commercial risks more manageable and provide stable returns.

In addition, minimum targets can be used to encourage specific products. In the example below the fund's objective is to provide local currency liquidity while achieving satisfactory portfolio diversification. An example for such a target would be:

- At least 20 % of the fund portfolio must consist of credit enhancement or local currency instruments.

Monitoring adherence to these limits is largely the task of the manager, whose performance is crucial to the success of a fund. Accordingly, risks of inadequate performance by the manager have to be addressed.

Management Risks

Investment funds of all types face the risk of mismanagement. To control this risk, funds apply structuring arrangements that provide performance incentives to the manager. These may include direct risk exposure through shares or notes held by the manager, methods of calculating fees, bonuses, waterfall and performance targets, and limited term contracts that provide for exit or renewal.

Some of these measures are usually adapted to the specific situation of the MFIF. For example, most funds must mobilise additional capital to reach critical mass, and incentives can be designed to encourage capital growth. At the same time investors such as DFIs or other dual objective investors who seek financial returns and social impact want to see their funds invested quickly, making rapid growth important. The management fee in this case might be calculated as a combination of a percentage of capital committed and a percentage of funds invested at a given point in time (i.e. the end of a fiscal year) sequenced over the first three years of the life of the fund.

Bonuses are a popular incentive all over the world. They may be calculated on the basis of net income and/or the achievement of certain portfolio objectives. Either of these may be structured in a linear manner or increased incrementally as targets are met. If exceptional flexibility is required to react to changes in volatile environments, targets may be agreed on an annual basis. However, in closed funds, additional restrictions may be appropriate to reduce investors' commercial risks. To ensure that the initial capital of the fund is not eroded, bonuses should be paid only if accumulated retained earnings plus capital are at least equal to the fund's initial capitalisation. Otherwise any net income should first be used to replenish the initial capital, which is a waterfall device. A strong incentive is to require the manager to pay a penalty calculated as a percentage of the shortfall.

Performance targets are essential for calculation of a bonus. All management contracts for MFI investments by KfW, whether through MFIFs or direct investments in MFIs, have performance targets. Performance indicators include:

- net income,

- profitability,

- portfolio quality (PAR – portfolio at risk),

- portfolio growth,

- cost of fund management and

- quantity and quality of staff.

These targets are monitored on a quarterly basis. Performance measurement against these targets and exposing the fund manager directly to the risk of the fund through an equity stake together constitute a major risk mitigation tool.

Finally, provisions should be made to terminate any management contract. A contract would generally have a fixed initial term and be renewable thereafter. Termination requires a cause and a notice period of no less than 30 days.

Downside Floors

For the majority of funds the withdrawal of an investor is problematic. Investors therefore reduce their risk through a downside floor, that is, through special rights that permit them to wind up the fund in the event of non-performance. From a structuring point of view, winding up is most easily achieved in debt funds because the assets may be sold or liquidated relatively quickly. Winding up an equity fund is more difficult: exit may take well over a year.

For example, the Global Microfinance Facility (GMF) includes provisions that enable the senior and mezzanine creditors to wind up the Facility. The senior lenders may exercise their right of cancellation if accumulated net losses (calculated in accordance with international accounting standards – IAS) are in excess of US$ 5 million, while mezzanine lenders can request acceleration of payment if accumulated net losses are in excess of US$ 6 million. The capital structure and the current asset size of GMF enables the senior lenders to request accelerated payment before any of their funds are at risk, while mezzanine lenders have a downside floor of 50 % of their total investment.

The AIM equity fund also has a provision for winding up if the fund fails to invest or commit to invest at least 50 % of the total commitments as of the third anniversary of the initial commitment, or if a majority of the shareholders approve a resolution for winding up. In the event that the fund is wound up, the board and holders of the majority of shares outstanding must approve a liquidation plan according to a divestment strategy under which the manager distributes all assets to the shareholders. If the divestment is successful, the investors would receive cash for shares redeemed by the fund. However, if the divestment strategy permits, a portion may be redeemed through in-kind payments. This option would be used only if divestment were not feasible within a reasonable period of time.

Waterfall Principles

Commercial risks may also be reduced by waterfall structures, consisting of several cascades that regulate the order of payment and distribution of profits. During the life of the fund, first priority is usually given to payment of operating expenses and fund management fees, subject to the restrictions noted above. Next in line, funds available for interest and dividend payments as well as reimbursement of capital are then distributed among the different classes of note or shareholders and usually also provide upside participation for investors bearing higher risks. The waterfall structure of GMF is complex because of the number of different classes of investors.

At the winding up of the fund, payments will be made in a prescribed order of priority and to the extent of available cash. An example of such an order for a structure including different classes of shares/notes could include the following ranking:

1. direct operating expenses of the special purpose vehicle,

2. management fee,

3. senior tranche interest and principal,

4. mezzanine tranche interest and principal,

5. management bonus,

6. junior tranche to the extent of their initial capital contributions,

7. common shareholders to the extent of their initial capital contributions,

8. return equivalent to 8 % IRR for the junior tranche, and

9. 40 % of all remaining residual or retained earnings to the mezzanine tranche and 60 % to the junior tranche.

This structure gives mezzanine investors an upside for the additional risk they take relative to those of senior investors. It also provides an upside for the greatest risk taker, the junior lender.

Similar waterfalls may be used in pure equity funds having different classes of shares, as will be the case in the European Fund for Southeast Europe (EFSE) (Ziller in this volume). If no dividend payments are made during the life of the fund, with earnings retained as cash reserves or to increase net worth, the waterfall will regulate the distribution of capital among the different classes at the end of the life of the fund. Since the manager generally holds some of the equity, the manager would be served last under any such waterfall.

Investing Liquid Funds

Investments other than those in portfolio companies or MFIs can provide additional income to the fund. However, the fund's management might be tempted to invest in high yield instruments bearing substantial risks. Liquidity limits and qualitative restrictions are used to deal with these possibilities. Minimum standards are usually applied to cash balances, which may be invested only in short-term first class instruments issued in OECD member countries by governments, banks, or by corporations with a rating of "P-1" or higher according to Moody's Investors Service or comparable rating agency. In addition, cash balances may be held in standard money market accounts in an OECD member country commercial bank that meets specific quality requirements.

Sales of Participations

DFI investors are selective in engaging co-investors. They have two concerns in this respect. The first is reputational risk. The second is protecting the original mission of the investment, which is microfinance. Generally, sales of participations to investment grade investors are considered acceptable if the objective is and will remain microfinance.

Due to these concerns, disposal of shares is normally restricted. An example of such a restriction is the limitation of share transfers to initial shareholders only for the first five years. Any other, exceptional transfers would have to be backed by agreement on all terms of the initial arrangement. Thereafter, existing shareholders might be given *preferential rights* to subscribe to issues of new shares. Other share transfer restrictions include but are not limited to *pre-emptive rights*, that are rights of first refusal for any transfer of shares, or by *tag along rights* requiring that shareholders willing to sell have to ensure that the buyer is prepared to buy all shares of this class on the same terms and conditions as originally offered to the potential seller. In addition, *piggyback rights* would give each shareholder the right to include its shares in any public offering. Rarely, however, would agreements include all of these restrictions.

Corporate Governance

Corporate governance of MFIFs may be less important in controlling risk than it is in direct investments in MFIs. But participation in governance remains a focus of DFIs because it allows some control of investment policy and procedures. Some DFIs will be satisfied by board representation, while others, mostly those with large exposures, want to exercise additional control through membership in investment committees. Depending on the requirements of the investors and of the group of investors, the number of bodies included in a governance structure and their importance may vary.

AIM has one of the most complex corporate governance structures providing a large number of checks and balances:

- The *assembly of shareholders* has control over the winding-up of the fund, mergers, acquisitions, termination of the management agreement and overall investment policies.

- The *board of directors* is the main decision making body and consists of investors or a group of investors who subscribe US$ 2.0 million in capital. It is responsible for the overall management of the fund.

- The *investment committee*, composed of representatives of the three largest shareholders, reviews portfolio investments recommended by the manager. If it unanimously approves an investment, the board of directors is notified. If the investment committee approves an investment by a less than unanimous vote, that investment decision must be reviewed and approved by the board. The board may also request a full review and approval of any investment. Divestment decisions are also reviewed by the investment committee.

- The *compliance committee* is composed of three persons, each of whom is nominated by one of the shareholders who have made the fourth, fifth and sixth largest commitments, other than the manager. It reviews asset and share valuations. It considers conflicts of interest and any other matters put to it by the board of directors or the investment committee. In effect it exercises control over the actions of the investment committee and the board of directors.

- The *donor committee* was established in connection with a TA facility. It is composed of two permanent members representing the original donors. The permanent members may select up to three additional members to represent donors that subsequently become parties to the TA facility. The donor committee decides on TA requirements proposed by the manager in conjunction with an investment.

Well-structured documentation requirements for each investment made by the fund also mitigate risk, ensuring a constant and sufficient flow of information to the investors. More importantly, documentation requirements exert discipline on the fund management by defining minimum standards for the analysis, evaluation and monitoring of individual investments and also by monitoring the manager according to performance standards. Documentation must include details on the type of instrument, the type of contract, amount of the transaction, currency, interest rate (nominal and effective), etc., as well as information on the project environment. A best-practise example of reporting requirements agreed upon by a group of like-minded DFIs (development finance institutions) investing in funds is attached as Annex 1.

In addition, TA (technical assistance) funds for portfolio companies are perceived as a major risk mitigant by allowing the fund to influence the policy and performance of the investee MFI in the same manner as for investments in individual MFIs as noted earlier.

Exits

Besides the question of how funds exit their investments, the question of how DFIs can exit the funds remains one of the biggest unresolved challenges. Generally preferred exits are: (a) a public listing of the fund or IPO (initial public offering), (b) a private sale of the original investors' shares in the fund, or (c) sales of the fund's investments and winding up the fund, with repayment of the share capital, including any retained earnings, to the shareholders according to their respective stakes.

IPOs are not currently feasible because markets for MFI equity are not sufficiently developed. At the same time the group of potential private investors is not sufficiently large for direct sales. Thus, shareholders must be prepared to hold their shares for an indefinite period. Even if both options already existed, it could be difficult to ensure that the focus on microfinance is perpetuated. For example, Citibank intends to invest in MFIs in Mexico. Will this result in mission drift or will Citibank be willing to engage in microfinance?

The last of the three options, winding up, is therefore the most likely to occur. Yet winding up is not consistent with the common objective of all DFIs to provide funds to MFIs in an efficient manner and to promote the sustainability of the industry.

Developing reliable exit mechanisms and instruments will therefore clearly be a focus of further DFI activities in microfinance. Towards this end contacts with financial institutions such as Commerzbank, already a big investor in microfinance, have been established.[2]

Conclusion

1. **KfW Entwicklungsbank's major risk reduction tool in MFI finance has been its ability to influence individual investments.** This is done by structuring its investments in funds and by its ability to control funds' investment policy. This resulted in an initial focus on equity funds and direct involvement in their governing structures.

2. **KfW Entwicklungsbank's strategy is to reduce its involvement in governance only as risk is reduced.** KfW therefore seeks to obtain sufficient comfort by guiding the actual fund structure. In this respect, GMF constitutes KfW's second generation of MFIFs because its mezzanine structure greatly reduces exit risks, with strong portfolio diversification to reduce portfolio risks while also providing an acceptable return. This, and the positive experience with GMF so far, will allow KfW to reduce its governance involvement in future funds having a similar structure. Also, as a debt fund GMF should be more successful in leveraging private capital than closed

---

[2] For an overview of the question of exit see also Köhn/Jainzik in this volume. They argue that the discussion of exit should include a review of the reasons why DFIs have invested in microfinance, whether these objectives have been achieved and, if not, whether private investors will continue to provide microfinance services to the original target group of clients.

funds funded mainly with equity, making this structure even more attractive to an investor such as KfW.

3. **Experiences with investors in funds show that public as well as institutional investors are still vitally important.** Public funding such as through BMZ's financial cooperation is required for first loss cushions, while institutional investors such as KfW Entwicklungsbank and other DFIs will pick up the mezzanine tranches or even the senior portion. This conclusion is consistent with the design of the GMF, where the structure provides substantial comfort for private capital in the form of a 50% risk cushion and cancellation rights when this is cushion depleted. Nevertheless, only one private investor, Crédit Coopératif, came forward during the first year the Facility was in operation.

4. **It is always possible to find private investors, but this requires intensive searches and has rarely brought more than two or three investors** investing US$ 500,000 or US$ 1 million each. While this is more than laudable, it does not constitute a substantial flow of private capital to MFI lending in lesser developed countries. Combined efforts, good results by existing funds and more sophisticated financing instruments will certainly engage private investors. But they will surely come as a complement to DFIs, not as a substitute for them. If private capital were willing to invest substantially in MFI assets, the exit problem would disappear.

5. Once private capital readily flows into these particular assets, **DFIs can shift their focus towards creating and developing new assets which** private investors are not yet willing to accept, as their risk-return profile is currently not known. This suggests that more structured funds are likely to be created.

Outlook and Trends

We are convinced that the future trend will follow two main paths:

- a growing number of more sophisticated structured funds similar to GMF and
- the emergence of pure public retail funds.

The objective of investors such as KfW Entwicklungsbank is and will continue to be the leveraging of private capital. In the short term more institutional investors will become involved. It clearly should be possible to provide attractive results to dual objective investors in microfinance while limiting their risk exposure. Lessons from GMF indicate that tenors of notes should be shortened and transferability should be easier. Clearly, private institutional investors have an interest in debt funding and possibly in contingent liabilities. Last but not least, a marketing campaign directed at asset managers should be implemented in order to create a better understanding of microfinance and its risks.

With due consideration of these experiences, KfW Entwicklungsbank is currently working on a number of funds that employ public or grant resources as first loss cushions, with KfW investing in mezzanine pieces, and offering senior tranches to private investors. In Southeast Europe such funds have evolved out of revolving facilities managed by KfW Entwicklungsbank. Here, the track record of investment performance should make the underlying assets more palatable to private capital. In a second step and given a volume of approximately € 500 million, ratings of the individual debt tranches will be possible.

In instances where KfW is less likely to find private investors, new structures could take the form of wholesale funds for a country or region. The initial structure would consist of two classes of assets consisting of a first-loss cushion and a second tranche. A third or senior class could possibly be added as the fund proves its ability to perform and as new interest develops from private sources of capital. The second tranche would thereby become a mezzanine tranche. The maturity of the senior tranche would be significantly shorter than the maturity of the mezzanine tranche.

In higher risk markets, public or grant funds would be invested in the equity of a wholesale fund, allowing DFIs to enter as senior lenders until a track record is established, at which time the DFIs may be replaced by local institutional investors.

Almost all existing funds are wholesale funds that could be described as closed shop investment companies. Their creation allows DFIs to realise efficiency gains that complement their support to individual MFIs. Yet, their structure is still fairly complex and their foundation is a lengthy process. The transaction costs of setting up these funds, of transferring shares or of bringing in additional investors remain on the high side. Investing in these funds therefore makes sense only if bigger amounts are at stake. For "ordinary" private individuals potentially willing to invest a couple of hundreds or even thousands of Euros, these funds are a no go.

Funds for microfinance can be significantly leveraged only if individual investors are enlisted on a broad scale. This requires the emergence of public retail funds like the responsAbility Global Microfinance Fund. These funds contain only very limited equity. Investments take the form of special assets through the sale of investment certificates either directly or distributed by co-operating banks. The investors will have no role in corporate governance. As in any other retail fund, they will be able to purchase and resell certificates only at prices officially announced on a daily basis. Due to the investment guidelines of these funds and their fairly high liquidity reserves, their certificates could be regarded as risky but also fairly liquid, assuming that transactions involve only a limited number of certificates. For MFIFs this type of fund will usher in a new era, representing a newer generation of funds. The emergence of this next generation of funds should be most welcome.

References

Allen, Franklin and Gale Douglas (2005): Systemic Risk and Regulation, CFS Conference on Risk Transfer between (Re-)Insurers, Banks and Markets

Allen, Franklin and Gale Douglas (1994): Financial Innovation and Risk Sharing. Cambridge, MA: MIT Press

Arping, Stefan (2004): Credit Protection and Lending Relationships, EFA Maastricht Meetings Paper No. 4551

Chiesa, Gabriella (2005): Risk Transfer, Lending Capacity and Real Investment Activity, CFS Conference on Risk Transfer between (Re-)Insurers, Banks and Markets

Draghi, Mario, Giavazzi Francesco and Merton Robert (2004): Transparency, Risk Management and International Financial Fragility, International Centre for Monetary and Banking Studies

Franke, Günter and Jan Pieter Krahnen (2005): Default Risk Sharing between Banks and Markets: The Contribution of Collateralized Debt Obligations, CFS Working Paper No. 2005/06

Glaubitt, Klaus, Hanns Martin Hagen and Haje Schütte: Mainstreaming Microfinance – Quo Vadis Microfinance Investments?, in this volume

Goodman, Patrick (2005): Microfinance Investment Funds: Objectives, Players, Potential; in this volume.

Köhn, Doris, and Michael Jainzik (2005): Microfinance Investment Funds – An Innovative Form of PPP to Foster the Commercialisation of Microfinance, in Matthäus-Maier, Ingrid, and J.D. von Pischke, eds., EU Accession – Financial Sector Opportunities and Challenges for Southeast Europe, Berlin/Heidelberg/New York: Springer.

Köhn, Doris and Michael Janzik: Sustainability in Microfinance – Visions and Versions for Exit by Development Finance Institutions, in this volume

Parlour, Christine and Guillaume Plantin (2005): Credit Risk Transfer, Pittsburgh, PA

Ziller, Dominik: The European Fund for Southeast Europe – An Innovative Instrument for Political and Economic Stabilisation, in this volume

Annex

REPORTING TEMPLATE for FUND MANAGERS

Good structured documentation requirements on the fund and for each investment ensure a constant and sufficient flow of information to the investors. They also exert discipline on the fund management by monitoring the manager and evaluating his performance.

The following template is designed to be a best practice example of reporting requirements for funds. It has been discussed amongst a group of like-minded donors with fund investment experience and reflect what we all would expect from a good professional fund manager. Of course, the template should be modified to reflect the characteristics of the respective fund.

---

1. Basic Fund Data

Reporting Frequency:

- After first closing, and thereafter as new information requires

Information:

1. Fund FY end
2. Fund reporting currency
3. Date of first closing and vintage year
4. Domicile, legal form and structure
5. Investment focus by stage and geography
6. Fund milestones:
   - Dates of first and final closings
   - Date of end of investment period, with extensions if any
   - Date of end of fund life, with extensions if any
7. Core investors (those with >=5 %)
8. Corporate governance:
   - Names of members of Advisory or other governing Board
   - Names of members of Investment Committee
   - Names of members of other committees
   - Change of key personnel in fund manager
   - Change of 20 % or more in ownership of the fund management
   - Name of auditor
   - List of other funds under management

Other material changes or events not noted above.

---

2. Summary of Fund Activity

Frequency:

- Level One: semi-annually
- Level Two: quarterly during investment period, then semi-annually

Information:

1. Total commitments; dates & amount of later increases and decreases
2. Total amount drawn and total amount remaining to be drawn
3. Total amount invested since inception and during current reporting period
4. Total amount realised since inception and during current reporting period
5. Total distributions to investors since inception and during current reporting period
6. Total amount of undrawn capital reserved, allocated or reserved or committed for follow-on investments
7. Cash multiple and gross IRR of the fund, including all investments, fees and other cash flows to and from investees and including the valuation of securities distributed to investors, but excluding unrealised gains and losses
8. Gross IRR of the fund, calculated on the same basis as the cash multiple
9. Gross IRR of the fund, including write-offs and all investments, fees and other cash flows to and from investees, treating current valuations as terminal value
10. Net IRR to investors, using all cash flows to the fund from investors and from the fund to investors, including fees, expenses, and amounts drawn for investments; calculated with and without current valuations as terminal value
11. Pipeline:
    - # of proposals undergoing due diligence
    - # of proposals presented to investment committee
    - # of proposals approved
    - # of investments made
12. Description of all defaults and opt-outs

Commentary:

1. Co-investments made by fund investors
2. Key man events and personnel changes at the partner level
3. Opening or closing of fund offices
4. Changes to legal documents or policies
5. Litigation, including lawsuits against the fund or the manager
6. Disclosure of related party transactions
7. Notification of fund's annual meeting
8. Brief summary of current political or economic events that can affect the fund

Other material changes or events not noted above.

----

3. Investee-by-Investee Summary

Frequency:

- Level One: semi-annually
- Level Two: semi-annually, except quarterly for current status

Basic information on each investee:

1. Name, location and legal domicile
2. Sector and country focus
3. Brief description of the business
4. Key shareholders and their %

Information at entry:

1. Date of first investment
2. Types of securities owned
3. Other fund exposure (such as guarantees, conversion rights, etc)
4. Investment details (options, special rights, restrictions on exit, etc.)
5. Latest audit qualified?
6. Fund strategy at entry:
   - Rationale going in (expansion, MBO, planned for roll-up, etc)
   - Stage at entry (seed, early, mature, etc)
   - Fund's role in the investment (the only fund, one of a group, lead, etc)
7. Board representation by the fund
8. Post-money valuation
9. Key ratios at entry (such as price/EBITDA)
10. Exit strategy as stated at entry

Information at exit:

1. Exit method (sale to strategic buyer, IPO, etc.)
2. Total exit proceeds
3. Cost of exited equity
4. Interest, dividends, and fee income received by the fund
5. Realised cash multiple
6. IRR: calculated (1) on same basis as cash multiple and (2) treating current valuation as terminal value
7. Date of latest exit

Current Status (if not completely exited):

1. Total amounts committed and disbursed to date
2. Total realised to date
3. Cost, valuation, valuation method, and valuation date of fund's unrealised investment

4. Rating (e. g., 1-5 with mid point of rating scale indicating break-even performance)

5. Fund ownership: USD/EUR and %

6. Fees paid to fund or manager

7. Brief commentary: significant events, performance versus plan

8. Exit strategy

9. Summary financials (see Annex)

Other material changes or events not noted above.

----

4. Capital Account

Note:

- Amounts should be shown at the level of the individual investor and as a total for the fund as a whole

- Time periods should include the current quarter and totals to date

Frequency:

- Level One: annually

- Level Two: At each drawdown during investment period; then semi-annually

Information:

1. Total capital committed

2. Capital called for:
   - Investments
   - Fees
   - Expenses
   - Other
   - Note: this list will vary depending on the legal structure, e. g., corporation, partnership, trust, etc.

3. Distributions to investors:
   - As return of capital
   - As capital gains
   - As dividends, interest, or fees

4. Fund investors by name with class of share or type of ownership and %

5. Spreadsheet of cash flows between fund and investors by month since inception

Other material changes or events not noted above.

----

5. Fees and Expenses

Frequency:

- Level One: annually
- Level Two: annually

Note:

- Time periods should be annual from fund inception
- Fees should be shown as earned/received, regardless of any cash flow netting

Information:

1. Fees and expenses from investees to fund manager
   Level One: total
   Level Two: by category, such as:

   - Arrangement fees
   - Director/monitoring fees
   - Broken deal costs paid to fund manager by investees
   - Other fees and expenses from investees

2. Fees and expenses from fund to fund manager
3. Level One: total
4. Level Two: by category, such as success fee, etc.
5. Fees from investors to fund manager, such as

   - Management fees
   - Other fees from investors

6. Carried interest from fund to fund manager

   - Amount subject to clawback, if any

Other material changes or events not noted above.

----

6. Fund Compliance Checklist

Frequency:

- Level One: annually
- Level Two: annually

Information for each compliance item:

- Description of item
- Detail of requirements
- Is the fund in compliance?
- Evidence of compliance, if appropriate

Examples of compliance items:
- Exposure limits by country
- Exposure limits by sector
- Exposure limits by % of fund
- Exposure limits by % of company
- Key man trigger
- Environmental & social constraints
- Borrowing limits
- Guarantee limits
- Auditing and reporting deadlines
- Cash management rules (such as limit on cash reserves)

Other material changes or events not noted above.

ATTACHMENT: PERFORMANCE TABLE TO BE SUBMITTED BY INVESTEES

(Three past years plus current year; data for illustration only)

Performance:	2003	2004	2005	2006 YTD
Revenues	15,0	20,0	22,0	-
EBITDA	7,5	9,0	9,0	-
Net Income	6,0	6,0	5,0	-
Current Assets	5,0	5,0	5,0	-
Non-Current Assets	35,0	40,0	45,0	-
	40,0	45,0	50,0	-
Current Liabilities	5,0	5,0	5,0	-
Non-Current Liabilities	5,0	5,0	5,0	-
	10,0	10,0	10,0	-
Equity	30,0	35,0	40,0	-
EBITDA Margin	50,0%	45,0%	40,9%	0,0%
Net Income Margin	40,0%	30,0%	22,7%	0,0%
RoAA	12,2%	14,1%	10,5%	0,0%
RoAE	15,0%	18,5%	13,3%	0,0%
Current Ratio	1,0	1,0	1,0	-
Leverage	25,0%	22,2%	20,0%	0,0%

The Management of Foreign Exchange Risk by Microfinance Institutions and Microfinance Investment Funds

Isabelle Barrès

Director for Strategic Development, The Microfinance Information eXchange (The MIX)

Introduction

Most microfinance investment funds (MFIFs) and other funders such as official development agencies finance their activities in US dollars (USD) or Euros (EUR), which may be called "hard currencies."[1] However, most microfinance institutions (MFIs)[2] operate in non-dollarised or non-Euro-based economies and lend local currency to their clients.[3]

Funding in one currency and lending in another, and the probability that the relative values of the two currencies will alter, creates foreign exchange (FX) risk.

---

[1] This chapter focuses on foreign microfinance investors surveyed jointly by ADA, CGAP and The MIX from July to October 2004 for the KfW symposium in November of that year. It also examines the funding and operating currencies of other microfinance investors (including local investors) using MIX Market 2005 data. The author thanks Julie Abrams, consultant to CGAP, Patrick Goodman, consultant to ADA, and Gautam Ivatury, CGAP for their assistance in gathering the data. Microfinance investors surveyed in this research are identified in Appendix 1.

[2] The term "MFI" is used broadly in this chapter to encompass institutions that provide small-scale financial services, such as loans, savings, insurance, remittances and other services (generally in amounts less than 250 % of GNP per capita). The term encompasses a wide variety of organisations: NGOs, credit unions, non-bank financial intermediaries, rural banks, etc.

[3] "Local currency" refers to a currency other than a "hard currency" (i. e., USD or EUR), even though some MFIs operate in countries where the local currency is the USD (i. e., Ecuador), or the EUR (i. e., Kosovo). This distinction is made because non-hard currencies tend to be more volatile, or have higher fluctuations and hence potential risk, than hard currencies. Nevertheless, some examples are given of EUR/USD transactions that show that the perception of stable hard currencies has been challenged in recent years, creating high costs for both MFIFs and MFIs.

Volatile currency exchange rate fluctuations in many countries where MFIs operate make FX risk a serious issue, but one that has often been accorded little urgency in microfinance. The accelerated development of microfinance through access to capital markets makes it imperative that foreign exchange be managed in ways that are consistent with best practice in finance. Until this is widely achieved, access to capital markets for the benefit of microfinance will be retarded.

Foreign exchange risk is one of many risks that MFIFs face. Interest rate risk is an additional risk that is related to FX risk. As currency values change, interest expense or income will also change. And, spreads between interest rates on both sides of the balance sheet may change, that is, interest rates on money borrowed in one currency by a microfinance institution, for example, may diverge from interest rates on money loaned to microentrepreneurs by the MFI. Each of these effects has implications for MFIF and MFI profitability. For purposes of economy, these second order exchange risks are not discussed further here in.

This chapter explores the nature of FX risk in debt funding by focusing on which party is likely to bear the risk of exchange rate fluctuations in different situations at different points in a funding transaction. The importance of hedging is noted, and mechanisms are listed that MFIFs and MFIs use to address their respective FX risks.

The relationships between currency and risk described below apply to equity funds, while in the case of guarantee funds the situation is reversed.[4] Equity investments, as capital, are always in the currency of the MFI. For the foreign equity investor, "foreign exchange risk becomes one of several risks associated with an investment rather than a central factor in making a loan."[5] Equity and guarantee funds, while not the focus of this chapter, are included in the Appendices with examples to identify when they face a currency risk and the hedging mechanisms they use.

How Does Foreign Exchange Risk Occur? Who Is Exposed?

Foreign exchange risk occurs when there is a mismatch in the currencies in which assets and liabilities are denominated (either at the MFI level, the MFIF level, or both), coupled with uncertainty about foreign exchange fluctuations. In theory, foreign exchange risk – or currency risk – is taken either by the MFI, the MFIF, or both, depending on their asset and liability structure.

---

[4] Guarantees are almost exclusively in the currency of the MFIF and enable the MFI to obtain local currency loans. FX risks are absent unless the MFIF offers guarantees in currencies that are different from its funding currency (i. e., FIG issues guarantees in USD, EUR and CHF [Swiss francs]), or if the MFI defaults on the loan to the commercial bank and the local currency *appreciates* vis-à-vis the currency of the guarantee (resulting in a claim on the MFIF that is larger than the amount of the guarantee). See Freedman, Paul L., Designing Loan Guarantees to Spur Growth in Developing Countries, USAID, 2004, page 11.

[5] Ibid, page 36.

The most common foreign exchange risk possibilities are summarised in Table 1. These combinations involve positions in Euros (EUR) and local currency, US dollars (USD) and local currency, and between EUR and USD, that comprise the currencies in which assets and liabilities are held by MFIs and MFIFs. Generalising, we assume that before the MFI receives funding, it has no currency mismatch. Its "operating currency," the currency in which its assets are denominated, is the same as its "funding" currency, which is the currency in which its liabilities are denominated.[6]

The funding and operating currencies are defined as follows:

- MFIF funding currency: the currency in which the MFIF borrows to fund its operations – the currency of the MFIF's liabilities;

- MFIF operating currency or MFI funding currency: the currency in which the MFIF lends to the MFI or the currency in which the MFI borrows from the MFIF to fund its operations, i. e., the currency of the MFIF's assets and the MFI's liabilities;

- MFI operating currency: the currency in which the MFI lends to its clients, i. e., the currency of the MFI's assets.

Table 1 assumes that the MFIF is funded in only one currency, it lends to 100 % of its MFI clients in only one currency, and the MFI lends to 100 % of its clients in only one currency.[7] This simplification is made to illustrate the mechanics of currency risk, and to identify who would be most likely to bear the risk of foreign exchange fluctuations. Another assumption is that the local currency will depreciate compared to the hard currency, even though in some cases the local currency appreciates and therefore creates a gain for the MFI that has foreign currency exposure.[8]

The example of change in value of the EUR against the USD is an interesting one to examine. Over a 2-year period, the EUR gained close to 40 % of its value against USD. This large change in the relative values of two "hard" currencies was underestimated by many MFIs and MFIFs. The EUR was launched in 2002 at USD 1.17, and subsequently fell to less than USD 0.90. Recently, however, the

---

[6] A mismatch between funding and operating currencies introduced by new funding will therefore necessarily increase FX risk. In reality, a new mismatch in the funding and operating currencies can offset an existing FX risk.

[7] The MFIFs listed as examples in the following section fall within that category: they are funded in one currency and lend in one currency only. In reality, because the MFIFs and the MFIs can be funded and operate in several currencies at a time, the overall risk to the MFIF and the MFI will depend on the proportion of assets and liabilities in each currency. Appendix 3 presents the breakdown by main funding currency and theoretical operating currency for the MFIFs studied in this chapter.

[8] See Women's World Banking, Foreign Exchange Risk Management in Microfinance, Occasional Paper, page 2, for analysis of past currency trends.

Table 1. Who Bears Currency Risk? Common Scenarios

Who bears the FX risk?	MFIF funding currency	MFIF operating currency/MFI funding currency	MFI operating currency
MFIF	**USD** **EUR** **EUR** **USD**	**Local** **Local** **USD** **EUR**	**Local** **Local** **USD** **EUR**
MFI [a]	**USD** **EUR** **EUR** **USD**	**USD** **EUR** **EUR** **USD**	Local Local USD EUR
NA – No risk (no asset/liability currency mismatch)	**USD** **EUR** **Local**	**USD** **EUR** **Local**	**USD** **EUR** **Local**
MFI and MFIF	**EUR** **USD**	**USD** **EUR**	**Local** **Local**
	Or **Through contractual arrangement**		

a) It is important to note that in this case, although the MFIF does not incur FX risk due to nominal exchange rate fluctuations, real exchange rate fluctuations in the MFI's country might affect its competitiveness and capacity to repay.

EUR has appreciated considerably against the USD, and many European MFIFs operating in EUR and lending in USD in dollarised countries in Latin America have incurred significant losses from the transactions.

The sharp appreciation of the EUR against the USD has created significant exchange losses on the EUR loans of many MFIs, which in some cases will require restructuring. The ASN-Novib Fonds is an example. It is an MFIF in the Netherlands that lends in hard currency (both USD and EUR), with most of its portfolio concentrated in Latin America. It is seeking opportunities in Asia and Africa if the foreign exchange risks can be hedged. In the past, the ASN-Novib Fonds made EUR loans to MFIs operating in dollarised economies, but the lack of hedging by its client MFIs and subsequent losses have forced ASN-Novib Fonds to discontinue unhedged EUR funding, which it considers too risky for the MFIs.[9] On the other hand, MFIs borrowing in USD and on-lending in EUR have experienced currency gains – their Euro-equivalent USD repayments of principal and interest have diminished considerably.

---

[9] For example, EUR loans were issued in 2002 to ANED and FADES in Bolivia, and Confianza and Proempresa in Peru.

Mitigating Currency Risk

Hedging: "A strategy used to offset market risk, whereby one position protects another. Traders and investors in foreign exchange hedge to protect their investment or portfolio against currency price fluctuations", First FX (*www.firstfx.com*).

Every risk can be mitigated by an appropriate hedging strategy. Hedging mitigates currency risk and takes many forms. Common methods used to mitigate currency risks are:

- Forward contracts;

- Futures contracts;

- Currency options;

- Currency swaps; and

- Back-to-back loans.

Hedging mechanisms are described in papers footnoted below that also offer examples of specific transactions where MFIs or MFIFs have hedged their risks.[10] This chapter does not describe these hedging mechanisms in detail, but brief definitions are summarised in Table 2.

Regardless of who bears the *direct* currency risk (i. e., direct losses from currency fluctuations), both parties are at risk for *indirect* losses resulting from currency risk. For example, if an MFIF suffers losses and downscales operations or changes the allocation of countries in which it invests, client MFIs may lose access to a funder that has been helpful in the past. On the other hand, MFIFs face increased credit risk (i. e., an *indirect* currency risk in this case), when MFIs have not hedged their currency risk and suffer subsequent losses that affect their profitability and long term viability. In this sense, some dimensions of currency risk are always shared between the MFIF and the MFI, regardless of which bears the direct risk, as portrayed in the examples above.

Because of *direct* and *indirect* FX risks, MFIFs and MFIs are working together to develop hedging mechanisms in countries where the capital markets may offer few of the hedging options that are available in developed countries.

---

[10] See, for example, Holden, Paul and Sarah Holden, Foreign Exchange Risk and Microfinance Institutions, The Enterprise Research Institute and MicroRate, July 2004; Bhatia, Romi, Social Enterprise Associates, Paper #3: Working Paper on Mitigating Currency Risk for Investing in Microfinance Institutions in Developing Countries, Jan. 2004, p. 5; Women's World Banking, Foreign Exchange Risk Management in Microfinance, Occasional Paper; Featherston, Scott, Elizabeth Littlefield, and Patricia Mwangi, Foreign Exchange Risk in Microfinance: What is it and how can it be managed? CGAP, forthcoming.

Table 2. Definitions of Common Methods of Hedging Currency Risks

Definitions
1. **Forward Contract** – A contract that obligates you to buy or sell a currency at a fixed rate on a specified future date. By linking this date to the date of your currency payment/purchase, you in effect lock in the exchange rate you want and eliminate the risk of future volatility. Contracts cannot be transferred.
2. **Futures Contract** – An exchange traded agreement to buy or sell a particular type and grade of commodity for delivery at an agreed upon place and time in the future. Futures contracts are transferable between parties.
3. **Currency Options** – A contract for a fee (premium + commission), sold by one party to another that offers the buyer the *right, but not the obligation*, to buy or sell a specified amount of one currency for a specified amount in another at an agreed-upon price during a certain period of time or on a specific date.
4. **Currency Swaps** – An agreement by two companies to exchange specified amounts of currency now and to reverse the exchange at some point in the future. A currency swap may not have an initial exchange, in which case it would involve one or more payments during the life of the swap, plus a final exchange.
5. **Back-to-Back Loans** – A loan between two companies in different countries that borrow offsetting amounts in each other's currency. The purpose of this transaction is to hedge against currency fluctuations.
Note: Back-to-back loans are now infrequently used, but were common when rigid exchange controls made it very expensive to convert an investor's home currency into another currency.

Source: Bhatia, Romi, Paper #3: Working Paper on Mitigating Currency Risk for Investing in Microfinance Institutions in Developing Countries, Social Enterprise Associates, January 2004, page 5.

To mitigate indirect currency risks, most MFIFs try to assess whether it is reasonable for their client MFIs to borrow in a certain currency. They examine their funding and operating currencies and monitor their overall foreign currency exposure on a regular basis as part of their due diligence process. MFIFs that have adopted these procedures include BIO, Cordaid, Etimos, Incofin, Luxmint-ADA, Rabobank and Triodos.[11] Exposure analysis varies, and is not used in every case. Informal cross-checking among MFIFs also helps raise their awareness of the foreign exchange exposure of their affiliates. Some MFIFs such as ASN-Novib Fonds have changed their policies to reduce MFI currency risks.

---

[11] Based on interviews conducted from July to October 2004 for the KfW Symposium. Appendix 1 identifies the institutions interviewed in this research. Triodos includes HTF, TDF, and TFSF.

MFIFs' Risk Mitigation Strategies

Before exploring MFIFs' currency risk mitigation strategies, an examination of their perceptions of foreign exchange risk and their actual exposure is helpful.

Perceptions Regarding Currency Risk

Interviews conducted by ADA, CGAP, and The MIX for the KfW symposium in 2004 shed some light on MFIFs' perceptions of FX risk.[12] The study found that perceptions of the degree of risk linked to currency fluctuations depend largely on direct currency exposure, although most MFIFs interviewed expressed great concern for the larger issue – whether or not they directly faced a risk – because of the potential repercussions of a loss incurred by MFIs as a result of transactions with an MFIF.

When asked: *"Is foreign exchange risk a big issue for the MFIs that you invest in?"*, MFIFs were almost unanimous in saying that foreign exchange risk is a major issue in lending to MFIs because it increases the risk of losses, regardless of who assumes the risk. MFIFs that shared this view included BIO, Cordaid, Lux-mint-ADA, Rabobank, and Triodos. Some MFIFs, including BIO, Cordaid, and PlaNet Fund, were nevertheless willing to assume greater FX risk, or were generally less concerned about it, for several reasons:

- Accepts greater currency risk due to funding received especially for that purpose;[13]

- Funding did not create a direct currency risk (i. e., EUR fund lending EUR to MFIs); and/or

- Hard currency funding was used as collateral to obtain local currency funding, and as such did not represent any currency risk for the MFIF or the MFI.

The potential currency losses linked to currency risk discussed previously contrast with the responses regarding risk mitigation. While levels of risk vary, not enough is being done from the perspectives of both MFIFs and MFIs. Many MFIFs and MFIs that should hedge because of the level of their exposure do not have hedging mechanisms in place, for a variety of reasons explored below.

---

[12] Several of the 54 MFIFs surveyed for the KfW symposium were interviewed (see Appendix 2). The joint survey team comprised of ADA, CGAP, and The MIX thanks the MFIFs that participated in the survey and interviews and agreed to share their results.

[13] A few examples include BIO and Cordaid. BIO will receive EUR 3 million per year for 4 years from the Belgian Government to make local currency loans to MFIs and SMEs, and will assume the entire foreign exchange risk. Cordaid offers loans in local currency in certain conditions. Sometimes the foreign exchange risk is such that Cordaid can predict that it will lose money, which it is willing to do up to a point because some of its funding comes from non-commercial sources.

Hedging Policy in Place?

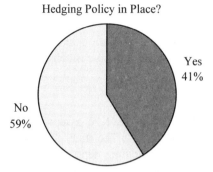

Figure 1. Microfinance Investment Funds' Policies

Importance of Hedging

Of the 64 MFIFs analysed for the KfW symposium and through The MIX Market, 49 provided the currency breakdown of their microfinance investment portfolios. Of these, 46 provided information about their hedging policies – or lack thereof.[14] Only a little over 40 % (19) of the MFIFs that gave details of their hedging policies indicated that they had a hedging policy in place.

As noted previously, not all MFIFs need to hedge. MFIFs that offer funding in their currency of operations have no FX risk and therefore do not have hedging policies in place.

Excepting the 7 MFIFs that were not exposed to direct currency risk,[15] 20 MFIFs, about 50 % of the 39 that faced exposure from currency risk, did not have hedging mechanisms in place, as illustrated in Table 3.

Table 3. Are MFIFs Hedging FX Risk?

	Should Hedge [a]	No Exposure, No Reason to Hedge	Total
Are Hedging	19	0	*19*
Are Not Hedging	20	7	*27*
Total	*39*	*7*	*46*

a) Whether or not an MFIF should hedge was based on current portfolio breakdown per currency. The dates for the portfolio breakdown correspond to the dates at which there was – or not – a hedging policy in place.

---

[14] See Appendices 4, 5, and 6 for details.

[15] See Appendix 6. For a list of MFIFs analysed by main funding currency and actual operating currencies, see Appendix 7. For details on portfolio breakdown by currencies for these same MFIFs, see Appendix 8.

Failures to hedge adequately created losses for several of the MFIFs studied, including many European microfinance investors, such as NOVIB (on local currency loans and participations in Ethiopia, Kenya, Mexico, Mozambique, Peru, Senegal, Sri Lanka, Tanzania and Uganda), Cordaid (on loans in Bangladesh, Bosnia and Herzegovina, Brazil, Colombia, the Dominican Republic, Ghana, India, Indonesia, Morocco, Peru, Philippines, etc.), and others.

How are exchange rate losses treated in accounting information? Some MFIFs show returns prior to exchange rate losses while others show returns after exchange rate losses. Lack of standardisation produces important differences in the overall return, often turning a positive return into a negative one. This difference should be taken into consideration when examining the financial statements of MFIFs. A forthcoming edition of the *MicroBanking Bulletin*, focusing on the supply side of MFI funding, will provide more details of issues arising from the lack of standardisation and transparency in MFIF reporting.

Hedging Practices

MFIFs that reported having hedging mechanisms in place indicated differences in their degree of hedging: some fully hedged currency risk, while many hedged hard currency risk but not their local currency exposure.

Examples of common hedging policies are:

- Hedging principal but not interest payments;

- When possible, matching funding and operating currencies;

- Use of currency swaps, currency options, forward contracts;

- Outsourcing FX risk management to a third party; and/or

- Portfolio diversification.

More details on the MFIFs' hedging practices are summarised in Appendix 4.

Why Do Some MFIFs Fail to Hedge?

The most common reason for not hedging currency risk is that MFIFs are willing to assume the risk.[16] MFIFs that had not hedged their currency exposure are identified in Appendix 5. Other MFIFs that were not hedging simply because they did not face direct currency risk are listed in Appendix 6. Some MFIFs also chose to bear the FX risk and not hedge, in order not to increase the costs of their loans and face the risk of losing potential customers.

---

[16] This applies especially to MFIFs that are less commercial in nature.

MFIs' Risk Mitigation Strategies

The Importance of Hedging

Appendix 3 indicates that a few investment funds, primarily social funds, are willing to assume direct currency risk by offering local currency loans to MFIs. However, most MFIFs invest in MFIs in hard currency,[17] passing the FX risk to the MFIs, which then bear the responsibility for hedging by obtaining a hard currency guarantee or buying a derivative security that neutralises their risk. A number of MFIFs are lending in hard currencies, sometimes recklessly, in countries where the devaluation risk is high and MFIs do not hedge.

To What Extent Are MFIs Hedging to Mitigate the Currency Risk That They Face?

Similar to the MFIFs, MFIs face varying levels of risk that depend not only on the mix of currencies they borrow and on-lend to their clients, but also on the volume of funds borrowed and/or on-lent in different currencies.

A recent survey conducted by CGAP and The MIX identified the funding structure and future funding projections of MFIs.[18] Of the 216 MFIs that responded to the survey, 80 indicated that they were currently using hard currency funding (USD or EUR) and indicated the amount.[19] Of these 80 MFIs, 8 operated in dollarised economies (Ecuador and El Salvador) or in Euros (Kosovo). The remaining 72 were exposed to either USD or EUR currency risk: 61 had an average exposure of USD 2.6 million and 11 had an average exposure of EUR 3.8 million.

An average of 48% of USD loans and an average of 36% of EUR loans were hedged. Nevertheless, these averages hide important differences in hedging practices amongst MFIs. More interesting is the distribution of hedging (Table 4).

In either USD or EUR exposures, 72 MFIs should have hedged: 54% were not hedging at all, while 24% were fully hedged. The remaining 16 MFIs (or 22%) partially hedged their currency risk. For more details on exposures and the percentage of hedging by the MFIs in the survey that were operating in a non-USD or non-EUR country, see Appendices 9, 10 and11.

---

[17] Per Ivatury, G. and J. Abrams, 92% of the international microfinance foreign investment debt is denominated in hard currency (The Market Opportunity for Microfinance Foreign Investment: Opportunities and Challenges, 2004 KfW Financial Sector Development Symposium). Even the mixed funds disburse about 80% of their funding in hard currency and 20% in local currency.

[18] The survey is available at: www.surveymonkey.com/s.asp?u=33938560773. The author thanks Julie Abrams, consultant to CGAP and Gautam Ivatury, CGAP for their collaboration on the "MFI Demand for Funding" survey.

[19] Because we are interested here in the details of the hard currency funding (amount, currencies, country), we focus only on the subset of 80 MFIs that provided full details. Of the 216 MFIs surveyed, 110 indicated that they had foreign currency loans.

Table 4. Distribution of Percentage of Hedging by 72 Respondents

x = % of Hedging	Number of Respondents	
	EUR	USD
x = 0 %	7	32
0 % < x ≤ 25 %	0	8
25 % < x ≤ 50 %	0	3
50 % < x ≤ 75 %	0	1
75 % < x ≤ 100 %	1	3
x = 100 %	3	14
Total	**11**	**61**

Most of the 216 surveyed MFIs had some exposure to currency risk through their transactions with an average of one foreign lender, and/or desired to increase their funding from foreign sources.[20] In addition, 68 (or 31 %) of the 216 MFIs surveyed indicated that foreign funders did not want to assume foreign exchange risk and that this was a challenge in obtaining foreign loans and equity. In addition, the sample results suggest that there is a high probability that MFIs that have access to foreign loans are not hedging properly. The hedging issue is therefore important: helping MFIs reduce currency risk will increase their interest in obtaining foreign lending and reducing FX losses.

Hedging Practices

Common hedging methods identified by MFIs include:

- Pass the risk to the clients through higher and/or flexible interest rates that follow currency movements;

- Use hard currency loans as guarantees for local currency loans with a local bank; and/or

- Convert loans in foreign currencies to loans in local currency through back-to-back operations that lower the currency risk but increase the costs.

When hedging, very few MFIFs use the common methods identified in Figure 1. The next section looks at common reasons why MFIs are not hedging.

---

[20] Of the MFIs surveyed, 38 % expressed interest in obtaining loans in USD or EUR. While foreign loans accounted for an average of 12 % of total liabilities, they would ideally like to see this increase to 14 % on average. The desired increase in foreign equity is much sharper: currently at an average of 7 % of total equity, MFIs on average would like to have up to 20 % foreign ownership.

Why Do Some MFIs Fail to Hedge?

MFIs that were not hedging, but that should hedge, failed to do so mainly due to the lack of vehicles for hedging in their local market, the costs linked to hedging, or lack of information regarding hedging. Additional reasons are:

- The risk is covered by the lenders (i. e., the amount borrowed can be paid back at the exchange rate prevailing when the funds were received);

- Hedging options are not available or are hard to find;

- They never gave it much thought;

- They are not sufficiently informed about hedging; and/or

- They manage the risk through asset/liability management: keeping foreign liabilities lower than foreign assets.

Similar to the MFIFs, the performance of MFIs is affected not only by the actual gains or losses incurred from foreign exchange, but also in the way these are accounted for. Adjustment methods used by external analysts such as rating agencies also contain considerable differences.[21] It is important to examine the specific accounting treatments when comparing the performance of MFIs.

Conclusion

Although FX risk occurs in almost every transaction between microfinance investors (especially foreign investors) and MFIs, too many MFIFs and MFIs are not hedging appropriately. Hedging is seldom used because common hedging mechanisms are not available in the countries where MFIs operate, or prohibitively costly for the small amounts of the transactions involved. While hedging increases transaction costs, lack of hedging results in losses that can be significant, especially for MFIs and MFIFs that do not have well diversified portfolios.[22]

In addition, MFIFs often compensate for FX risk by increasing their interest rates to MFIs to cover potential losses. FX risk therefore increases the lending costs for the MFIs (and ultimately, for their clients), regardless of whether or not

---

[21] Different adjustment methodologies are presented in Nègre, Alice and Fabio Malanchini, Use Caution When Analyzing Adjusted MFI Performance Data: Adjustment Methodologies May Have Different Impacts, *MicroBanking Bulletin,* Issue No. 10, March 2005, page 7: "… some MFIs or analysts will record the gain/loss on the income statement when the asset is sold or the liability is liquidated; others will record it as non operating revenue (expense); and still others will record it only on the balance sheet as an increase (decrease) to the relevant asset and liability accounts, offset by an equal increase (decrease) to equity."

[22] While some MFIFs are diversifying their portfolio to spread the FX risk, MFIs have limited options, often borrowing in USD and/or EUR.

they have access to local currency loans. Unless MFIFs are able to assume more of the FX risk linked to their lending to MFIs, other funding instruments such as guarantees may be more appropriate for MFIs that face small margins.

"Best practices" for hedging by MFIFs should include strategies of when to hedge, how much to hedge, how to hedge. Sharing experiences with successful and innovative hedging mechanisms, such as FX insurance funds, would greatly encourage MFIFs to absorb more of the FX risk that MFIs are so ill equipped to address,[23] reducing costs for MFIFs and MFIs.

---

[23] Some examples include hedging only if more than "x"% of the portfolio is invested in other currencies, hedging only currencies where there is a major exposure and there is an active developed forward market, cross-hedging currencies against highly correlated major currencies, hedging all currency exposure "x"%, etc.

Appendix 1: Names, Acronyms and Abbreviations

Other than Microfinance Investment Funds

ADA: Appui au Développement Autonome
CAD: Canadian dollar
CGAP: Consultative Group to Assist the Poor
CHF :   Swiss Franc
MFI: Microfinance Institution
MFIF: Microfinance Investment Fund
MIX: Microfinance Information eXchange
FX: Foreign Exchange
EUR: Euro
USD: United States dollar

Microfinance Investment Funds

ACCION Gateway: ACCION Gateway Fund
AfriCap: AfriCap Microfinance Fund*
AIM: ACCION Investments in Microfinance
Alterfin: Alterfin c.v.b.a.
ANF: ASN-Novib Fonds*
AWF Development Debt: AXA World Funds – Development Debt Fund
BIO: Belgian Investment Company for Developing Countries*
BO Securities I: BlueOrchard Microfinance Securities I, LLC*
CAF: Corporacion Andina de Fomento
Calvert Foundation: Calvert Social Investment Foundation Community
                       Investment Notes*
Cordaid: Stichting (Foundation) Cordaid*
CreSud: CreSud SpA
DB MDF: Deutsche Bank Microcredit Development Fund
DID – Fonidi: Développement International Desjardins – Fonidi Fund
DID – Guarantee: Développement International Desjardins – Guarantee
                       Fund
DID – Partnership: Développement International Desjardins – Partnership
                       Fund
DOEN: Stichting (Foundation) DOEN-Postcode Loterij/Sponsor
                       Loterij

EBRD:	European Bank for Reconstruction and Development
Etimos:	Consorzio Etimos S.c.a.r.l.*
FIG:	Fonds International de Garantie
Finnfund:	Finnish Fund for Industrial Cooperation Ltd.
FMO:	Netherlands Development Finance Company*
FWWB:	Friends of Women's World Banking
GMF:	Global Microfinance Facility
Gray Ghost:	Gray Ghost Microfinance Fund LLC
HTF:	Stichting (Foundation) Hivos-Triodos Fund
ICCO:	Inter Church Organization for Development Co-Operation*
IDF:	Idyll Development Foundation
IFC:	International Finance Corporation*
Incofin:	Incofin cvso*
I&P Développement:	Investisseur et Partenaire pour le Développement
KEF :	Khula Enterprise Finance Limited
KFW/DEG:	Kreditanstalt für Wiederaufbau/ Deutsche Investitions-und Entwicklungsgesellschaft mbH
Kolibri:	Kolibri Kapital ASA
LABF:	ACCION Latin America Bridge Fund
LA-CIF:	Latin American Challenge Investment Fund, S.A.
LFP:	La Fayette Participations, Horus Banque et Finance
Luxmint-ADA:	Luxmint – Appui au Développement Autonome*
MFDF:	MicroFinance Development Fund
MicroVest:	MicroVest I L.P.*
MIF/IADB:	Multilateral Investment Fund of the Inter-American Development Bank
Oikocredit:	Oikocredit Ecumenical Development Cooperative Society*
OTI:	Opportunity Transformation Investments, Inc.
PCG:	Partners for the Common Good
PKSF:	Palli Karma-Sahayak Foundation
PlaNet Fund:	PlaNet Finance Revolving Credit Fund*
ProCredit Holding:	formerly Internationale Micro Investitionen Aktiengesellschaft (IMI-AG)
PROFUND:	ProFund International*

PT UKABIMA:	PT. Usaha Karya Bina Mandiri
Rabobank:	Rabobank Foundation*
responsAbility Fund:	responsAbility Global Microfinance Fund
RFC:	Rural Finance Corporation
Sarona:	Sarona Global Investment Fund, Inc.*
SFD:	Social Fund for Development
SGIF:	Sarona Global Investment Fund, Inc.*
ShoreCap Intl.:	ShoreCap International, Ltd.
SIDI:	Solidarité Internationale pour le Développement et l'Investissement
TDF:	Triodos-Doen Foundation
TFSF:	Triodos Fair Share Fund *
UNCDF:	United Nations Capital Development Fund
USAID Credit Guarantees:	United States Agency for International Development/Development Credit Authority Credit Guarantees

Investors surveyed in this research.

Appendix 2: The 64 Microfinance Investors Analysed

KfW Survey (total = 54)	
Existing Microfinance Investment Funds (total = 38)	
ACCION Gateway Fund (c)	Hivos-Triodos Fund
ACCION Investments in Microfinance (b)	Incofin
ACCION Latin America Bridge Fund (a)	Investisseur et Partenaire pour le Développement
AfriCap (b)	Kolibri Kapital ASA
Alterfin c.v.b.a.	La Fayette Participations, Horus Banque et Finance (b)
ASN-Novib Fonds	Latin America Challenge Investment Fund, S.A.
AXA World Funds - Development Debt Fund	Luxmint-ADA
BlueOrchard Microfinance Securities I, LLC	MicroVest I L.P.
Calvert Social Investment Foundation Community Investment Notes	Oikocredit
Consorzio Etimos S.c.a.r.l.	Opportunity Transformation Investments, Inc.
CreSud SpA	PlaNet Finance - Revolving Credit Fund
Deutsche Bank Microcredit Development Fund	ProCredit Holding
Développement International Desjardins - Fonidi Fund (c)	PROFUND
Développement International Desjardins - Guarantee Fund (a)	responsAbility Global Microfinance Fund
Développement International Desjardins - Partnership Fund	Sarona Global Investment Fund, Inc. (d)
Dexia Microcredit Fund	ShoreCap International, Ltd. (c)
Fonds International de Garantie (a)	Solidarité Internationale pour le Développement et l'Investissement (SIDI)
Global Microfinance Facility	Triodos-Doen Foundation
Gray Ghost Microfinance Fund LLC	Triodos Fair Share Fund

(a) Guarantees. (b) Equity/Quasi-equity. (c) Mixed, currently invested only in equity. (d) As of December 31, 2004, the Sarona Global Investment Fund has dissolved operation. Sarona invited its investors to roll their investments over to a MicroVest mPower Note being offered through Calvert Social Investment Fund. For further information on the mPower Note, please contact info@microvestfund.com or www.microvest.com.

Source: Joint KfW Survey by ADA, CGAP, and The MIX, July – October 2004; MIX Market 2005.

Appendix 2 (continued)

KfW Survey (total = 54)

Development Agencies, Foundations and NGOs acting as Investors in Microfinance (total = 16)

Belgian Investment Company for Developing
  Countries (BIO)
Cordaid Foundation
Corporacion Andina de Fomento
Doen Foundation
European Bank for Reconstruction and
  Development (EBRD)
Finnish Fund for Industrial Cooperation Ltd.
  (Finmfund)
Inter Church Organization for Development Co-
  operation (ICCO)

International Finance Corporation (IFC)
KfW/DEG
MIF/IADB
Netherlands Development Finance Company
  (FMO)
NOVIB
Partners for the Common Good
Rabobank Foundation
Unitus
USAID/Credit Guarantees (a)

MIX Market (total = 10)

Additional Microfinance Investors (total = 10)

Citigroup Foundation
Friends of Women's World Banking
Idyll Development Foundation
Khula Enterprise Finance Limited
MicroFinance Development Fund

Palli Karma-Sahayak Foundation
PT. Usaha Karya Bina Mandiri (PT UKABIMA)
Rural Finance Corporation
Social Fund for Development
United Nations Capital Development Fund

(a) Guarantees.

Source: Joint KfW Survey by ADA, CGAP, and The MIX, July – October 2004; MIX Market 2005.

Appendix 3: Microfinance Investors, by Main Funding Currency and Operating Currencies (for 64 Microfinance Investors)

MFIF Operating Currency (c)	MFIF Main Funding Currency		
	USD	EUR	Other
USD only	Calvert Foundation, Citigroup Foundation, DB MDF, Gray Ghost, IDF, LABF (a) — LA-CIF, PCG, SGIF, USAID/Credit Guarantees (a)		
EUR only		PlaNet Fund	
Local currency only	AfriCap (b)		**Indian Rupee:** FWWB, **South African Rand:** KEF, **Bangladeshi Taka:** PKSF, **Indonesian Rupiah:** PT UKABIMA, **Moldovan Leu:** RFC, **Yemeni Riyal:** SFD

(a) Guarantees. (b) Equity/Quasi-equity. (c) These correspond to currencies offered by the MFIFs. Actual currencies used for operations do not always correspond to the full MFIF product offering (i.e., an MFIF can theoretically invest in local and hard currencies but is currently invested only in USD). MFIF Operating Currency = currency in which the MFIF lends to MFIs; MFIF Main Funding Currency = Main currency in which the MFIF is funded.

Source: Joint KfW Survey by ADA, CGAP, and The MIX, July – October 2004; MIX Market 2005.

Appendix 3 (continued)

MFIF Operating Currency (d)	MFIF Main Funding Currency		
	USD	EUR	Other
Mix of USD, EUR, and other currencies, including other hard currencies, but mainly local currencies	ACCION Gateway* (c) AIM (b) BO Securities I** CAF CreSud Dexia Microcredit Fund GMF IFC MFDF MicroVest MIF/IADB PROFUND OTI responsAbility Fund ShoreCap Intl.* (c) UNCDF Unitus*	Alterfin ANF AWF Development Debt** BIO Cordaid DOEN EBRD Etimos Finnfund** FMO ICCO Incofin I&P Développement* KfW/DEG Kolibri Kapital ASA LFP* (b) Luxmint-ADA NOVIB Oikocredit ProCredit Holding Rabobank SIDI Triodos (HTF, TDF, TFSF)	**Canadian dollar:** DID – Fonidi Fund* (c) DID – Guarantee Fund* (a) DID – Partnership Fund **Swiss franc:** FIG (a)

(a) Guarantees. (b) Equity/Quasi-equity. (c) Mixed, currently invested only in equity. MFIF Operating Currency = currency in which the MFIF lends to MFIs; MFIF Main Funding Currency = Main currency in which the MFIF is funded. (d) These correspond to currencies offered by the MFIFs. Actual currencies used for operations do not always correspond to the full MFIF product offering (i.e., an MFIF can theoretically invest in local and hard currencies but is currently invested only in USD). * = MFIFs that can theoretically invest in a mix of MFI operating currencies but currently invest only in local currencies. ** = MFIF that can theoretically invest in a mix of MFI operating currencies but currently invest only in USD. See Appendices 7 and 8 for more details.

Source: Joint KfW Survey by ADA, CGAP, and The MIX, July – October 2004; MIX Market 2005.

Appendix 4: Currency Risk Management Policies for 19 Fully or Partially Hedged MFIFs

Alterfin	Matches funding currency with operating currencies in most cases (i.e., borrows in USD for loans in USD). (a)
ANF	Provides mainly hard currency loans (hence focus on Latin America and Eastern Europe). All USD loans are hedged against the EUR for principal, not for interest payments. Exceptionally, may provide local currency loans.
BIO	USD/EUR hedges are obtained through swaps and forwards. Local currency equity holdings are not hedged.
Etimos	Hedging policy applies only to capital, not to interest. The loans in local currencies were hedged by grants that were received for this purpose by the Italian central and local governments. Paid hedging instruments for loans in USD.
CreSud	100% EUR/USD hedge (less than 10% of the portfolio denominated in EUR).
Dexia Microcredit Fund	No local currency loans, foreign exchange hedging mechanism assistance setup if required. Portfolio mainly funded in USD. Foreign exchange contracts in order to hedge 100% CHF and EUR classes, as well as EUR portfolio.
DID – Partnership	Hedging contracts for loans, no hedging for equity investments.
Incofin	All USD denominated loans have been hedged since 2003. Its valuation rules stipulate that participations and shares are valued at acquisition cost unless sustained loss or value depreciation is apparent: equity investments are not hedged. Apart from the risk of the exposure, an assessment is made of the appropriateness of the asset-liability management techniques in place within the MFI. Particular attention is given to the hedging of currency exposures, where the risk of creating open positions is assessed in view of the specific monetary situation (often local currencies are pegged to USD or EUR, commonly by using a "crawling peg") and the possibility to off set.
IFC	The Corporation conducts its operations for its loans, time deposits and securities and borrowings in multiple currencies. The Corporation's policy is to minimise the level of currency risk by closely matching the currency of its assets (other than equity investments and quasi-equity investments) and liabilities by using hedging instruments. The Corporation's equity investments in enterprises located in its developing member countries are typically made in the local currency of the country. As a matter of policy, the Corporation carries the currency risk of equity investments and quasi-equity investments and funds these investments from its capital and retained earnings.
MicroVest	Tries to hedge currency risk wherever possible.
NOVIB	USD and local currencies were previously not hedged. A hedging policy is now in place and NOVIB hedges all USD repayments with maturities shorter than 2 years. In addition, NOVIB hedges around 60% of local currency loans strongly influenced by the USD with maturities shorter than 2 years.

Appendix 4 (continued)

Oikocredit	Protection against currency losses through the Local Currency Risk Fund (LCRF) and an interest rate calculation mechanism that takes into account the currency risk. The interest rate mechanism ensures *on average* a return on local currency loans equivalent to the return on similar loans in Euros regardless of currency fluctuations on these local currency loans. The LCRF was established with funds from members and functions as a buffer fund for exchange rate fluctuations or as a type of "exchange rate risk insurance". Most exposure in USD is hedged by currency swaps or foreign forward contracts.
responsAbility Fund	responsAbility Fund has two hedging policies: one for funds flowing in from investors: the fund's currency is USD and hedged EUR and CHF classes are available to investors; another for the investments of the rAGMF: investments are primarily in USD. Investments can be partially in EUR and are always hedged versus USD. Local currencies are permitted on a limited basis.
Triodos (HTF, TD, TFSF)	Triodos adopts a diversification strategy, with loans in a variety of local and hard currencies. The spreads between Triodos' cost of funds and its on-lending rate to MFIs are sufficient to cover foreign exchange losses in the long run, and even with the increase in the value of the EUR its funds have done well in the long term. *Hivos-Triodos Fund and Triodos-Doen Foundation*: since 2002 the USD/EUR risk has been hedged by forward transactions. Positions in other currencies are not hedged but the funds try to cover exchange rate losses by a sufficient spread between interest rates charged in local currency and costs in EUR. *Triodos Fair Share Fund*: the USD/EUR and MNX/EUR risks are hedged by forward transactions. Positions in other currencies are not hedged.
SIDI	SIDI is specialised in the financial support of potentially strong MFIs. In some cases, these institutions are not yet financially viable when SIDI starts financing. Given this target group, its specific needs, and SIDI's vision, SIDI accords priority to equity investment and local currency loans. Two thirds of the portfolio is in equity, of which most is in local currency. For the remaining one third, over half is in local currency. In order to use these two financial instruments without directly incurring associated exchange losses, SIDI has set up a hedging fund, the FID (Development Incentive Fund). An internal review (2001) of the costs and benefits of the equity investments showed that in all cases but 2, after 12 years the gain in the market price of the shares more than overcomes the loss from currency devaluation.
Unitus	Does not hedge equity. Loans are made in local currency. FX hedges and exposure are outsourced to a third party.
USAID/Credit Guarantees	All currency hedging for guarantees is done by the U.S. Treasury.

(a) Although Alterfin borrows in USD to match its funding and operating currency, this chapter – for the sake of simplification – focuses on the MFIF's main currency. (b) For more details, see Women's World Banking, Foreign Exchange Risk Management in Microfinance, Occasional Paper, pages 13-14, and Oikocredit Annual Report 2003, page 29.

Source: Joint KfW Survey by ADA, CGAP, and The MIX, July – October 2004.

Appendix 5: Currency Risk Management Policies for 20 MFIFs That Face Currency Risk But Do

ACCION Gateway (c)	Does not hedge its local currency equity investments.
AIM (b)	Does not hedge its local currency equity investments.
AfriCap (b)	Equity and quasi-equity investments are made in local currency and the fund assumes currency risk.
AWF Development Debt	No hedging.
Cordaid	No hedging. High foreign exchange losses for the past two years due to EUR/USD exchange rate (about USD 2 million a year). No losses in 2004.
DOEN	No hedging policy.
DID – Fonidi (c)	No hedging strategy for equity investments.
FIG (a)	All guarantees are issued in hard currencies (USD, EUR and CHF).
ICCO	No hedging policy.
I&P Développement	Lending in EUR, USD, or local currency (with currency risk shared among borrower and lender). No hedging for equity investments.
KfW/DEG	No hedging.
LABF (a)	Makes dollar denominated guarantees for local currency borrowings by MFIs.
LFP (b)	No hedging policy.
Luxmint-ADA	Investments are made in USD or EUR. The USD-EUR FX risk is taken by the fund.
MIF/IADB	No hedging policy currently, but reviewing different mechanisms for future implementation.
OTI	OTI is mainly an equity fund and does not hedge equity. However, within the Opportunity International group, a separate loan guarantee fund helps affiliates obtain local currency loans. This is Opportunity International's approach to hedging debt for affiliates.
ProCredit Holding	Financial statements are in EUR. USD/EUR currency risk for equity investments is not hedged. The local currency risk is managed in the institutions in which we invest by EUR/USD indexed lending to our customers.
PROFUND	The fund does not enter into any hedging contracts.
Rabobank Foundation	Since Rabobank Foundation's main objective is to eradicate poverty, it is targeted to small, new initiatives and uses local currency loans as a development instrument. Rabobank Foundation therefore runs the currency exchange risk.
ShoreCap Intl. (c)	Preferred but not required.

(a) Guarantees. (b) Equity/Quasi-equity. (c) Mixed, currently invested only in equity.

Source: Joint KfW Survey by ADA, CGAP, and The MIX, July – October 2004.

Appendix 6: Currency Risk Management Policies for 7 MFIFs That Do Not Hedge Because They Face No Currency Risk

Calvert Foundation	Lends only in USD to MFIs that can comfortably manage the foreign exchange risk (e.g., where the economy is dollarised to some degree and the MFI has dollar assets and liabilities). In countries where FX risk is a greater concern, Calvert Foundation places dollars on deposit to serve as collateral for local currency loans.
DB MDF	The MFI must deposit the DB MDF funds as collateral for obtaining a further leveraged loan in local currency from a local bank. The MFI earns market interest on this USD-based deposit. If the interest earned is higher than the interest payment due on the local currency loan. The DB MDF loan remains in USD unless the MFI defaults on the loan to the local commercial bank, thereby avoiding foreign exchange risk. Local currency market-rate loans must have a minimum leverage ratio of 2:1.
Gray Ghost	No hedging required.
DID – Guarantee (a)	No hedging strategy due to the uncertainty of disbursement (no transactions in the fund yet).
PCG	No hedging policy.
PlaNet Fund	There is no currency hedging as the loans are granted in EUR. Local currency funding will be soon in place in India (through deposits as guarantees for local currency loans from the local subsidiary of an international bank). PlaNet is starting to make USD loans to MFIs in dollarised economies in Latin America, and the EUR/USD risk is taken by the fund.
SGIF	No equity hedge. Currently hedge only CAD/USD, as most loans are in USD. May use EUR as SGIF expands into Eastern Europe, and would need EUR/USD hedge. (b)

(a) Guarantees. (b) SGIF is funded mainly in USD, but also in CAD. This study focuses on the currency risk that occurs in the transaction between the MFIF and the MFI. For simplification, the study focuses on the *main* funding currency of the MFIF. As this example indicates, there are cases where the MFIF is funded in more than one currency, and should hedge even if its main funding currency and its operating currency are the same.

Source: Joint KfW Survey by ADA, CGAP, and The MIX, July – October 2004.

Appendix 7: Microfinance Investors by Main Funding Currency and Actual Operating Currencies (Based on 2003 or 2004 Portfolios of 46 Microfinance Investors)

MFIF Operating Currency	MFIF Main Funding Currency		
	USD	EUR	Other
USD only	BO Securities I** Calvert Foundation DB MDF Dexia Microcredit Fund Gray Ghost LABF (a) PCG SGIF USAID/Credit Guarantees (a)	AWF Development Debt** Finnfund**	
EUR only		PlaNet Fund	
Local currency only	ACCION Gateway* (c) AfriCap (b) ShoreCap Intl.* (c) Unitus*	I&P Développement* LFP* (b)	CAD (Canadian dollar): DID – Fonidi Fund* (c) DID – Guarantee Fund* (a)
No detailed data available	Citigroup Foundation IDF LA-CIF		Indian Rupee: FWWB South African Rand: KEF Bangladeshi Taka: PKSF Indonesian Rupiah: PT UKABIMA Moldovan Leu: RFC Yemeni Rival: SFD

(a) Guarantees. (b) Equity/Quasi-equity. (c) Mixed, currently only invested in equity. MFIF Operating Currency = currency in which the MFIF lends to MFIs; MFIF Main Funding Currency = Main currency in which the MFIF is funded. * = MFIFs that can theoretically invest in a mix of MFI operating currencies but currently invest only in local currencies. ** = MFIF that can theoretically invest in a mix of MFI operating currencies but currently invest only in USD. See Appendices 3 and 8 for more details.

Source: Joint KfW Survey by ADA, CGAP, and The MIX, July – October 2004; MIX Market 2005.

Appendix 7 (continued)

MFIF Operating Currency	MFIF Main Funding Currency		
	USD	EUR	Other
Mix of USD, EUR, and other, including other hard currencies, but mainly local currencies	AIM (b) CreSud IFC MicroVest MIF/IADB OTI PROFUND responsAbility Fund	Alterfin ANF BIO Cordaid DOEN Etimos FMO ICCO Incofin KfW/DEG Luxmint-ADA NOVIB Oikocredit ProCredit Holding Rabobank SIDI Triodos (HTF, TDF, TFSF)	**CAD (Canadian dollar):** DID – Partnership Fund **CHF (Swiss franc):** FIG (a)
No detailed data available	CAF GMF (c) MFDF UNCDF	EBRD Kolibri	

(a) Guarantees. (b) Equity/Quasi-equity. (c) Launched in April 2004. MFIF Operating Currency = currency in which the MFIF lends to MFIs; MFIF Main Funding Currency = Main currency in which the MFIF is funded.

Source: Joint KfW Survey by ADA, CGAP, and The MIX, July – October 2004; MIX Market 2005.

Appendix 8: Portfolio Breakdown by Actual Operating Currencies for 46 Microfinance Investors (Based on 2003 or 2004 data)

MFIF Main Funding Currency	Name of MFIF	Date	USD	EUR	Other hard currency	Local currency (b)
	Funding Exclusively in USD					
	ACCION Latin America Bridge Fund (a)	Dec-03	100%	0%	0%	0%
	BlueOrchard Microfinance Securities I, LLC**	Dec-03	100%	0%	0%	0%
	Calvert Foundation	Jun-04	100%	0%	0%	0%
USD	DB MDF	Dec-03	100%	0%	0%	0%
	Gray Ghost	Oct-04	100%	0%	0%	0%
	Partners for the Common Good	Dec-03	100%	0%	0%	0%
	Sarona Global Investment Fund, Inc.	Sep-04	100%	0%	0%	0%
	USAID/Credit Guarantees (a)	Sep-04	100%	0%	0%	0%
	Funding Exclusively in EUR					
EUR	AWF**	Sep-04	100%	0%	0%	0%
	Finnfund**	Sep-04	100%	0%	0%	0%
EUR	PlaNet Fund	Dec-03	0%	100%	0%	0%

(a) Guarantees. (b) If different than USD or EUR. ** = MFIF that can theoretically invest in a mix of MFI operating currencies but currently invest only in USD. See Appendixes 3 and 7.

Source: Joint KfW Survey by ADA, CGAP, and The MIX, July – October 2004; MIX Market 2005. Note that the portfolio breakdown is captured at a specific point in time (see "Date", above). The portfolio composition – and place of the MFIFs in the table – can change based on the theoretical operating currencies in which MFIFs lend to MFIs, presented in Appendix 3. Investments include investments in MFIs and/or networks and other MFIs.

Appendix 8 (continued)

MFIF Main Funding Currency	Name of MFIF	Date	USD	EUR	Other hard currency	Local currency (d)
	Funding Exclusively in Local Currencies (other than USD and EUR)					
USD	ACCION Gateway Fund* (c)	Jun-04	0%	0%	0%	100%
	AfriCap Microfinance Fund (b)	Dec-03	0%	0%	0%	100%
	ShoreCap Intl.* (c)	Dec-03	0%	0%	0%	100%
	Unitus*	Dec-03	0%	0%	0%	100%
EUR	I&P Développement*	Jun-04	0%	0%	0%	100%
	LFP* (b)	Sep-04	0%	0%	0%	100%
CAD	DID – Fonidi Fund* (c)	Mar-04	0%	0%	0%	100%
	Funding in a Mix of Currencies					
USD	ACCION Investments in Microfinance (b)	Sep-04	21%	0%	0%	79%
	CreSud	Sep-04	93%	7%	0%	0%
	Dexia Microcredit Fund	Dec-03	94%	6%	0%	0%
	IFC	Sep-04	73%	0%	0%	27%
	MicroVest	Jul-04	89%	0%	0%	11%
	MIF/IADB	Dec-03	71%	0%	0%	29%
	OTI	Jun-04	50%	50%	0%	0%
	PROFUND	Jun-04	9%	91%	0%	0%
	responsAbility Fund	Jun-04	74%	26%	0%	0%

(a) Guarantees. (b) Equity/Quasi-equity. (c) Mixed, currently invested only in equity. (d) If different than USD or EUR. * = MFIFs that can theoretically invest in a mix of MFI operating currencies but currently invest only in local currencies. See Appendices 3 and 7.

Source: Joint KfW Survey by ADA, CGAP, and The MIX, July – October 2004; MIX Market 2005. Note that the portfolio breakdown is captured at a specific point in time (see "Date" above). The portfolio composition – and place of the MFIFs in the table – can change based on the theoretical operating currencies in which MFIs lend to MFIs, presented in Appendix 3. Investments include investments in MFIs and/or networks and other MFIFs.

Appendix 8 (continued)

MFIF Main Funding Currency	Name of MFIF	Date	USD	EUR	Other hard currency	Local currency (d)
	Funding in a Mix of Currencies (continued)					
EUR	Alterfin	Dec-03	71%	13%	0%	16%
EUR	ASN-Novib Fonds	Dec-03	67%	33%	0%	0%
EUR	BIO	Jun-04	42%	46%	0%	12%
EUR	Cordaid Foundation	Dec-03	17%	31%	0%	52%
EUR	DOEN Foundation	Dec-03	0%	88%	0%	12%
EUR	Etimos	Dec-03	55%	44%	0%	1%
EUR	FMO	Dec-03	0%	61%	0%	39%
EUR	Hivos-Triodos Fund	Dec-04	34%	21%	0%	45%
EUR	ICCO	Dec-03	0%	56%	0%	44%
EUR	Incofin	Sep-04	26%	63%	0%	11%
EUR	KfW/DEG	Oct-04	24%	76%	0%	0%
EUR	Luxmint-ADA	Dec-03	79%	21%	0%	0%
EUR	NOVIB	Dec-03	48%	19%	0%	33%
EUR	Oikocredit	Jun-04	43%	22%	0%	35%
EUR	ProCredit Holding	Sep-04	73%	20%	0%	7%
EUR	Rabobank Foundation	Jun-04	34%	10%	7%	49%
EUR	SIDI	Dec-04	23%	6%	0%	71%
EUR	Triodos-Doen Foundation	Dec-04	56%	22%	0%	22%
EUR	Triodos Fair Share Fund	Dec-04	61%	28%	0%	11%
CAD	DID – Partnership Fund	Jun-04	97%	0%	0%	3%
CHF	FIG (a)	Dec-03	84%	16%	0%	0%

(a) Guarantees. (b) If different than USD or EUR.

Source: Joint KfW Survey by ADA, CGAP, and The MIX, July – October 2004; MIX Market 2005. Note that the portfolio breakdown is captured at a specific point in time (see "Date" above). The portfolio composition – and place of the MFIFs in the table – can change over time based on the theoretical operating currencies in which MFIFs lend to MFIs, presented in Appendix 3. Investments include investments in MFIs and/or networks and other MFIFs.

Appendix 9: Unhedged Foreign Currency Loans (39 selected MFIs)

Country	Amount	Currency
Azerbaijan	300,000	USD
Bangladesh	124,470	USD
Benin	36,225	USD
Benin	1,300,000	EUR
Bolivia (4 MFIs)	58,085,260	USD
Bosnia and Herzegovina (2MFIs)	9,062,628	EUR
Bosnia and Herzegovina	3,982,450	USD
Bulgaria	1,888,195	USD
Cambodia	100,000	USD
Congo, Democratic Republic of the	10,000	USD
Dominican Republic (2 MFIs)	578,000	USD
Georgia	300,000	USD
Haiti	750,000	USD
India (2 MFIs)	942,148	USD
Jordan	150,000	USD
Kyrgyzstan	4,000,000	USD
Mexico	100,000	USD
Morocco	625,570	USD
Morocco	5,200,000	EUR
Nepal	40,000	USD
Nicaragua	650,000	USD
Peru (5 MFIs)	9,864,983	USD
Philippines	19,570	USD
Togo (3 MFIs)	297,904	EUR
Uganda (2 MFIs)	350,000	USD
Venezuela	195,000	USD

Exchange rate USD/EUR = 1.2557. This Table omits USD loans to MFIs in completely dollarised economies and EUR loans to MFIs operating in EURs: 5 USD loans to Ecuador for a combined amount of USD 2,674,946, a USD loan to El Salvador for USD 500,000, and a EUR loan to Kosovo for EUR 2,845,261.

Source: "MFI Demand for Funding" survey by CGAP and The MIX, 2004.

Appendix 10: Partially Hedged Foreign Currency Loans (16 selected MFIs)

Country	Amount	Currency	Percentage Hedged
Cambodia	510,000	USD	5 %
Malawi	440,530	USD	5 %
Nigeria	50,000	USD	5 %
Paraguay	1,335,873	USD	5 %
Tanzania	10,000	USD	5 %
Colombia	683,000	USD	10 %
Cambodia	2,500,000	USD	15 %
Uganda	3054121	USD	20 %
India	5,000	USD	40 %
Kyrgyzstan	755,814	USD	50 %
Nicaragua	390,000	USD	50 %
Mongolia	1,725,000	USD	75 %
Cambodia	1,500,000	USD	80 %
Armenia	400,000	USD	85 %
Bosnia and Herzegovina	800,000	EUR	90 %
Peru	45,000,000	USD	95 %

Exchange rate USD/EUR = 1.2557. This Table omits one USD loan to an MFI in El Salvador (dollarised economy) for USD 65,400.

Source: "MFI Demand for Funding" survey by CGAP and The MIX, 2004.

Appendix 11: Fully Hedged Foreign Currency Loans (17 selected MFIs)

Country	Amount	Currency
Bosnia and Herzegovina (2 MFIs)	12,927,566	EUR
Colombia	415,000	USD
Croatia	500,000	USD
Egypt	200,000	USD
Guatemala	100,000	USD
India	658,196	USD
Mexico	9,583,333	USD

Country	Amount	Currency
Morocco	12,750,000	EUR
Nicaragua (2 MFIs)	1,017,187	USD
Pakistan	800,000	USD
Peru (2 MFIs)	2,444,839	USD
Tanzania	2,195,000	USD
Uganda	375,000	USD
Zimbabwe	6,000	USD

Source: "MFI Demand for Funding" survey by CGAP and The MIX, 2004.

CHAPTER 9

Governance, Transparency, and Accountability in the Microfinance Investment Fund Industry[1]

Robert Pouliot

Chief Analyst, RCP and Partners, Geneva

Introduction: Improving Fiduciary Practice

Fiduciary governance of the microfinance investment fund (MFIF) industry is at a crossroads. Best practice and fiduciary governance require serious improvement to win the trust of an entirely new class of institutional investors. A new breed of managers have become "swing funders" of microfinance, increasingly able to influence interest rate movements, while investors are kept in the dark about the true nature of this asset class, its risk levels and the "social hazards" imposed upon them.

This paper proposes practical ways to address these problems. In combination with the glossary at the end of the book, it examines the two sides of fiduciary governance: exogenous factors affecting investment professionals, such as its poor regulatory environment, and the importance of defining this new asset class on the basis of a clear risk/reward profile; and endogenous factors related to the daily practice of fiduciaries and how they meet the contractual expectations of investors.

The exogenous dimension includes the confusion surrounding the whole microfinance asset class, which is undermined by social hazards that weaken fiduciary practice and threaten its credibility among institutional investors. The asset class remains unclear, blurred by factors that make it difficult for outside investors to determine risk levels. Microcredit investment is essentially conducted over-the-counter (there is no exchange or liquid market as yet) for both fixed-income and equity securities of microfinance institution. Some managers claim microfinance investment is a "money market plus" product (providing a yield equal to the money market rates *plus* some additional percentage or a dual objective investment seeking a financial return *plus* development impact). Others say that it is much closer to the least efficient markets of private equity, showing an enormous performance gap exceeding 10%. If it is mission-oriented, it is impossible to determine how much investors "leave on the table" in the form of development im-

---

[1] 2005 © Rating Capital Partners SA.

pact rather than financial return. This ambiguity is deepened by the uneven standards applied to microfinance institutions (MFIs) by rating agencies. Some ratings are credit driven, while others have a fiduciary focus, with no common denominator of risk or risk measurement for funders, whether financial or social.

The endogenous case arises from the fair to poor fiduciary practice by fund managers. The lack of performance valuation and presentation standards makes it virtually impossible for investors to compare funds by their risks and rewards. Furthermore, some emerging MFIF professionals do not seem to distinguish the wide risk disparity between equity and fixed income (that is, debt) management. Fiduciary practice includes fund structure, risk control systems and compliance, investment processes, price setting, quality of reporting, integrity and comparability of data. These variables are the most critical components of the three key concerns of any serious investor: governance, transparency and accountability. Until these conditions meet generally accepted and recognised fiduciary practice (GARFP) standards, the level of trustworthiness and reliability will not trigger the flood of capital that so many people hope for.

The explosive growth of the MFIF industry since 2002 on the fixed income (debt) side and the current trend towards much greater leverage might expose or create fiduciary problems that could reduce investor interest for some time to come. To strengthen the credibility of the MFIF industry, this chapter recommends to bilateral and multilateral organisations five major lines of action: defining the asset class, defining the fiduciary risk, setting key assumptions, setting fiduciary practice, and measuring fiduciary risk. In addition, it prescribes fiduciary rating for all management firms offering microcredit investment funds, and advocates a charter of fiduciary rights (Annex).

Setting the Context: External and Internal Fiduciary Causes for Concern

Risk management is rapidly evolving in fiduciary practice. Formerly, it focused strictly on the investment portfolio, based on quantitative measurement against market benchmarks. Risk management practice gradually moved upstream during the late 1990s to identify the major sources of high and low performance by asset managers within the fund industry, recognising that people and systems could not be divorced from overall governance, checks and balances, risk control, fund raising and compliance. The nascent MFIF industry, hardly more than 6 years old, is emerging from a start-up phase. It is attracting institutional money, especially from pension funds. The better-managed MFIFs have experienced meteoric growth, with assets under management more than trebling since 2001. This creates concern about how the industry will cope with such rapid growth without improvements in fiduciary practice. While fiduciary practice has progressed, it has yet to become fully credible in the eyes of mainstream institutional investors. Rapid changes are required.

Exogenous Threats to the Asset Class

Microfinance is a unique asset class in the investment management industry. Seven exogenous factors put its credibility at stake.

- Confusion between credit and fiduciary risk remains widespread. A majority of MFIF professionals fail to recognise that, due to average low returns, their practice is probably the main cause of under-performance.

- The MFIF market, fixed income and equity, is highly inefficient. No real performance benchmarks exist and few funds are comparable, making it difficult to determine how much value MFIF professionals really create beyond what the market readily provides.

- There is clearly no consensus on the level of riskiness or on the benchmark rate of return for this asset class. Until a common range is agreed, this asset class is unlikely to be broadly accepted by institutional investors, their consultants and trustees – let alone their clients.

- The implicit recognition by several managers that investors are giving away part of the gross return in favour of sustainability and social development benefits creates confusion about the returns that can be expected from this asset class. Large institutional investors do not know whether microfinance is a mission-oriented investment with clear financial goals, or an ethical fund with returns discounted in favour of non-financial values. While giving the appearance of an immature asset class, such debate makes the task of allocating assets even more difficult for institutional investors.

The risk measurement scales of most rating and evaluation services used by the MFIF industry are still weak and confusing. Moreover, the Inter-American Development Bank (IDB) and the Consultative Group to Assist the Poor (CGAP) have provided rather poor supervision in accrediting rating services and optimising quality control. As a result, wide disparities persist in rating judgments and little or no correlation exists between ratings and interest rate spreads. Some ratings are fiduciary, others are credit-driven. Some measure risk, while others provide financial ratios but no overall risk judgment. None provides an adequate country credit risk assessment.

- The average MFIF size is far too low to attract institutional investors: the vast majority have assets of less than the threshold of US$/€ 20 million. Prudence causes institutional investors to limit their holdings in any single fund, usually to less than a 5% stake. An investor following this rule would restrict its investment to US$/€ 1 million in an MFIF with assets of US$/€ 20 million. This could make the position too costly in terms of transaction costs, such as fiduciary reporting and analysis, biting into the low return of most funds. Small size implies management fees of 2.5% to 3.5%, high by industry standards, which, added to relatively costly transactions, tend to inflate the total expense ratio (TER).

Box 1. 10 Key Distinctions Between Fiduciary and Corporate Governance

Fiduciary	**Corporate**
• Shareholder driven	• Organisation driven
• Mission focus to meet investors' expectations	• Arbitrage among various stakeholders
• Trust sensitive	• Credit sensitive
• Ensure trustworthiness	• Ensure creditworthiness
• Principles-based	• Rules-based
• Principal vs. agency concerns	• Check & balance focus
• Priority to accountability	• Priority to compliance
• Sustainability-driven	• Performance-driven
• More practice-centred	• More operation-centred
• Data integrity/reliability	• Organisation transparency

Gomper, Ishii, and Metrick (2001) constructed a broad index of shareholders' rights (Governance Index), and documented a positive correlation between the governance index and long-horizon returns (quoted by Governance & Risk, from George Dallas of S&P).

- The multiplicity of actors and funders grouped under the "social development" label and the variety of their agendas prevent the market for this asset class from achieving the discipline and standardisation required by professional trustees. "Soft" and "hard" money investors have different risk appetites and yield expectations, although the soft investors' agendas are often muddled.

Endogenous Threats to the Asset Class

Four key endogenous fiduciary constraints prevent MFIFs from reaching medium-to-high net worth retail investors and institutional investors.

- The immature stage of most investment tools and systems used by MFIF practitioners has kept fiduciary standards far below those of the larger fund management industry. It has also fuelled doubts about whether micro fund management might simply boil down to large or multinational MFIs' (microfinance institutions) lending to local MFIs disguised as investment vehicles.

- Reporting is generally poor. Even the more transparent firms fail to provide the disclosure expected by investors in conventional vehicles. The absence of clearly identifiable market benchmarks, other than basic cost-plus indices such as LIBOR+2% or LIBORx2 and TERs, add confusion to the risk profile and the opportunity cost of this new asset class.[2]

- The lack of performance presentation standards, either agreed among the leaders of the industry or reflecting the Global Investment Performance Standards (GIPS) promoted by the CFA Institute[3] and most European and Asian financial analysts' societies, makes comparison virtually impossible. This adds to the bleak perceptions institutional investors may have of this asset class.

- The investment process is hardly documented and can be summarised as lending to MFIs based on an established diversification policy, with little or very low expected returns unrelated to their effective risks.

Defining the Asset Class: Where Does Microfinance Belong in the Investment Universe?

Strangely, key features of the microfinance investment universe have led some specialists to classify this asset class as money market plus. Key features that misleadingly suggest such a definition include: little or nil volatility, like money market instruments; predominately short term, with an average duration of 18 months, seldom exceeding the 36-month short term limit;[4] the cash nature of the business with a high transaction turnover due to short duration; and the low default record. For example, Dexia and LACIF, relatively large MFIFs, have never recorded any loss from an insolvency of an investee. IGF experienced several losses on loans to small MFIs (as a result of guarantees being called by banks), but its shareholders have never suffered a capital loss.[5]

---

[2] LIBOR is the London Inter-Bank Offered Rate. LIBORx2 = twice the LIBOR rate.

[3] Previously known as the Association for Investment & Management Research, based in Charlottesville, Virginia. The CFA Institute is an international, non-profit organisation of more than 70,000 investment practitioners and educators in over 100 countries. Its mission is "To lead the investment profession globally by setting the highest standards of education, integrity, and professional excellence."

[4] In contrast, the Lehman Emerging Market Bond Index, which includes over 100 issuers, had an average duration of 3.7 years with an average annual return on its global composite index of 7% from March 1998 to mid-2004.

[5] The average tenor (maturity) is 19 months for Dexia's Micro-Credit Fund and for LACIF loans in Latin America, 18 months limited to 24 months. A recent loan of US$ 2.5 million made by LACIF had a 3 year maturity. A trend towards much longer maturities is discernable, best illustrated by BlueOrchard. The initial Dexia fund it started had a maturity cap of 3 years, according to Luxembourg regulations. The second responsAbility Global Fund it took over in 2003 from a group of Swiss banks allows maturities of up to 5 years. And the 2004 collateralised debt obligation (CDO) fund agreement concluded with the US OPIC offered maturities as long as 7 years. Such lengthening will have a direct impact on duration and MFIF portfolio sensitivity within the next three years. Marking-to-market will be unavoidable.

Box 2. Where Does Microfinance Investment Fit?

There are four major investment classes:

- Conventional – listed securities, bonds and money markets.

- Alternative – hedge funds, private equity/venture capital, real estate, etc.

- Mission-oriented investments – with sustainable development, environmental, social, religious or other value constraints.

The first three, listed above, primarily seek financial performance that is either relative (compared against benchmarks) or absolute (avoiding losses and maximising returns).

- Ethical, mission oriented seeking value satisfaction – feeling good by helping people – before financial returns. The return can only be relative to a mission; measurement must take into account the benefits left on the table, or how the investor's financial concession is recycled into tangible benefits (financial, material, social, etc.), making asset allocation even more difficult to achieve in an efficient way for institutional investors.

Where does MFIF belong in the investment universe?

The micro fund management asset class is mission-oriented and belongs to the alternative asset class in the high yield end of the over-the-counter issued debt and equity market.

MFIF instruments are indeed distinct from conventional OECD money market instruments. The money market plus approach is also flawed because it ignores the risk of emerging money and bond markets where:

- Macro-volatility of local markets is highly dependent on international interest rates. Moreover, local markets, which MFIs increasingly tap for funding, are very inefficient.

- Tropical weather (storms, hurricanes, floods, etc) can have devastating effects on financial markets and on MFIs.

- MFIs' foreign currency exposure can threaten solvency. Funding locally generated by depositors is growing, but this increases MFIs' exposure to local systemic risks.

- Steady increases in maturity and duration are starting to introduce liquidity pressure in the market, making it difficult for an MFIF to pull out or liquefy its exposure prior to maturity.

The MFIF industry has the following characteristics: It has a high-yield fixed income stream (including the guarantee market but excluding funds invested in equity). It is based mainly on low grade issuers of promissory notes, CDs (certificates of deposit) and guarantees in emerging markets. The asset class is closer to entrepreneurial finance than to conventional corporate finance. It is part of the unlisted world of private equity markets and small to medium enterprises (SME). When it stakes start-ups it is close to venture capital. It is an alternative asset class.

Box 3. Ten Key Differences Between Two Types of Risk	
Credit Risk	**Fiduciary Risk**
• Asset intermediation	• Systems/processes
• Fixed income revenue in symmetry with client interest	• Variable fee revenue in asymmetry with client interest
• Economic cycles	• Capital market cycles
• Shown ex-post on balance sheet	• Shown ex-ante on P&L
• More downstream	• More upstream
• Medium-term inertia	• Short-term inertia
• More quantitative	• More qualitative
• Results centred	• Best practice centred
• Excludes fiduciary governance	• Includes corporate governance
• Banking regulation	• Securities regulation

Another feature of the industry is fiduciary behaviour in packaging MFIF products in ways that often tend to be confusing, if not misleading. For example, "social development" for marketing reasons may simply justify a lower return than could normally be expected on this asset class. MFIF operations may indeed have a social dimension and impact, but the investments should first and foremost be essentially financial, unless investors are willing to leave some of their gains on the table. In that case, funds should qualify as "ethical," which denotes zero returns or a return equal to the rate of inflation.

Given the definition of alternative asset classes, the return should be stated in absolute terms against a benchmark. In other words, if a benchmark is negative, it would not be enough to beat the benchmark by posting a smaller negative performance (as is the case with so many so-called actively managed conventional funds). MFIFs should always record a positive return with no drawdown unless a default is recorded. Management should be active, seeking to create value rather than trying to replicate an index. The only alternative would be a passive approach with funders co-investing alongside funds. However, this is not recommended; if things go wrong, a serious accountability problem arises.

Defining the Fiduciary Risk: Debt, Balanced Portfolio, and Equity

A microcredit fund may appear homogeneous, but as in the case of liquid securities, managing bonds often proves to be very different from managing shares. Private equity distinguishes early, mid- and late stage investments, and the range of sub-asset classes in microfinance requires different skills, systems and techniques.

Box 4. Risk Definition of Three Sub-classes of Microfinance Investments		
Lowest Risk	**Medium Risk**	**Highest Risk**
Debt Securities and Guarantees	Balanced Portfolio	Venture Capital (early seed stage equity)
Key challenges	*Key challenges in addition to those of lowest risk*	*Key challenges in addition to those of lower risks*
Liquidity	Corporate governance	Very early stage/seed risk
Solvency	Long illiquidity (>7 years)	Very capital intensive
Yield curve management	Exit planning	
Portfolio mix, diversification	Financial engineering	
Leverage		
Key risk features	*Key risk features in addition to those of lowest risk*	*Key risk features in addition to those of lower risks*
Currency risk	Post-early stage MFIs are going concerns, seeking mezzanine/development capital	Little alignment of interests with social entrepreneurs
Country risk		Confusing status of start-up/ early stage MFIs
Specific risk of funding structure – hard to assess	Soft front-end equity risk with high-end debt risk	Reaching going concern status
Lack of secondary market		
Confusing ownership of MFIs	Confusion in evaluating two risks: equity and debt, with different surveillance requirements	
Little alignment of interests among investors		

Debt Securities and Guarantees: Too Nice to Fail?

The low specific risk and high yield of the microfinance asset class offers a unique investment for OECD investors seeking exposure to the private equity fixed income market of emerging countries. Key features include fiduciary leniency, volatility, illiquidity, strong monitoring, and outstanding growth.

Fiduciary Leniency

Unlike other segments of emerging markets, MFIs enjoy exceptional protection from aid providers: cheap funding, credit insurance, emergency assistance in natural catastrophes, training institutes, subsidised rating facilities, etc. To some extent, they are "too nice to fail," supported by a sort of moral safety net that has never been quantified and is not found in any other emerging market sector. But this rose bed should be considered with suspicion to avoid fuelling moral hazard and a false sense of fiduciary discretion.

MFI Monitoring

MFI monitoring is exceptionally strong, conducted by the sponsors that create the "too nice to fail" security blanket. Similar to venture capital industry practice, coaching, supervision and tracking have actively reinforced "alignment of concerns" that remains short of true symmetry in effective alignment of financial interests. But unlike venture capital, investee managers are poorly rewarded for their contribution to their financial performance, despite a very impressive value creation track record. Incentives in the form of equity, stock options, purchase rights or a basic carried interest (share of the profits) are rare in this asset class. Its main difference from venture capital is that the MFI entrepreneurial element lies in its ownership of the mission instead of capital. This creates a clash over fiduciary governance. Mission is indeed the privy of shareholders and cannot be set by any other stakeholder. In the NGO world the entrepreneur tends to abandon his financial rights for his mission and often confuses his role of agent with that of principal.

Volatility

In contrast to many other segments of emerging markets, MFIs appear to be less sensitive to local and regional economic cycles because their clientele depends heavily on subsistence consumption. However, as MFIs tranform into small to medium size commercial banks, they tend to lose their interest rate insensitivity and their volatility begins to emerge.

Liquidity

The absence of secondary markets for MFI debt and the lack of any significant benchmarks against which these instruments can be marked-to-market considerably reduce the volatility of the investment exposure. However, intrinsic underlying volatility cannot yet be properly recorded and data may be insufficient to meet new IFR (international financial reporting) and US GAAP standards. On the other hand, volatility is dampened by the rather short duration of most loans to MFIs. In fact, there is a secondary market where fair market value may be assessed. First, some MFIFs use put options that would force an MFI to repay their loan immediately in case a triggering event occurs. The put means that the alternative to the loan is either another loan to an MFI or the interest rate prevailing on local bank loans to MFIs. Second, although MFI CDs or commercial papers are not tradable on the local market, any spread resulting from the difference between current loans to MFIs by MFIFs and local commercial bank loans to MFIs should indicate the real value of the MFIF investment.

Rapid Growth

The outstanding growth of MFIs, ranging from 20 % to 40 % per annum, dwarfs any other asset class in emerging markets. Remarkably, equity exposure has been neglected by financial investors, especially at the seed and start-up stages, in contrast to the developing stage where an MFI takes off after reaching sustainability.

MFIF Debt Securities' Emerging Market Status

While offering low specific risk and high yields, microcredit investment is high risk compared to emerging market sovereigns (government debt) and blue chips. But the low risk feature will dissipate if investment funds move into second tier or lower quality MFIs in order to maintain their spread and protect their yield. (Many funds' yields have dropped since 2002.) For instance, if a fund targets a gross yield of 6-month LIBOR+6% for its loans to MFIs and has a TER of 3% (LACIF had 3.5% in 2003), it creates a loss for the investor. But how? An investor could earn 2.5% on a treasury bill. Is it really worthwhile for him to move into emerging markets and earn an extra 2.5% on a privately held MFI, often with a highly confusing ownership structure, exposed to risky emerging markets which may be subjected to risk premiums ranging from 4% to 8%? Put differently, an MFIF client earning 2% to 3% is essentially an ethical investor who gives away between: a) 1% to 2% of extra income that could be earned directly from the MFI; and b) 4% to 8% of extra income that could be earned from country risk. If that is the actual "social development tax" imposed on investors, it will be difficult to attract institutional investors unless MFIF professionals are willing to reduce TER to half of its present level. This could be dangerous because it could lower the quality of research and due diligence.

Box 5. Risk-Adjusted Returns

Two Leading Funds and Three Indices (%)

Period	BlueOrchard	LACIF	Lehman	JPMorgan	ESBI-Citi
2000	-0.24	-18.29	-1.99	5.00	4.88
2001	2.18	4.69	-6.12	-7.07	-7.31
2002	1.90	21.86	-1.01	3.68	4.56
2003	1.87	15.30	18.12	21.12	23.28
2004 6 mos.	1.07	5.44	-1.94	-9.14	-7.40

The risk-adjusted return calculated here is known as the Sharpe Ratio. It is the return minus all the sweat (or risk) required to achieve the return. The purpose here is to see whether MFIFs offer a better return than three market indices. The ratio calculates effective value creation beyond two risk levels: *creditworthiness*, using as proxy a risk-free 6-month deposit with a prime bank, and *volatility* or fluctuation of the investment value (see Glossary for definition). Subtract the risk-free interest rate or LIBOR from the return of each fund or index. This difference indicates what the manager (or the market for the indices) generates beyond a risk-free investment. BlueOrchard achieved a 4.07% return in 2002; deducting the average LIBOR rate of 1.97% leaves 2.1% of real value, which is called excess return. Then, volatility of the MFIs' return on a monthly basis, 0.21%, is subtracted, leaving a net of 1.90% for all the risk the investor has taken. The high returns of LACIF are due to heavy leverage (>3x).

Risk-Stripping and Gearing to Increase Yields

There are two ways – risk stripping and borrowing – for investors to capitalise on gearing (or leverage) without falling victim to moral hazard caused by excessive risk, specifically through the unexpected erosion of capital.

Risk Stripping or Federative Investment

The first requirement in risk stripping is to draw a line between financial and social yields. The financial yield is the objective of institutional investors. The social yield is the objective of soft investors such as IFIs (international financial institutions, e. g. the World Bank or KfW), other donors and major private aid providers. This division is best achieved by designing special fund classes for capital from soft investors seeking "social yield rates." Such rates would neutralise all country risk through the participation of bi- and multilaterals, leaving a return for institutional investors based only on the specific risk of the MFI. Such "stripped fund classes" would enable funds to raise leverage capital more easily by transferring the yield to private investors such as pension funds, which could more easily attain a return reflecting the true risk profile of the asset class.

The danger of stripping is not that one class of investors subsidises the other (the bi- and multilaterals would subsidise anyway), but that the managers would stop trying to optimise their own total return by relying too heavily on shareholder arbitrage, blurring the distinction among the classes of investors and foregoing a more rational MFI portfolio mix incorporating a sound investment yield curve. In short, financial leverage creates moral hazard by reducing the incentive to produce an appropriate pricing model. Finally, there is no free ride: leverage increases any losses that front-end equity holders would have to face, which is why they get a higher return.

Gearing Is Not a Proxy for Best Practice

The second way to leverage is for the investment vehicle to borrow funds to guarantee redemption liquidity for investors seeking exits, but more importantly, to provide a gearing booster to the overall yield. Such leverage creates better resource allocation by using low cost funds or risk-averse money to invest more risk-tolerant money as in higher yield instruments. However, it should never be a substitute for sound investment management processes and for the quest for absolute return on core assets. As no stable leverage models have yet been developed using gearing ratios, a 1:1 leverage limit should be imposed until research proves otherwise.

The Diseconomies of Scope and High Risks of Balance Portfolios

As the investment banking side of the MFIF industry develops, venture capitalists will discover that exposure to this asset class at start-up levels may be quite expensive because of transaction costs. To obtain better returns, some investment funds are considering using their knowledge of MFI fixed-income markets to initiate equity deals. This could make sense, as most of the 26 funds recorded by CGAP invest in both asset classes, that is, debt and equity. When due diligence is undertaken and the relationship for buying debt is already established, the same information would support investment in equity. This would help reduce the high transaction cost, especially for second and third tier MFIs. However, several key issues arise, as follows:

- First, this approach is appropriate for very small portfolios having a closed group of investors. But it nonetheless requires two kinds of specialists: one on credit, the other on pure equity and start-ups. It would be unwise and dangerous for a fixed-income specialist to drill down into equity schemes where the style, approach, systems, techniques and skills are simply far too different.

- Second, the twin capital approach can become a minefield of conflicts of interest. The "equity venture" unit would need fixed-income assets to leverage its position and the fixed-income managers may require subordinated equity for comfort. Cross investment can often distort risk assessments and independent analysis. Maintaining fire walls becomes impossible where the segregation of investment streams is a sine qua non for success. Venture capital and private equity firms can easily secure leverage for their investees because the money does not come from their shareholders but rather from a bank or other independent third party creditors.

- Third, when these mixed funds grow, they are unlikely to attract institutional investors because of the mix of investment styles and potential conflicts of interest. Attribution analysis, breaking down the main sources of performance, would be too difficult to be meaningful.

Box 6. MFIs vs. Early Stage Venture Capital: How Investment Criteria Differ

MFIs	Main features	Venture Cap
Yes	Fast sector growth ≥25 %	Yes
No	Strong edge/unique technology	Yes
No	High multiple gain at exit	Yes
No	Internal Rate of Return ≥25 %	Yes
No	Low capital intensity	Yes
Low	Leverage	Nil
Yes	Open to debt	Not much
Difficult	Alignment of interest	Reasonable
Plenty	Social hazards	No

- Finally, it might be easier and less problematic to use puts and calls to convert debt into equity; or through preferred shares. This is widely used in venture capital where the primary driver is equity, not debt. Although exit opportunities remain the most critical issue, this approach could provide a protective floor (in the form of preferred shares) or "yield boosters" (in the form of convertible loans) producing returns that many fund managers would be thrilled to achieve.

Equity Securities: Intensive Capital and Extensive Resources to Bear Very High Risk

If the MFIs are lower risk than normally perceived on the fixed income side, the reverse is true for the equity segment. MFIs are probably one of the most difficult enterprises to start up and develop with entrepreneurial finance, for several reasons:

- First, various microfinance agendas and purposes often have nothing to do with commercial start ups and financial performance, and its high moral and social content attracts managers and "feel good" people, some with an NGO or charity background, who are a poor fit in the world of entrepreneurship. It may be much easier to overcome an entrepreneur's tenacious obsession centred on an invention or patent in order to build a profitable company than it is to subordinate moral and social considerations in a microfinance institution so that it can create value through profits. Austrian author Stefan Sweig calls this the "confusion of sentiments" that distracts the start-up entrepreneur from becoming commercially viable. Corporate and fiduciary governance practice can suffer because the microfinance mission is viewed as essentially social rather than financial and results from a transfer of values.

- Second, fiduciary alignment of interest is difficult, involving the entire chain of investors – from the venture capital fund investor to the direct investor of the start-up MFI and to creditors – and MFI management. Without meaningful financial incentive programmes and adherence to an expected return target, the investee's management may experience serious compliance problems.

- Third, MFIs have a voracious appetite for capital because of their high growth rates (20-40% per year), and follow-on financing is exponentially more demanding than in traditional venture capital. Yet, the operating leverage potential remains relatively small and initial capital is often too low to justify the extensive resource requirements (such as time, labour, systems, valuation tracking) relative to conventional venture capital.

- Fourth, to reach business objectives a venture capital approach to microfinance requires extensive due diligence and great attention to governance through supervision and investee reporting.

- Finally, microfinance remains illiquid for at least 7 to 10 years. This makes valuation issues more complex under the new "fair market value" treatment required by IFRS and US GAAP. This complication is compounded because there are very few listed MFIs or merger and acquisition transactions that could serve as proxies or benchmarks for value. In addition, exit is quite difficult in a monoculture market where the whole equity portfolio is a single asset class.

Setting Key Criteria for the Success of the MFIF Industry

Three factors should govern the criteria used to evaluate the performance of microfinance investment funds and their managers in order to achieve good governance, transparency and accountability for investors. First, MFIF firms should be judged by the same professional criteria as other investment houses active in capital markets. The culture of the microfinance industry is fundamentally credit driven: most microfinance investment managers have little investment experience or knowledge of modern portfolio theory and fiduciary prescriptions. They tend to operate as commercial bankers, with a very pro-active deal-making focus. However, for microfinance to be recognised as a true alternative asset class by institutional investors, a code of fiduciary best practice will have to be developed to ensure consistency and professionalism.

Second, reference to social investment is used to assess the coherence and consistency of the investment management with its strategic goal and expected return. "Social investment" is far too broad a term to justify its unquestioned acceptance. For some, it suggests "ethical" investment, which means making a financial sacrifice or incurring an opportunity cost to gain entry to the asset class. For others, social investment suggests that the investor should be selective in allocating capital without having to make any financial sacrifice. It can also simply mean an investment style and a way of dealing with the asset class investees. For accountability, the social component should be clearly defined and the impact it may have on the expected financial return should be disclosed. For example, if the financial benchmark suggests that a portfolio should earn 10 % when it earns only 5 %, the gap should be clearly defined in terms of real social benefits achieved. Without this clarity, managers achieving poor returns could simply hide their lagging performance by citing vaguely defined "social benefits" or "moral values." "Helping the poor" should not justify poor results. As Jacob Yaron asked, "Is banking for the poor necessarily poor banking?"

Third, the MFIF asset class must define the level of risk and benchmark (or opportunity cost) against which performance and volatility should be measured. This asset class remains ill defined in terms of risk and opportunity, and also in terms of its true financial characteristics. Clear benchmarks based on international standards could improve the allocation of this asset class by institutional investors and their advisors. An investment policy requires an allocation strategy which

---

Box 7. Governance, Transparency, Accountability

- Governance is the mode of ruling an organisation, focusing on compliance with the mission set by owners or stakeholders.

- Transparency is the provision of useful, consistent, accurate, timely and relevant information – a disclosure practice that is independent of results.

- Accountability is the mode of reporting by which performance is measured against governance policies and transparency standards.

---

synchronises assets with future liabilities (as in annuities, pension, insurance coverage, etc.). Allocation is based on historical yields of each asset class and the correlation of each of these classes among themselves. If the MFIF asset class remains fuzzy, justifying specific allocations is very difficult and the contribution to the overall asset pool will remain too uncertain to attract large numbers of investors.

Governance

"Governance" is used in many contexts. It is used here as the overall mode of ruling an organisation to ensure that systems and structures are in place to provide conformity with the reasonable expectations of a relevant interest group of shareholders and possibly other stakeholders. This definition draws a very clear line for day-to-day management and insists on three basic approaches, whatever the corporate form: policy setting, compliance checks and balance tests, and supervision of management in the implementation of the mission set by the board on behalf of investors.

Fiduciary governance refers to how an organisation deals with its shareholders, in contrast to debt (or bond or money market) investors. The first allegiance of any corporation must be to its principals, known as shareholders. The extent of such allegiance will be directly proportional to the public exposure of shareholders. A corporation publicly listed on a stock exchange will obviously have much greater fiduciary responsibility (and thus risk) towards thousands of its investors than a privately-held or family-owned corporation. This does not imply that shareholders of publicly-quoted and privately-held corporations should not be treated equally, but the arbitrage required to deal with creditors and equity holders will vary according to each party's contribution to the financing of the corporation or institution. (Calculation of the ratio of equity to debt should treat debt on a net basis, after deducting tangible assets, to take capital intensity into account. Capital intensity varies relatively systematically by industry or activity.) For example, a commercial bank is heavily credit driven due to its relatively high gearing ratio of 12 times its capital, giving it an 8.5 % capital ratio against an average of 40 % to 60 % for non-financial corporations.

Governance of an organisation engaged in trust finance, such as an MFIF, is predominantly fiduciary as its total resources (capital of shareholders plus the mandate of third party investors) are unsecured with an absolute value at risk. Even if the portfolio contains only fixed income instruments, investors are normally exposed to absolute risk (systematic or beta risk), especially when the portfolio is marked-to-market and its securities are traded on a daily basis.

As a result, fiduciary risk is probably the biggest component of all risks faced by investors in microfinance. Because returns are so low, fiduciary governance – the way these funds are managed – has more impact on the funds' performance than the actual investments per se. Endogenous factors, such as weak portfolio mix, under-pricing of investments, poor yield management, and high expense ratios, explain most of the poor return on this asset class. Exogenous factors such as currency risk, market risk, and specific risk have a smaller impact.

Corporate governance has two levels of concern in the context of microfinance investment. First, corporate governance in an investment management firm refers to the way the firm exercises its rights and how it influences the MFI borrower or investee. If no secondary market exists or if put options are not commonly used to force MFIs to repay their loans before maturity because of fiduciary breaches, investment funds cannot vote with their feet and exit easily from an MFI. This is despite the fact that the asset class remains short term with average loan maturities hardly exceeding 12 to 15 months. This means that the pre-investment due diligence stage must be quite rigorous.

Second, corporate governance also refers to the way MFIs exercise their own corporate power. MFI ratings, especially of credit, may act as a proxy. However, fiduciary ratings are often insufficient or inappropriate for the least developed MFIs which have not reached sustainability or financial autonomy. Furthermore, no real corporate governance standards exist within the microfinance rating community.

Transparency

Transparency serves many purposes. The most critical reason for transparency is to establish trust in a relationship where there is no obligation to produce any specific result. Although transparency is no proxy for performance, it influences the manner in which the fiduciary achieves a return expected by the investor. Transparency requirements are directly proportional to the extent of fiduciary responsibility.

Fiduciary systems and processes are used to implement investment strategy. It includes systems and processes and decision-making in order to achieve the expected target return. For example, the JP Morgan Emerging Market Bond Index includes both sovereign and corporate issuers. It suggests that between 1998 and 2004 emerging market debt should have earned the ultimate end-investor 10.8 %, with a range from 9.2 % for Latin America to 14.2 % for Africa. So should investors in microfinance funds earn less than if they had invested in emerging market government debt or local blue chip listed companies in these markets?

Top-Down Aggregation or What the Market Can Bear

One approach to answering this question is a top down building-block process whereby going lending rates to MFIs are used as benchmarks. Little consideration is given to the components of such rates or how they may be distorted by inefficient market forces. Fund managers using a top down approach set the price the market can bear. Any ex-post risk segregation of these components (including a risk-free base, the currency risk, the country or market risk and then the specific risk of the MFI to which a loan is made[6]) gives a semblance of rationality to their overall risk-taking. No true risk scaling is applied to set the price before the loan is granted to the MFI.

MFIF professionals use MFI ratings merely as diligence tools and risk indicators because they are little more than audits. Some ratings, such as those assigned by PlanetRating and Microfinanza, are more fiduciary driven, which implies less stable rating processes, with less stable defined as situations in which a single set of data could lead different analysts to assign different judgments or ratings. Others are more credit driven, such as MicroRate, M-Cril and most other credit rating agencies. However, these rating procedures are not sufficiently comprehensive to serve as a basis for estimating the spreads to be applied to the securities issued by MFIs. Of course, comparing or mixing fiduciary ratings and credit rating is not a valid basis for estimating or measuring spreads. This reflects in part the differences among emerging markets and among the rating methodologies.

Furthermore, dedicated MFI rating agencies do not even distinguish between local and foreign currency risks, which implies no real difference between the two. Amongst all rating agencies accredited by the IDB-CGAP Rating Fund, S&P and Fitch are the only ones that draw a distinction between the two risks, reflecting the leading agencies' general practice of unbundling their ratings. In the rating industry, there is no such thing as a single credit rating that ignores the distinction between local and foreign currency. The only time that microcredit rating agencies draw a line between foreign and local currency risk is when they make an asset-liability management diagnosis to assess an institution's vulnerability to foreign exchange movements. But this has nothing to do with pricing a loan that incorporates currency or country risk.

Bottom-Up Aggregation

A bottom-up approach shows how an MFI risk becomes residual (to low risk money and country risk) and enables institutions of equal-to-lower quality to pay the same or less than their peers in better rated countries. The process builds up the end price by including all driving components. The country risk is an intrinsic component of the MFI pricing mechanism. Since most emerging markets' business cycles, including local consumption trends, are extremely sensitive to interest rate

---

[6] These components are all expressed in basis points, which equal hundredths of a per cent.

Box 8. Why Nicaraguan MFI Risk is Cheaper than Lower-risk Peruvian MFIs		
Cost of risk breakdown	**Peru**	**Nicaragua**
Cost of cash – low risk money	US$ 6-month LIBOR = 3 %	US$ 6-month LIBOR = 3 %
Cost of country risk (including LIBOR)	"BB" rating of S&P = 8 %	Current loans: 10 %
Normal cost of specific MFI risk	2 % to 3 %	3 % to 4 %
TOTAL cost of risk to MFI	3 %+5 %+3 % = 11 %	3 %+7 %+4 % = 14 %
However, due to inflow of soft money and inefficient markets, no MFI would pay 14 % in Nicaragua. The limit would be closer to 12-13 %, which means that the MFI risk, if calculated as a residual risk, costs only 2-3 % (12 %-7 %-3 %) or equal to the best risk of MFIs in Peru.		
Effective cost of specific MFI risk	3 %+5 %+**2-3 %** = 10-11 %	3 %+7 %+**2-3 %** = 12-13 %

movements in international capital markets,[7] investment funds have to consider two important price drivers: a) the effective risk level of country markets hosting MFIs, and b) the opportunity cost of OECD investors, especially in emerging market alternative asset classes.

The limitation to any topping-up is essentially due to an inefficient market with excess liquidities, where lenders are ready to accept lower rates to place their money. Add to this the funnelling of cheaper money from soft lenders and you end up with an "MFI glass-ceiling" effect. Therefore, the Peruvian MFI may actually pay equal or more for its own specific risk than its Nicaraguan peer. Put differently, because the country risk of Nicaragua is higher than that of Peru, it leaves less room the bear the specific institutional risk.

Price Distortions in Social Investing

The pent-up demand for "safe plus" social investments is currently so high among institutional investors that other considerations are ignored. But as competition builds and fund raising by MFIFs increases, investors' performance expectations will become more and more demanding.

---

[7] A study conducted in 2001 by Pablo A. Neumeyer and Fabrizio Perri ("Business Cycles in Emerging Economies: the role of interest rates") shows that in Argentina interest rate shocks alone can explain 50 % of output fluctuations and can generate business cycle patterns consistent with the major booms and recessions in the last 20 years. The study was conducted at the Universidad T. di Tella, CONICET, New York University and Princeton University.

The absence of generally accepted benchmarks that could serve as reference points to assess the performance of investments in microfinance can also influence private investors' expectations about returns from MFIFs. The expected returns for a composite fixed-income fund exposed primarily to Latin American MFIs ranges between 3 % and 15 % for similar risks, showing the huge risk/return appreciation gap prevailing among managers.

Compare the Dexia Micro-credit Fund's average return of 4.66 % between 2000 and 2004 with LACIF's average return of 0.5 %-6 % for debt to 11.02 % for equity holders over the same period, Dexia investors are completely at risk, effectively pure equity investors. However, they enjoy much greater liquidity because they can move in and out at no cost each month, and diversification of the portfolio is worldwide against the strictly regional LACIF portfolio. Also, Dexia investors are not exposed to any leverage, although this is changing now that the fund will borrow to improve its liquidity position (not for gearing purposes). Pure equity investors at LACIF have received in excess of 15 % per annum over the last two years. Other LACIF "investment lenders" earned more than 6 % on preferred shares, 5 % on subordinated tranches, and 0.5 % to 5.5 % on senior debt. These returns are possible because LACIF is not a fund but a finance company that exposes its equity holders to a 3.6 leverage ratio, which is however partially insured by USAID. On a strict fixed-income basis, aside from concessional investors, all debt holders of LACIF were actually earning 200 to 300 basis points more than all clients of Dexia from 2002 to 2004 while enjoying a senior ranking that no investor with Dexia could ever obtain.

Risks of lending to MFIs that are both mispriced and misvalued will reinforce the expectation that returns should be low because high returns would be politically incorrect or simply unjustified in microfinance. This view may retard the expansion of investment in microfinance because low returns are not competitive with other emerging market opportunities. As long as the microfinance industry remains outside mainstream capital markets and privately held, its investment asset class will belong to the private equity sector, whether for fixed-income or equity investments. This means that the valuation process should conform to the performance calculation standards of the Private Equity Industry Guidelines Group (PEIGG)[8] and of the International Limited Partner Association (ILPA), and the presentation standards recently issued for Global Investment Performance Standards (GIPS).[9]

---

[8] See "PEIGG Reporting and Performance Measurement Survey Results," February 1, 2004 as well as the Guidelines issued by PEIGG in December 2003.

[9] The new provisions took effect in January 2005. The Global Investment Performance Standards (GIPS) are presentation standards initiated in the US in the early 1990s and extended abroad during the late 1990s. Their purpose is to prevent manipulation of performance data in marketing. They cover five areas: input data, calculation methodology, composite construction, disclosure and presentation/reporting. They particularly insist on an annualised Since Inception-Internal Rate of Return (SI-IRR), using daily or monthly cash flows and period-end valuation of unliquidated remaining holdings. Investment houses must also provide two sets of performance records: returns net and gross of management fees for each year since inception.

Compliance with these norms would be largely consistent with the core principles and fair market value approach promoted by the British Venture Capital Association and the European Venture Capital Association (EVCA), which promote a principles-based approach as opposed to the US rules-approach to accounting provisions. Close cooperation by the MFIF industry with the new Emerging Markets Private Equity Association (EMPEA) could help tremendously in streamlining standards and best practice.

Accountability

Accountability is communicated through attribution analysis, benchmarks, the total expense ratio and asset/liability management. Attribution analysis evaluates the abilities of asset managers, identifies where and how money is earned or value is created, and generates a dialogue between asset managers and investment clients. It requires the provision of reliable, periodic performance information to investors and other stakeholders. Risk/return attribution becomes essential when accountability is defined as how performance is measured against key governance policies (mission, milestones, resources, etc.) and transparency rules. In short, attribution analysis quantifies the decisions made by managers and helps directors, trustees and investors detect any change in investment style or policy.

Total expense ratio attribution analysis cannot be achieved unless proper benchmarks are available to segregate risks and returns as independent opportunities. Benchmarks should normally be approved by the board of directors or an independent valuation committee that includes a majority of investors or trustees selected by investors. As benchmarks do not have expenses (a stock market index does not presume any brokerage commission), benchmark comparisons should be made on a gross and net basis, according to general IPS prescriptions. On a gross basis, the performance should include all expenses incurred to achieve the return.

Asset liability management requires well structured portfolio management to optimise return and contain risks to achieve the target risk/return expectations of investors.

Setting Fiduciary Practice: Defying Golden Rules of Modern Portfolio Theory

Modern portfolio theory claims that the more mature a capital market is, the more efficient it becomes and the more difficult it is to beat. The microfinance market belongs to one of the most difficult and inefficient markets. For both debt and equity, conditions can vary wildly from one country to another with under- and overrated markets. Volatility is high in the medium term. MFIF professionals must constantly make their own judgments and arbitrage their portfolio across markets to achieve diversification goals and manage their yield curve efficiently. Actually, a portfolio of MFI investments may create more value through diversification and

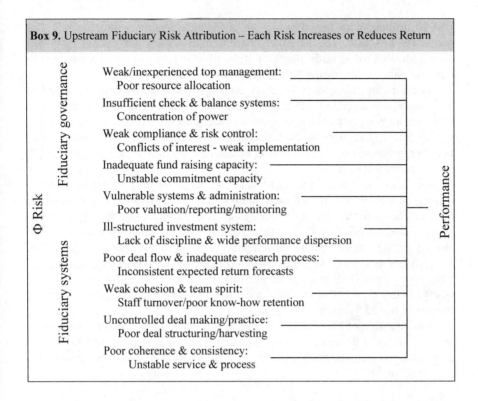

Box 9. Upstream Fiduciary Risk Attribution – Each Risk Increases or Reduces Return

yield management than through lending to specific MFIs – a culture very different from that of conventional credit markets.

Investment managers face poor visibility in microfinance because of the absence of key investment tools such as benchmarks, market indices and sub-indices by geographic areas and MFI quality tier levels, pricing practice and agendas, poor to nil attribution analysis practice, and comprehensive and integrated databases on current outstanding loans and durations. And very few regulators recognise the microfinance asset class as such and its particular risk profile, although the first microcredit investment fund, launched by Dexia in 1998, is fully regulated by Luxembourg authorities.

MFIF professionals generally run their portfolios based on the naked eye rather than on the more professional radar screens and detection support systems used to guide hedge funds, or on conventional fund management practices where markets are better organised, structured and serviced. For this reason, the next wave of support and technical assistance programmes from bi- and multilaterals should assist the MFIF industry through training, encouraging joint venturing between boutiques and more established investment management houses, rather than by providing capital directly.

To manage market risk versus specific risk, diversification rules normally recommend a minimum of 20 to 30 lines (or investments) per portfolio tranche of

US$ 10 million, with less than 5 % in any single security. Since country risk dominates this asset class, market concentration should not exceed 20 % and should ideally tend towards a limit of 10 %. BlueOrchard has demonstrated excellent discipline in this respect for the Dexia Micro-Credit Fund.

Time horizon and duration are short. Average loan maturities do not exceed 18 to 24 months as a general rule with minima and maxima of 12 to 36 months. This preserves a strong grip over loan renewals, maintains diversification and optimises risk control. Until proper benchmarks become available and mark-to-market practice is enforced, the market beta effect of duration has little impact on the microfinance investment industry.

Size factors are significant in MFIFs. The large majority of MFIFs are loss making on a RAROC (risk adjusted return on capital) basis for the team handling the portfolio or for the investors in the fund. The minimum size for a fund should be € 25 million/US$ 30 million in the fixed-income class and € 10 million/US$ 15 million on the equity venture capital side. By comparison, the average size of hedge funds is US$ 12 to US$ 15 million, with far less operating expense and transaction costs. Despite those norms, there are MFIF firms that lose money on assets of US$ 35 to US$ 40 million under management, even though management fees are in the 2.5 % range.

Administration of MFIF is less secure because only a few funds use depository banks as proxy custodians: there are no real custodians worthy of the name in this asset class to challenge asset managers' valuation processes and provide real custody of securities.

Suggestions to Bi- and Multilaterals: To Avoid a Major Upset

To make the MFIF industry more attractive to institutional investors and contribute to reduction of exogenous and endogenous fiduciary risks that cripple the industry today, bi- and multilateral agencies promoting microfinance should take five practical steps.

- *Make fiduciary rating mandatory and introduce a fiduciary charter*: Promote better fiduciary practice through annual rating of fiduciaries' trustworthiness and their compliance with a minimum set of reporting and presentation standards. There is an explosion of investment funds sponsored by various organisations of different stature and mission, most of which have little experience in investment management. Their only legitimacy comes from their closeness to the microfinance industry or their sponsorship of specific MFI initiatives.

  A charter of fiduciary rights should be seriously considered in 2005, the UN Year of Microcredit. A charter could advance the MFIF industry's fiduciary commitment. All investment management firms should be invited to adhere to the charter and share the same commitments towards retail investors. The charter would include three major components: optimum disclosure, reliable trusteeship and sound governance. (See Annex.)

- **Review the capital structure model of investment funds**: Participate in the capital restructuring of funds to improve capital allocation efficiency and maximise leverage synergy among different funding classes. Leading bi- and multilaterals have imposed models which are far too credit-driven and insufficiently fiduciary-oriented. Fund structures, often outmoded, are built along the lines of finance companies (LACIF, BlueOrchard Microfinance Securities I, Cyrano's Global Microfinance Facility) with very little flexibility for investors to move in or out, or making capital movements too expensive and constraining. Essentially, these are "club funds" in contrast to open funds such as the Dexia Micro-Credit fund. To attract both non-taxable and taxable investors, offshore vehicles should be considered as a means of reducing costs.

- **Build investment capacity**: Encourage MFIF houses to strengthen their investment process, fiduciary governance and systems. This requires a gradual change of focus by "soft" or "development investors" so that their priorities shift away from direct funding of first and second tier microfinance institutions to indirect funding, via investment funds. This strategic shift would enable these investors to build investment capacity and know-how that is likely to attract private and wealthier institutions. This fits well with CGAP's peer review of donor practice in microfinance.

  Capacity building should improve accountability by soft investors. Although their activities may be transparent, the performance and effective value created by their contribution may not be measured adequately based on industry standards. By channelling a growing share of their money through funds, this class of investors would automatically improve accountability. Their stronger focus or concentration of fund flows would give these funders much greater impact on MFI governance. Indeed, some microbanks are confused by signals from different types of investors.

  By pooling their funds with those of private investors, "soft" funders could still retain a "soft status" through subordinated loans, low interest guarantees, preferred shares, equity layers, and similar instruments while creating economies of scale and bringing more comfort to large institutional investors. The second major benefit of this pooling or federative approach is to tailor the capital structures of funds to the risk/reward appetites of different classes of investors. The main disadvantage is liquidity: it is more cumbersome to enter or exit such funds. Pure segregated funds represent good fiduciary practice because they operate on a less Byzantine playing field.

- **Reinforce technical assistance and speed up R&D in new management tools**: Soft investors should provide technical assistance to fund management through programmes designed to raise managerial capacity and ability and improve fiduciary practice, in the same way that these investors have supported MFIs. The MFIF industry lacks a wide range of critical management

---

Box 10. Seven Investment Tools that Should be Created

- A World Global MFI Index of fixed-income instruments based on maturity, size and geographic criteria. Target 50 institutions, with regional breakdown, for fixed income and for equity.

- A World Global MFI Index of local currency banking rates for loans to MFIs with conversions back into US$ and €.

- Currency indices by country and by region for the top 25 MFI markets, with regional breakdowns to provide measures of volatility and value-at-risk.

- Default monitoring of MFIs.

- Performance standards for valuation and presentation purposes.

- Attribution analysis models setting basic benchmark criteria against which returns can be disaggregated to evaluate the contribution of each investment component.

- Mandatory credit rating with voluntary fiduciary rating.

In addition to improving market visibility, these tools could facilitate attribution analysis and encourage the emergence of badly needed administrative and custodial services for funds.

---

and analytical tools that could reduce endogenous fiduciary risk. These include benchmarks, attribution analysis models, risk determination and monitoring, market indices, and mandatory registration of all borrowings in a central database.

- ***Training, alliances and joint ventures***: Help develop training programmes in fiduciary practice and encourage alliances and joint ventures of MFIF professionals with well-established investment firms to speed up the transfer of know-how and best practice. A precedent is the experience of several Asian countries that accelerated the development of their asset management industries in the late 1990s.

Roadmap to Measuring Fiduciary Risk: How and Why

In summary, better fiduciary practice requires more attention to fiduciary risk and its management. Fiduciary ratings and a system-wide view would be immensely helpful.

Rating Investment Management Firms

The best accountability test for an MFIF house is annual rating of fiduciary risk. This aims to improve governance, transparency and accountability so that this asset class is professionally managed and in a position to attract hard-core institutional money. These criteria, embedded in an annual fiduciary risk rating process, will help define best practice standards across the MFIF industry, establish a clear typology of funds and provide the tools required by investors to anticipate their risk and fine-tune their expected return. It is difficult to justify credit risk rating of MFIs lending less than US$ 5 million while the fiduciary risk of MFIF management firms investing 5 to 10 times as much is ignored.

In contrast, performance ranking of funds should be avoided until return calculations and presentation standards are adopted by the industry. Without standards, performance ranking would only add more confusion, putting quantitative returns ahead of their proper interpretation through fiduciary practice, risk considerations and qualitative factors.

. Rating is quite urgent. The new generation of investment firms will probably be the future backbone of the microfinance secondary capital market, as shown by the recent collateralised debt obligation entity set up by BlueOrchard and Developing World Markets Inc. with the Overseas Private Investment Corporation (OPIC). The entity was set up in July 2004 with 7-year loans made to large, first tier MFIs in several countries for a total of US$ 40 million. These loans were funded directly by debt and equity holders and indirectly by OPIC through a guarantee of 75 % of the overall funding. The fund has a leverage of 28 times debt against equity.

Extension of the CGAP-IDB Fund rating programme to the investment management firms (not to the funds per se) could improve overall fiduciary standards and best practice. The rating would clearly focus on fiduciary – not credit – risk and would provide a standard measure of risk for all investors, especially for institutional and public investors subject to fiduciary compliance rules. Furthermore, the rating would bring the MFIF firms closer to the conventional asset management industry where major names such as Deutsche Bank's DWS, Invesco, UBS, Robeco and AIG have received fiduciary risk ratings. Rating is done annually and can change during the year in response to events likely to affect the risk profile of the organisation.

Leading bi- and multilaterals would apply the same procedures used by MFIF professionals who avoid investing in unrated MFIs. The programme could be phased in over a period of 12 to 18 months so that investment organisations could improve their systems and operations accordingly. Initial confidential ratings could be carried out on a trial basis to develop the information and benchmarks useful to top management.

What Fiduciary Rating Is All About

As the rating scale shows in the Glossary at the end of the book (*see fiduciary risk*), fiduciary rating is about measuring the probability that an investment management firm may fail to meet the contractual expectations of investors. It covers two dimensions: fiduciary governance and systems.

Fiduciary governance covers the entire structural risk of an organisation from the board of directors to the top management to key areas such as middle and back office support, fund raising/marketing and client care, risk control and compliance. Its prime intent is to provide coherence for the whole organisation, covering:

- Management, checks and balances, controls and systems.

- Mission and overall consistency of goals set by the board of directors or trustees

- Risk control, compliance and legal structure with clear accountability for compliance officers straight through to the board of directors.

- Client care and marketing, as well as conformity with asset/liability management standards of each client account.

- Administration (middle/back office support, including IT) to review failed transactions, valuation processes and incidences of misvaluation. These do not yet apply to the MFIF industry because it does not adhere to mark-to-market rules.

Fiduciary systems cover the whole process risk of an organisation from the decision-making process of the investment system to research, deal flow, investment transactions, position management and final liquidation/exit of the investment. It is meant primarily to provide consistency of performance, covering:

- The entire investment system chain.

- Deal flow and research. Together with yield management, deal-flow management is the most critical point of any fiduciary system in the MFIF industry. Similar to private equity and venture capital, deal-flow sourcing and ongoing relationships with investees are essential to maintain diversification and good risk management.

- Cohesion and team spirit provide the stability and sharing of know-how that is essential for sustained good performance.

- Deal making (trading) and practice (entry/exit) are critical in equity venture capital but also quite important in the fixed income field.

- Performance consistency aims to produce consistent returns year after year, regardless of their volatility (that is, cost) against market movements and other exogenous factors.

Annex – Charter of Fiduciary Rights

The charter would establish three major rights:

a) Disclosure:

i   Fiduciary contract: Investors have the right to full contractual protection[10] based on a clear description of all the rights and obligations involving their investment.

ii   Fiduciary reporting: Investors have the right to full and continuous disclosure of purpose, goal, cost and risk of any investment they make.

iii   Fiduciary compliance: Investors have the right of full disclosure of any conflict of interest by fiduciaries overseeing their investment.

b) Trusteeship:

i   Fiduciary responsibility: Investors have the right to full protection of their assets.

ii   Fiduciary practice: All investment decisions must be made according to generally accepted ethics, practice and conditions, in accordance with a specific investment policy statement.

iii   Fiduciary audit: Investors have the right to full data and to fiduciary integrity so that they may evaluate investment conditions and return on the basis of agreed quantitative methods and presentation standards.

c) Governance:

i   Fiduciary breach: The right of fiduciary audit, certification or rating[11] to ensure that full fiduciary responsibility is inherent in an investment mandate[12] so that the investors' trust is not breached.

Note: Technical terms are defined and illustrated in Annex B.

[10] Protection does not mean a guarantee, nor does it imply that losses cannot occur. It simply means that at all times, the goal of protecting the investor's assets is the prime consideration of any investment manager before profit can be made. Only investors can waive primary fiduciary duty.

[11] Professional examination and verification of documents and data regarding the flow, management, intermediation, administration or custody of funds on behalf of third party clients for the purpose of rendering an opinion as to the fairness, accuracy, consistency and conformity of fiduciary practice in that organisation. The scope of the examination covers front, middle and back office activities, overall governance, compliance and sustainability as well as including verification of investment performance data and of the organisation's due care in the management of its human resources and the selection and monitoring of external service providers.

[12] An investment mandate refers to a contract to manage an investment fund in a fiduciary capacity.

    ii Fiduciary governance: Fiduciaries have a duty of diligence and of good governance that requires them to take all means necessary to protect the investors' interest.

Fiduciary recourse: Investors have a right to legal recourse in the event of fiduciary breach. An arbitration clause should be mandatory in fiduciary contracts.

PART III:

The Future of Investment in Microfinance

Introduction to Part III

Part III peers into the future of investment in microfinance. In Chapter 10 Doris Köhn and Michael Jainzik of KfW describe life-cycle issues in creating financial institutions that serve the poor. They discuss a number of different ways in which development financiers such as KfW have enlisted existing institutions in this cause. Based on this experience they argue that the promotion of new institutions designed specifically to serve the poor is a better solution. However, development financiers that invest in new microfinance institutions will at some point want to exit, selling their shares. Exit is an unresolved issue that is attracting increasing attention, and Köhn and Jainzik explore the advantages and disadvantages of various exit possibilities.

Transformation can be a step towards exit. Chapter 11 describes a transformation of existing funds that support a broad variety of purposes and projects for Southeast Europe. Transformation in this case consists of amalgamating existing funds into a new fund that should be operational before the end of 2005. The result is expected to create efficiencies and also to provide possibilities for new initiatives and leverage. Dominik Ziller, Deputy Head of Division at BMZ, describes the architecture of the fund in detail. Challenges that could weaken the new fund are addressed by a structure of rules and incentives that are designed to enable the fund to operate efficiently, on a sustainable basis, and with an uncorrupted mission or purpose. Financial engineering is used to leverage KfW's ownership and support in ways that will attract finance from other financial institutions and investors.

Klaus Glaubitt, Hanns Martin Hagen and Haje Schütte of KfW provide a wide-ranging summary of the development of microfinance and its off-spring in Chapter 12. The lessons provided are valuable and offer a basis for further progress. Within this wider scope, they highlight KfW's strategy of complementarity – of working on several fronts simultaneously within a single sector. Consequently, this strategy provides a basis for comparing all of the ways in which institutional development has been fostered in microfinance: greenfielding, upgrading, downscaling and linkages with wider markets. A policy and project design framework with four components is discussed, incorporating product development, institutional issues, policy and legal issues, and institutions and investors. This framework is used to identify current and future challenges and also serves as a guide for KfW's continued efforts at the frontier.

In Chapter 13 Bob Pattillo, an innovative private investor in microfinance, offers a dual-objective perspective that focuses on financial returns and on social returns. He goes even further, reflecting on an introspective view of what well-designed and well-placed investment can accomplish. His richly abstract vision includes returns that are both tangible and intangible and that affect many parties.

Chapter 14, by Ernst Brugger, a pioneering figure in private microfinance investment, summarises KfW's 2004 Berlin Symposium dedicated to microfinance investment. He views microfinance investment funds as critical vehicles linking microfinance institutions with mainstream financial markets. Institutional investors and commercial banks are likely to be attracted to microfinance because of its low risk, its weak correlations with global markets and its potential size. In addition, it offers nonfinancial returns attractive to dual-objective investors. At the same time, local currency financing, longer maturities and institutional development will speed the integration of microfinance investment into the mainstream. MFIFs will have to provide efficient products incorporating leverage and securitisation, networks based on equity participation and reporting that is responsive to dual-objective investors.

The closing chapter by Hanns-Peter Neuhoff of KfW takes an historical perspective on the challenges of using finance as an instrument to promote economic and social development. The role of leading public sector development banks such as KfW has changed, but still remains essential for economic and social progress where there has been little before. The development banker's job is to continue to provide leadership at the frontier by structuring initiatives that the private sector is not yet willing to entertain on its own, but in which it can be included and of which it becomes the natural owner in due course. This mission of discovery and refinement by both public and private sector financiers requires diligent institution building, competitive behaviour and a constant concern for corrective actions if wealth is to be created in environments that are stubbornly poor.

CHAPTER 10

Sustainability in Microfinance – Visions and Versions for Exit by Development Finance Institutions

Doris Köhn[1] and Michael Jainzik[2]

[1] First Vice President Europe, KfW Entwicklungsbank
[2] Project Manager, KfW Entwicklungsbank

Success calls for justification. If microfinance institutions were a failure, nobody would envy development financiers that pour money into them without receiving any financial return. But now they are profitable: many microfinance institutions (MFIs) have proved that this business can be done in a financially sustainable way. Sometimes they are even very profitable while still reaching the target group and contributing to poverty alleviation.

This creates a new issue: Why should development finance institutions continue to be involved in these projects after achieving success? Why not sell their equity stakes in MFIs to private investors so that public money can be used for other development ventures, leaving private investors to keep successful MFIs running? Are not private investors even better investors in MFIs since they can tap the capital market, have more financial know-how and suffer less bureaucracy than development financiers?

The issue of exit is becoming a new mantra in microfinance, innately linked to its accelerating commercialisation. Development financiers usually emphasise exit strategies, and the exit of development finance from a microfinance institution is defined here as sale of equity to a private investor that is not a development finance institution.[1]

---

[1] Equity is a crucial form of involvement: It gives development financiers decision making power in the governing bodies of microfinance institutions. It bears the risk of losing the investment, and the chance for gains. In general, development finance institutions use three different forms of financial support to microfinance institutions: technical assistance, (structured) loan products and equity. Technical assistance usually is intended for a limited time only, and loan products may have lives of their own. It is only equity that has the capacity for continuity and also for termination of the relationship between the microfinance institution and the supporting development finance institution.

In our view, exit is not a goal in itself. We discuss when and why development finance institutions should sell their holdings in microfinance institutions, handing over their stake to other investors, or when and why they should stay engaged. In order to find a satisfactory answer, we first have to determine the motives and reasons that lead development finance institutions invest in microfinance in the first place. What is the case for public support of MFIs?

Market Failure and Sustainable Financial Intermediaries

The involvement of development finance institutions in microfinance is based on the fact that the market does not offer adequate financial services to the poor. Banking reality differs from the perfect market model of neoclassical economic theory, where banks have all information needed to accurately assess potential borrowers' actual and future repayment capacities and their willingness to repay. In reality, banks apply screening devices and decision-making techniques to assess potential credit risk and make credit decisions under the conditions of imperfect information. These imperfect assessment techniques can lead banks not to lend at all to certain groups of customers whose risks are perceived as too high or too difficult to assess – instead of offering loans to these customers at higher interest rates that cover their risk. As a consequence, the market can fail to serve particular groups.[2]

The case for public action in microfinance may also be derived from the credit-rationing argument in economic theory, as described above: The poor are not served, although they are willing to pay interest rates high enough to cover the overall costs of the services. But there may be more promising investment opportunities for commercial banks or they systematically overestimate the risks or underestimate the gains of lending to the poor. Or they simply lack the knowledge of how to deliver profitable services to the poor. In addition, they may be restrained by regulations, such as those governing collateral requirements.

This "market failure argument" is not specifically aimed at developing countries or transition economies. It also holds true for industrialised countries with developed financial markets and calls for specific state or public action in order to make market mechanisms work. In the United States, for example, in 1977 the Community Reinvestment Act (CRA) was adopted by Congress after banks had "redlined" slum areas which did not promise adequate returns, and closed branches and declined to lend in these areas. Now supervisory authorities verify if banks make adequate efforts to lend in poor areas.[3]

---

[2] In economic theory, key arguments were first provided by Stiglitz/Weiss (1981).

[3] A political rush to abolish this law or to soften the requirements and controls has caused apprehension that banks may again leave these low-income areas because returns are below average. High social and economic costs for the respective areas are expected.

In developing and transition countries the poorer part of society usually represents a very large part of the population, but cannot obtain financial services from commercial banks because the banks often lack the technologies to serve that target group efficiently.

Establishing Banks to Overcome Market Failure instead of Designing a Set of Rules

Instead of forcing private banks to act, as in the US example above, development policy has for many years tended to support banks that are willing to serve disadvantaged groups of customers. In contrast to developed financial systems, developing and transition countries' regulation and supervision of banking activities is rather weak. This makes it much more difficult to set rules for banks and enforce compliance in ways that make markets work. Thus, establishing specific target-group oriented banks appears to be an effective economic policy measure for serving disadvantaged people.[4]

However, the first experiences with target group oriented financial institutions were not too promising either: Many traditional government-owned development banks in developing countries turned out to be a failure. Subsidised services led to heavy market distortions, while nepotism, bureaucratic procedures and inadequate credit technology led to bad credit portfolios. The banks ended up with losses that created a permanent strain on the state budget.

Thus, development finance institutions sought ways to work together with private banks. Their overall performance seemed to be a better foundation for microfinance programmes. Experience from this "down-scaling approach" is mixed, but definitely more promising than working with development banks. In a number of private commercial banks credit products for microentrepreneurs have been introduced successfully, usually by supporting the establishment of new credit departments with technical assistance, while making loans to the banks for refinancing their microcredit business. But even in successful down-scaling programmes, like the EBRD-funded Russia Small Business Fund, there are doubts that the product is implemented firmly in a way that will continue after development financiers leave: "Questions remain, however, about whether the programmes are sufficiently robust in various partner banks to continue in the same manner, given the opportunity costs perceived by these banks, without the involvement of international financial institutions that have funded this effort

---

[4] This argument is contestable: Setting up an adequate set of rules for private actors may be more efficient in the long run. Setting up banks may be very popular for politicians and other public agents, because it shows that they have the power to act even though the outcomes of their policy may be limited. These and other arguments are not discussed in this article.

to get it underway."[5] Maintaining target group orientation without the direct influence of development finance institutions is the theme of this chapter.

As a complement to the down-scaling approach, the greenfield approach has been applied.[6] Development finance institutions have founded completely new banks, acting as shareholders and designing the banks (or non-bank micro-finance institutions) in a unique way. The basics of the approach are – and this is the core market orientation principle in microfinance – to establish financial institutions which do not rely on any kind of on-going public financial support whilst serving the target group in an effective and efficient manner.[7] This structure was recognised as suitable for reaching sound sustainability in microfinance operations.

Usually development financiers talk about "sustainability" when they refer to target-group oriented programmes that become financially self-sustaining as well as institutionally enduring. To make this concept operational in microfinance, three main dimensions can be identified.

First, the MFI certainly needs to have risk-adequate profitability (see Box 1). Second, the institution has to be able to maintain its level of operations, i. e. the capacity to maintain its human capital and to have adequate staff to respond to or influence market developments so that the microfinance institution stays on the financial frontier. And last but not least, it must maintain its target group orientation, and – even better – enhance market dynamics in a way that creates incentives for other institutions to offer the same or similar services to the poor.

In an exit scenario, the first two aspects, having to do with conditions for permanence, seem to be less critical: Any investors will most likely want to support the institution's operational capacities in order to produce continuing profits.[8] However, this might not be the case if the investor were a competitor.

---

[5] Wallace (2004), p. 82. Wallace was director of EBRD's Group for Small Business that launched a number of down-scaling programmes in Southeast European and Central Asian transition countries.

[6] The contribution by Glaubitt, Hagen and Schütte in this volume describes these approaches in greater depth. They view down-scaling as central in mainstreaming micro-finance, i. e., they deem it necessary to move private banks into microfinance in order to increase outreach.

[7] As a third approach, development financiers support the up-grading of credit NGOs into target-group oriented banks or other regulated entities. These microcredit organisations have often been founded by charities. In order to grow and increase their outreach, many of them now intend to commercialise and to transform into banks. This may help them attract commercial funding and – depending on the respective law – attract savings and offer other banking services not permitted for non-banks.

[8] Interest alone is not enough: the capacity to do so is also essential. We assume that only reasonably experienced investors will have the chance to acquire shares when development finance institutions sell.

Box 1: Dimensions of sustainability in microfinance institutions

(i)   Financial sustainability (=profitability)

(ii) Institutional sustainability

- Level of human resources maintained and increased (personnel development etc)

- Capacities to develop new products

- Operations: Ability to redesign and adapt organisational and IT structures continuously in response to market and produce developments

(iii) Lasting positive sector impact

- Maintaining the target group orientation

- Enhancement of competition and market dynamics

(i as precondition for ii and iii)

Maximum Yield vs. Development Goals

But the third dimension – lasting impact – seems the most imperilled by exit, which could jeopardise the sustainability of a microfinance programme established with tax-payers' money. A retail business with small and micro customers is a cumbersome and costly business, and in microfinance institutions it is undertaken to produce a positive development impact. It is not undertaken as the world's most lucrative venture. Development financiers expect a risk-adequate return from MFIs which may be below the returns of other banks but high enough to ensure the MFIs' future development and cover the development financiers' costs.[9] In contrast, private, pure commercial investors seek maximisation of return – most likely by reducing or "freezing" target group orientation if it appears to be less profitable than other banking activities. Or to put it in different terms, development financiers may be satisfied with lower financial returns than private investors in order to maintain their socially oriented mission.[10] At the same time, development finance institutions are likely to be more patient investors and accept longer amortisation periods and later divestment dates.

---

[9] The Swiss Development Cooperation Unit, the State Secretariat for Economic Affairs (seco) assumes that a net return of around 10 % p.a. for microfinance investments funds is possible. See seco (2005), p. 6.

[10] Historical evidence seems to support such an argument: Even in developed countries in Western Europe one can say, *grosso modo*, that middle class and poorer clients are often served by non-shareholder value-oriented financial institutions such as the public savings banks and co-operative or mutual savings banks.

Private Investors' Motivation for Maintaining Target Group Orientation

If equity is sold to a private investor, will "mission drift" occur, and if so, how can it be avoided? Neuschütz (2004) recommends that development finance institutions sell their shares to the right investor, i. e. "a strategic investor who will not abandon the original business purpose" because there is a "common set of values and objectives" between private investor and public seller.[11] If a buyer subsequently changes the character of the microfinance institution, he could be obliged to repay all or some portion of the donor money contributed to the project. But apart from the fact that such a clause would require costly monitoring and assessment, it might make it more difficult for development institutions to find private buyers for the shares.[12] This comment of an experienced equity financier raises the concern that not many potential private investors would be willing to lock themselves into the mission of microfinance.

The Commercial Investor

Purely commercial investors such as national or international commercial banks or venture capital funds have good reasons to invest in microfinance institutions, especially if they can become a majority shareholder or at least a strategic investor.

For instance, commercial investors might be willing to pay a high price for a microfinance bank that has a banking licence which they might otherwise not be able to obtain from the supervisory authority. They may also acquire a well-established brand and an excellent reputation. And last but not least, they can acquire qualified staff and management. All these aspects have an important value for every investor, not only for those who want to succeed with microfinance, but also for those who intend to refocus the acquired bank's strategy and business model for their own purposes.

Development finance institutions are not investment banks. Development finance institutions are not supposed to sell a microfinance institution to whomever comes along with enough money. The promotional institutions' public mandate requires them to seek an acceptable investor who will continue the target-group oriented business.[13] There are a number of doubts whether an exit in the form of privatisation by commercial investors would preserve and enhance microfinance activities.

But what means can be employed to commit a private investor to maintain the target-group orientation? Or are there economic reasons that will convince the

---

[11] Neuschütz (2004), p. 108. Neuschütz is Vice President of DEG, a mission-driven investment bank within KfW Bankengruppe.

[12] Neuschütz (2004), p. 108.

[13] See also Wallace (2004), p.87.

Box 2: Options for selling shares of microfinance institutions

- MFIs' national IPO (stock market)

- Sale to local commercial banks (private placement)

- Sale to international commercial banks (private placement)

- MFIs' consolidation into a group (and later international IPO of the holding)

---

commercial investor to keep the microfinance orientation after the purchase of shares? The charter or articles of association can be changed by a (sometimes qualified) majority of the shareholders. The present management can be replaced by the shareholders. Current profit from microfinance operations may not be high enough to satisfy management and shareholders.

Selling shares in a microfinance institution may in principle offer a number of different options or different buyers, with potentially different consequences for target group orientation. Box 2 lists typical forms of sale which can be discussed as options.

Private placement in the form of a sale to a buyer without an initial public offer (IPO) is the most likely. It has the advantage that the development finance institution as seller can influence who will be the (first) buyer and negotiate conditions as proposed by Neuschütz above. From our experience, commercial investors usually intend to acquire the majority share in a company – or at least a qualified minority – in order to be able to enforce their business interests.[14] With a new majority shareholder, doubts about maintaining the target group orientation become serious, both for national and international commercial investors as potential buyers. We have no evidence that there is a difference in attitude between national or foreign financial investors' motivation in this regard. Patriotic pro-microfinance policies by local investors may be part of the potential buyers' courting, or a ruse created by the sellers to vindicate their sale, but, given certain exceptions, they are rather unlikely to be sincere.

Selling the MFI's shares in the stock market may lead to a different situation: First, the buyers may be different from commercial banks. A small investor does not then have the power to alter the company's character. Thus, it can be assumed that small investors are a priori more satisfied with the performance potential and orientation of the company they invest in – otherwise they would not invest. Thus, not only the power but also the disposition to support fundamental strategic changes

---

[14] There are strategic considerations which can motivate commercial banks to hold minority stakes in microfinance institutions, such as cross-selling (e.g. international payment services) or access to other business opportunities. See Baechle (2004) for Commerzbank's approach. But this broader strategic vision seems to be the exception rather than the rule.

may be less in the case of small investors compared to strategic investors. Second, without strategic investors and with widely distributed shares, the position of the management is generally much stronger. A specific strategic orientation like microfinance will last as long as the management's commitment, which is not necessarily tied to maximisation of profit. Instead the motivation of management may consist of non-financial incentives, such as working in the "right institution" and the potential social recognition. On the other hand, a strong position by the management combined with a less assertive shareholder structure can lead either to the strengthening or abandonment of microfinance – as the result of the management's discretion. To summarise: having owners who appoint a supervisory board with the "right representatives" seems essential to guarantee a stable mission in the case of an IPO.

In any event, the authors are not aware of an IPO being used as the exit vehicle for investors in a microfinance institution, and we doubt that this will be the most common way. One central reason is that stock markets in developing and transition countries are usually not sufficiently developed to execute this option. Also, most MFIs are much too small to go public on a stock exchange.

Dual-Objective Investors

Apart from the "pure commercial investors" discussed in previous paragraphs, there are other private investors who make multifaceted investment decisions which are not based only on financial return.

Social investors might be in a position to buy out development finance institutions' shares in MFIs. Social investors want risk-adequate financial returns, but the return can be lower than the maximum possible return for an investment with additional social benefits. Apart from well-meaning individuals, these include institutional investors who bundle individual investments. Particularly in the case of institutional investors, "reputational return" is often a component which is important for investment decisions.

A number of privately owned microfinance equity investment funds or similar entities have been set up.[15] A number of them are completely private and attract individual investors who are interested in commercially successful as well as socially sound ventures. Others are mixed forms of private participation and initiative by development financiers.[16]

In principle, these funds may afford a realistic opportunity to sell shares in MFIs to a committed long-term investor. But two main factors make them appear not yet suitable: First, only a few funds invest in equity. Second, most of these funds are rather small; they would not be able to buy into the share capital of microfinance institutions on a large scale.

---

[15] See Goodman in this volume.

[16] See Köhn and Jainzik (2005) on microfinance investment funds as a form of Public Private Partnership.

Strategic Concepts of Microfinance Investment Funds

Microfinance investment funds have a limited appetite for MFI equity. Funds that are designed to attract the general public have a strong preference for more liquid and short-term investments than the market offers today.[17] But funds for institutional investors usually are put together for a defined period of time – and loans and guarantees can be aligned accordingly, whereas equity may not be ready for sale.[18]

Funds that invest in equity often do not intend to acquire significant or majority stakes in microfinance institutions. The strategy rests on two main considerations: First, investment funds usually strive for a diversified portfolio and are reluctant to invest too much in one venture, especially when the fund is rather small. Second, significant and particularly majority stakes clearly entail a higher responsibility and involvement.

Only a few funds have made the strategic decision to go beyond being a minority investor, and to act as a holding company with a controlling influence on the MFIs they have invested in. Usually these funds or investment companies have in fact developed and matured together with a group of microfinance institutions, forming a network of such institutions.[19] ProCredit Holding, earlier operating as Internationale Micro Investitionen (IMI), is the most prominent example of an investor that intends to take over majority stakes in microfinance institutions and hold these shares long-term.[20] Thus, it offers a perspective for minority investors in particular microfinance institutions within the ProCredit network to sell their participations to ProCredit Holding.

Until now, none of these majority investors are quoted on a stock exchange. And, as in ProCredit Holding, international financial institutions, bilateral development financiers or other public entities still play an important part. This may be partly due to the fact that these non-quoted funds still need committed long-term investors to support their long-term portfolios. But it may also be due to the fact that development financiers as equity investors in microfinance have unique functions which go beyond the pure injection of cheap and patient capital.

---

[17] Only a limited number of instruments have been explored so far that could make investments in microfinance more suitable for the public. Principle Protected Notes, for instance, may be an intermediate instrument to swap longer-term investments into tradable papers. Principle Protected Notes are structured so that parts of the investment are in risk-free bonds, enabling the issuing bank to guarantee the repayment of principle to the note-holder. The minor part of the investment, which would produce the note-holder's return, is put into risky investments in commodities or stocks – in our case the stock of microfinance institutions.

[18] As Goodman notes in this volume, the more commercially oriented microfinance investment funds invest almost exclusively in loans.

[19] See Köhn and Jainzik (2005) for a characterisation of microfinance funds.

[20] See Alexander (2005) for an overview of ProCredit Holding and its strategy. Further examples of funds that intend to act in ways similar to a holding are Acción Investments in Microfinance (AIM), La Fayette Participations and ShoreCap International.

The Role of Specific Knowledge and the Weight of Investors

Microfinance is still a difficult field. It requires specific technical and financial knowledge and the capacity to persevere since innovation in technology and dynamic environments permanently create new challenges.

MFIs and capital investments in them are last but not least a product of institutions and people who not only had the knowledge, but who also believed in the idea and developed and supported the growth of the industry. And this is somehow a core issue with regard to exit and privatisation: How can this spirit be kept? Strong promoters and a major part of the avant-garde in microfinance can be found in non-government organisations and the development finance institutions that mobilised funding for microfinance projects and paid for technical assistance.

Stereotypes often describe the private parties as the only active promoters and motivating force. The internet homepage of ProCredit Holding also projects this view, but points out the functions of its public shareholders, too: "The private owners are the company's driving force. The public-sector owners, having charters that commit them to development policy objectives, reinforce our micro and small enterprise target group orientation, contribute to disciplined control, have a longer-term orientation, and offer a different and stimulating perspective on the business issues we face."[21]

We would like to elaborate and explain these features, drawing on our experience from participating in supervisory bodies of microfinance institutions and from supporting microfinance institutions as part of KfW's work and mission.

In both the representation on supervisory boards and the active portfolio management (for single microfinance institutions as well as for investment funds), development financiers apply their knowledge about financial institutions and financial sectors. As a development finance institution, KfW not only supports the microfinance institutions in which it is a co-owner. We often also have a number of financial sector programmes in the respective countries and we closely follow political and economic developments – probably with a wider view than any single MFI might have. And we may also follow developments more intensively than other shareholders who are not engaged in microfinance and financial sector development to the same extent. KfW, in common with other development financiers, can draw on professional experience and its involvement in new, world-wide developments in microfinance, and use this input in strategic and management decisions. Besides, KfW as one of Germany's biggest financial institutions also has solid banking knowledge in specific fields such as securitisation, risk management and other areas which can be explored for the benefit of microfinance.

The specific nature of this activity enables KfW, along with other development financiers, to provide valuable focused input for the development of microfinance institutions which goes far beyond pure provision of capital. Instead, development finance institutions can offer "intelligent capital" that produces additional benefits.

---

[21] See www.procredit-holding.com, "business philosophy".

Promotional institutions are bound by their public mission. KfW's mission leads it to reinforce the orientation towards poverty alleviation. As demonstrated by sometimes controversial, but productive supervisory board meetings, representatives with extensive financial knowledge and substantial interest in microfinance are valued and in great demand. These checks and balances through public owners have been an important intangible asset for microfinance institutions.

Furthermore, development finance institutions have a longer-term orientation than private shareholders may have, and they are also extraordinarily stable. They have been in existence for decades before the first microfinance institutions were founded. This institutional stability among their owners is an important selling point when microfinance institutions want to solicit private investors or obtain other sources of capital.

Last but not least, having development finance institutions as shareholders can make life easier for MFIs. Microfinance institutions are usually not part of a countries' business networks or clans, interlocked business groups or political countertrade. This makes them more vulnerable to political and economic attacks, since they do not have as many "friends" as other companies. Development financiers may provide a certain balance because governments are usually reluctant to heavily provoke players like EBRD, IFC or KfW.

All of the functions fulfilled by development financiers in microfinance institutions seem rather unique. We do not yet see private investors that can fulfil these functions to the same extent and quality.

From the perspective of a microfinance institution, it does not seem very wise to lightly disregard the additional benefits that development finance institutions routinely provide as shareholders. The benefit of having private shareholders, in particular the probability that they will create better access to additional capital, could be easily outweighed by the negative impacts of a hasty exit of public institutions. Instead of viewing shareholders as either private or public, MFIs should rather seek both types of investors and combine the specific benefits of each.[22]

From our perspective, private investors are welcome to join the club and increase their presence in microfinance. Additional capital and potentially new business relations are suitable bases for increasing microfinance institutions' development impact. Until now, private investors' interest in microfinance remains rather limited. Development finance institutions such as KfW have invested a lot of effort as a facilitator that can guide private partners into microfinance. The entry of private investors into microfinance – commercial as well as social investors – has been slow even where support was provided. Hence, helping them play

---

[22] And even if development finance institutions were to withdraw from a particular MFI, the microfinance institution should have an interest in keeping development financiers present in the sector: they play a role in positively influencing the working environment, for instance by supporting the creation of a suitable legal framework or by supporting competitive structures in the financial sector.

a bigger role and become serious players will certainly take more time and effort – both on the part of the private investors as well as from the development financiers.

The Target Group Issue Again

From the perspective of development finance institutions, MFIs have to be viewed as vehicles for reaching the target group effectively and efficiently. In this regard, we would like to highlight a critical efficiency argument. Development financiers usually have invested a significant amount of funds and effort to make MFIs work and become effective means of poverty reduction and of the realisation of other development goals. If poverty can be addressed through participation in a micro-finance institution or network, why should development financiers withdraw? If we manage to strengthen an electricity company within the scope of a develop-ment project so that it is able to fulfil its tasks, we are usually happy to work to-gether with this partner in new programmes, and we try to strengthen the ties as long as "development assistance" remains useful and feasible. Why should we withdraw from fruitful cooperation in the financial sector? Rather, we should be interested in further strengthening our relation to MFIs as vehicles for reaching our target group and fighting poverty.

From the target groups' perspectives it is not terribly important whether devel-opment financiers support microfinance by grants, loans or equity. And they do not care either if services are provided by public or private entities. Ultimately, services for the poor simply have to be provided, and provided efficiently. In the financial sector, all evidence shows that development financiers remain indispen-sable. This is, after all, why development finance institutions *get into* micro-finance. In the medium term, private investment in microfinance will – hopefully – play a bigger role. But it seems to remain the development financiers' task to guide private investors, for instance through public-private partnerships, and by inspiring further investments in microfinance.

Completely replacing development financiers in microfinance through take-overs by private players seems to be – if at all – a vision for the future.

References

Alexander, Helen: "Sustainable Microfinance Banks – IMI as a Public Private Partnership in Practise," in: Matthäus-Maier and von Pischke (2005), pp. 289 – 302

Baechle, Jan: "Equity Participation in Microfinance Banks in Southeast Europe and Georgia – A strategic option for a Large Private German Bank?" in: Matthäus-Maier and von Pischke 2004, pp. 135 – 139

Glaubitt, Klaus, Hagen, Hanns Martin and Schütte, Haje: "Mainstreaming Micro-finance – *Quo Vadis* Microfinance Investments?" in this volume

Goodman, Patrick: "Microfinance Investment Funds: Objectives, Players, Potential", in this volume

Köhn, Doris and Jainzik, Michael: "Microfinance Investment Funds – An Innovative Form of PPP to Foster the Commercialisation of Microfinance," in: Matthäus-Maier and von Pischke 2005, pp. 323–335

Matthäus-Maier, Ingrid and von Pischke, J.D. (eds.): *The Development of the Financial Sector in South-East Europe*, Berlin/Heidelberg/New York: Springer 2004

Matthäus-Maier, Ingrid and von Pischke, J.D. (eds.): *EU Accession – Financial Sector Opportunities and Challenges for Southeast Europe*, Berlin/Heidelberg/New York: Springer 2005

Neuschütz, Volker: "Institutional Development and Commercialisation – Optimal Exit for Equity Financiers," in: Matthäus-Maier and von Pischke 2004, pp. 101–111

seco: Microfinance – the deployment of seco instruments in the area of microfinance in: http://www.seco-cooperation.ch (2005)

Stiglitz, J.E. and Weiss, A.: "Credit Rationing in Markets with Imperfect Information," *American Economic Review*, Volume 71, No. 3, 1981, pp. 393–410

Wallace, Elizabeth: "EBRD's Micro and Small Enterprise Lending Programmes: Down-Scaling Commercial Banks and Starting Greenfield Banks," in Matthäus-Maier and von Pischke 2004, pp. 79–87

The European Fund for Southeast Europe: An Innovative Instrument for Political and Economic Stabilisation

Dominik Ziller

Deputy Head of Division, Federal Ministry for Economic Cooperation and Development (BMZ)

The European Fund for Southeast Europe (EFSE) is being formed from four existing local funds that mainly promote micro, small and medium-sized enterprises (MSMEs) and households seeking improved housing through qualified financial institutions in Southeast Europe. The new fund is expected to be chartered as an independent institution by December 2005. The purpose of this innovative instrument is to enhance the economies of Southeast Europe by providing finance to micro and small enterprises. The Fund is designed to be a sustainable example of an effective partnership between the public and private sectors (PPP). Its creation conveniently coincides with the United Nations' International Year of Microcredit.

This chapter begins by describing the strategic role of MSME promotion in the economic and political stabilisation of Southeast Europe. This exposition incorporates the development-policy perspective of the international community. The second part of this chapter examines the strengths and weaknesses of the approach taken thus far by the four existing local funds. The third part presents the options that have been explored in the development of this strategy. Finally, the concept of a regional fund and the framework that emerged from discussions by its founders is explained, along with details that remain to be clarified.

The Role of SME Promotion in the Stabilisation of Southeast Europe

The Situation in Southeast Europe After the Balkan Wars of the 1990s

The economic level of the former Yugoslavia was relatively high compared to the Eastern European states, but the political opportunities offered by the fall of the iron curtain at the beginning of the 1990s were not translated into economic gains. Instead, ethnic and religious hostilities, suppressed for decades by the multi-ethnic state of Yugoslavia, flared up again. These led to military confrontations and the rapid break-up of Yugoslavia into a number of small states. During this conflict, the economies of the successor states declined drastically, creating an economic disaster characterised by:

- the destruction of and damage to manufacturing facilities during the military conflicts

- the destruction of and damage to public utilities, e. g. energy and water supply infrastructure, and also to the transport sector

- the burden on public and private budgets from the costs of the war and of reconstruction

- the loss of long-standing markets in Eastern Europe due to the opening up to the West and access to products of higher quality

- manufacturing facilities that became obsolete due to lack of investment in maintenance and modernisation, which widened the quality gap and further weakened competitiveness

- the retention of the Yugoslav model of highly subsidised public utility tariffs, which could no longer be financed from state revenues, so that the systems became derelict and were cannibalised or maintained on a greatly reduced scale

- the displacement and flight of ethnic groups, which led to considerable losses of human capital in some regions

- the policy that retained government control of the socialist economy which remained uncompetitive, especially in Serbia under Milosevic, while weakening the nationalised financial sector through nepotism and corruption

- the breakdown of the Serbian economy that weakened neighbouring economies

As a consequence of these developments the economies of the Western Balkan states shrank by up to 70 % by the end of the 1990s. Eastern Balkan countries were much less affected although regional trade greatly diminished and Bulgaria, Romania and Moldova suffered from the withdrawal of strategic investors. In 1998/1999, the economies of most of the states of Southeast Europe consisted primarily of unprofitable public or "collective" production facilities, most of which were no longer able to operate in a cost-efficient manner and almost all of which employed far more workers than were actually required.

A financial sector existed, at least in theory. The book values on banks' balance sheets were highly unrealistic – credit institutions were essentially bankrupt. Hardly any capital was available for investment or for the creation of new private enterprises because the banks were unable to recapitalise themselves through international financial markets due to their poor condition and high risk of loss. Energy and municipal or district heating and water supply were on the brink of collapse and transport infrastructure was very fragile.

The combination of a planned economy, continuing ethnic and religious unrest, inadequate infrastructure, an ailing financial sector and the lack of a sound economic environment (suppliers, buyers, etc.) prevented a rapid revival of investment capital flows from abroad. Consequently, it was rather unlikely that exogenous factors or outside forces would succeed in reviving the economy.

On the positive side, the education level remains comparatively high in most Balkan states. The population is relatively young with many qualified and motivated people who are strongly committed to democratisation and to the establishment of market economy structures – at least since the end of the Milosevic regime. Moreover, the region is rich in raw materials. The donor community has therefore been faced primarily with the task of using this potential for economic reconstruction as rapidly and efficiently as possible so that EU standards can be achieved.

An important element in this endeavour is the popular expectations in Southeast Europe. Citizens hope that the commitment to the market economy will quickly and lastingly improve their living conditions, as is occurring in Eastern Europe. If these expectations are not realised, the region could not only revert to communism and the planned economy, but also to renewed ethnic conflicts and violence.

The Solution Proposed by the International Community

To deal with this highly challenging task, the international community created the Stability Pact for Southeast Europe in Cologne on July 10, 1999. Under this agreement, target countries and regions in Southeast Europe, bilateral donors, and multilateral and international institutions agreed to cooperate in finding coordinated, comprehensive solutions to the most pressing problems of the region. It was clear that the overall objective of the pact – political stabilisation – would not be possible without rapid and lasting economic stabilisation. Working Table 2 of the Stability Pact, which is in charge of economic reconstruction, was of particular importance from the beginning. Three main pillars quickly emerged.

First, it was necessary to supply basic goods such as energy and drinking water, and rehabilitation programmes for these purposes were launched. The initial focus was on emergency aid, such as restoring the grid for electricity imports, but the initiative soon shifted to introducing durable, self-sustaining structures. In some states this process has been completed. In others, especially Kosovo, Serbia, Montenegro, Albania, Bosnia and Herzegovina, the process is still underway and the international community is still supporting infrastructure restoration and development. Rapid and sustainable improvement of living conditions has enabled large portions of society to experience the real benefits of democracy. In addition, functioning supply networks are a precondition for the foreign direct investment that the region urgently requires for economic recovery.

Second, in order to stimulate local recovery and to attract foreign investment, it was essential to create an economic system functioning along the lines of the Central European model of a social market economy, and to do so as quickly as possible. Numerous advisory programmes have supported the elected legislatures of Southeast Europe in setting up a corresponding framework governing trade law, corporate law, customs legislation, tax laws, contract law and property law; parallel efforts assisted the executive powers in applying these new regulations. This approach has been successful: the EU determines the basic lines of institutional development, while European and bilateral cooperation (e. g. German Technical Cooperation) develop the framework. Moreover, the privatisation of public and "collective" production was promoted in order to create economically sound enterprises, to save as many jobs as possible while creating attractive investment opportunities for foreign investors. This agenda has been completed in some regions, while in others it is still in process – especially in Kosovo, where its unresolved status poses major problems.

Third, strong focus was placed on the promotion of the local economy. This was based on the realisation that attracting foreign investors and restructuring large companies would not generate sufficient economic growth without the participation of efficient MSMEs. Experience gained in Germany demonstrates that small and medium-sized enterprises are able to create a large number of jobs, and that the capital generated by such enterprises is usually reinvested in the domestic economy. In contrast, profits generated by large international groups are highly volatile and mobile. In addition, the relatively high level of education in the Balkans and the pronounced entrepreneurial initiative of the population offered a good basis for developing viable MSMEs. The main problem was that this initiative was not being channelled into the creation of new enterprises or the expansion of existing ones. Due to the precarious condition of the financial sector of Southeast Europe after the Kosovo war, potential founders of new businesses had little opportunity to realise their ambitions because banks were unable to provide investment capital. This led donors to develop an innovative promotional model, described in the following section.

A Strategy to Promote a Revolving Fund for MSMEs

First Approach

Remarkably, all stakeholders engaged in MSME promotion agreed on a common approach right from the start. It consisted of two main components:

- First, new microbanks were founded as partner banks in those states and areas where no existing banks seemed eligible for long-term cooperation in the promotion of the MSME sector. KfW on the initiative of the German federal government, with other donors as well as with Commerzbank and IPC as private partners, helped to create these new microbanks. Where viable local banks existed or were later created, their suitability as partner banks was assessed through a due diligence procedure. If the result was positive they were included in the promotional programmes. Locally recruited employees of all partner banks were trained as loan officers with a special focus on micro and SME finance.

- In parallel with the selection and creation of banks, four "European Funds for the Promotion of MSME" administered by KfW were established, one each for Bosnia and Herzegovina, Kosovo, Montenegro and Serbia. The EU endowed the first of these, the European Fund for Bosnia and Herzegovina, with a significant amount of loan capital. (The name is slightly misleading: these vehicles were technically not real funds, but rather similarly-designed parallel credit lines for microfinance, SME and housing modernisation.) Next to the EU, further funding was provided by Germany, Switzerland, Austria and the Netherlands. These funds issued credit lines to qualified financial institutions (commercial banks and non-bank-microfinance institutions at a close to market interest rate).

Credit is provided on the condition that it is used exclusively for loans to the target groups of MSMEs and to private households for the improvement of housing conditions. All qualified financial institutions are selected in each country/entity in order to encourage competitive behaviour that will result in the interest advantage being passed on to the final borrowers. As the loans are repaid to partner banks by the final borrowers, the proceeds must be repaid to the fund. A particularly attractive and innovative feature in the design of the funds is that their resources are available on a revolving basis. Consequently, the funds are reused for further loans.

As a result of the comprehensive training programme for loan officers and the reliability of the due diligence procedures, the default rates are almost zero at the level of the target group of final borrowers and also at the level of the partner banks. In fact, interest income has increased fund resources slightly, a process that should continue indefinitely. The success of the MSME credit lines has led some donors to provide additional financing to establish similarly structured credit lines for agricultural enterprises. Additionally, the German government has created a similarly structured but regionally focused "Apex-Fund" for MSME promotion, which is to be available to other countries in the region. Altogether, these funds' total portfolio approximates EUR 130 million.

Strengths and Weaknesses

The results of the projects are highly positive. The number of loans issued to final borrowers in all Southeast European states exceeds expectations by far. The revolving feature has made it possible to issue more than 45,000 loans amounting to more than EUR 250 million[1]. About 230,000 jobs have been created or safe-

---

[1] As at December 31, 2004.

guarded through the promotion of MSMEs. Also, the financial sectors of the partner countries have been greatly strengthened. The emergence of new or strengthened financial institutions has made it easier for governments to close poorly performing banks. In the special case of Kosovo, the new microfinance bank was the only bank in the territory for nearly one and a half years after its founding early in 2001. Since then it has significantly contributed to the development of a highly stable financial sector that is now comprised of seven banks, four of which are partner banks.

In many cases the newly created partner banks serve as blueprints for additional activities of private banks. The partner banks have also become important employers. The continuous training of loan officers and the migration of some of them to other banks has generally strengthened the lending business in the region. More surprising is the confidence, illustrated by deposits placed by citizens in the newly created microbanks and private partner banks. Consequently they have become able to extend their activities beyond microfinance, providing a wide range of banking services. However, deposits are still mostly short-term: long-term deposits will have to be obtained to enable the banks to engage in long-term lending. Until now, only fund resources (and equity) can be used for this purpose.

However, experience has exposed three limitations to this support scheme:

- First, the four funds that currently operate are "political" rather than "real," including about thirty different lending lines. The coexistence of these organisationally independent funds with different sponsors leads to efficiency losses. It is only reasonable to provide loans in relatively large tranches to the partner banks, which they repay in instalments. This means that each fund must have sufficient inflows from loan repayments before they can issue new loans. With no common institutional structures, the different funds cannot be pooled, but rather build up in about thirty lending pipelines. Their individual balances allocated for specific purposes are too small to be disbursed as new loans.

- The structure is administratively inefficient: thirty fund lines are managed separately, thirty different accounts have to be kept, thirty separate reports have to be compiled for various donors. This could jeopardise sustainability in the long term because management costs are too large a burden on such a small-scale design. However, these inefficiencies contrast to the overall structure in which they operate, which is very efficient. In 2004 the Consultative Group to Assist the Poorest (CGAP), in a global comparison, praised the design and approach of the European Fund, as an example of best practice in donor coordination. In light of this testimonial, and given the potential for sustainable development in Southeast Europe, efforts to achieve better institutional efficiency should go further.

- Second, the region where the current Funds are operating is still underbanked and has an enormous growth potential. Other donors and financial institutions have expressed interest in participating in European Funds but require clarification of the exit strategy before committing new funds to this instrument.

- Third, in principle, the funds could have an unlimited life, continuing long after the original developmental purposes are achieved. There is also no reason why the partner countries should not be given an instrument to promote economic growth in general – similar to the Marshall Fund for Germany after World War II. However, should a structure be set up with no expiration date when donors control the strategy of the fund and the use of the money? For this reason the four funds were established for a limited term, ending between 2006 (Kosovo) and 2012 (Bosnia and Herzegovina).

- However, a prolongation seems as reasonable an option as the creation of a new instrument. Due to the rapidly approaching termination date of the Kosovo fund, the selection of a successor model is urgent. The new model should develop an exit strategy for the donors while increasingly giving the partner countries more control over uses of the fund while maintaining its developmental purpose. This question is important not only because of the approaching expiration date, but also because the European Fund for Kosovo is currently the only source of long-term funds for local banks and micro-finance institutions that engage in MSME lending. The closure of the Fund would have grave consequences for the development of the banking and the MSME sectors in this still crisis-prone territory. No other source is available to strengthen the MSME sector.

A review conducted by donors in 2003[2] examined these problems and concluded that an institutionalisation of the funds would significantly contribute to the solution of these problems. A new institution with its own legal status would enable the donors to withdraw individually and at a moment of their own choosing, depending on when they considered the developmental purpose to be fulfilled or sufficiently institutionalised so that their direct involvement would no longer be required. Control could then be transferred to the partner countries. In addition, it would be advisable to pool most of the funds, thereby improving their efficiency, and obtaining additional participation by other donors, development banks or private investors.

A working group was set up to discuss these possibilities. The group included KfW as the fund manager, the other donors involved, and a team of external experts. Very quickly three options emerged.

---

[2] The concept was explored by Klaus Glaubitt and Haje Schütte, "Providing Long-Term Funds to Local Financial Institutions – The European Refinancing Funds in Southeast Europe", in Ingrid Matthäus-Maier and J.D. von Pischke, eds., *The Development of the Financial Sector in Southeast Europe: Innovative Approaches in Volatile Environments*. Heidelberg and New York: Springer Verlag, 2004. pp. 61–77.

Institutional Alternatives: Foundation, Development Bank or Separate Fund

The Foundation Option

Some members of the working group initially favoured establishing a foundation headquartered in Germany or Luxembourg, which would have the advantage of stability. Incorporated as a special fund, a foundation's mission could be protected by its articles of association or corporate charter, and could have a perpetual life. The funds subscribed could be utilised only for the purpose specified by its founders. Misappropriation would be quite difficult. Even after donors' withdrawal, the purpose of the foundation would be preserved, making it possible to transfer the responsibility of the management boards to the partner states at an early date. This is a "safe" and sustainable solution: even if the funds were depleted through poor management, they could never be disbursed for non-statutory purposes. Finally, as a foundation in Germany, for example, neither the funds contributed nor the interest they generate would be taxable. The foundation's capital could not be depleted by third parties.

But the gains from stability can very quickly become a disadvantage. If the purpose of the foundation is rigorously limited, it is very difficult to adjust its outreach to advancements in the financial sector. Finding the right balance at the outset between preventing misappropriation on the one hand and scope for flexibility to adapt to future developments on the other, would require a balancing act, but with a high risk of failure. In the dynamic environment of Southeast Europe, developments are often so fast and unexpected that it is difficult to foresee what institutional changes and strategic challenges will arise in the longer term.

In addition, a foundation might not be able to attract new donors because they could not influence a structural design that cannot be modified. Engaging private investors would be completely out of the question because money subscribed and any interest earned could never be withdrawn. A foundation would also have difficulty obtaining a banking licence that would permit it to conduct business using funds that were not assets of the foundation. Finally, in some states like Bosnia and Herzegovina a foundation headquartered abroad is not allowed to conduct any credit operations, making it completely impossible to serve the banks in these states. For these reasons the foundation model was rejected following thorough discussion.

Establishing a Development Bank

As a second option, the working group briefly considered creating a new regional finance institution such as a development bank. An institution of this sort headquartered outside the partner countries would have the advantage of clear shareholder structures and transferability of the shares to the partner states or suitable trustees at any time. It would also be relatively straightforward to develop a clear decision-making structure that could respond to trends and develop new instruments to meet demand, such as loan guarantees or deposit insurance. Besides, it would also be conceivable to attract new funds from other public sector donors – though hardly from private ones. Raising funds in international capital markets would be possible only if the institutions could earn an acceptable rating.

However, it was unclear whether the institution could obtain a tax-exempt status: under no conditions would it be acceptable for the state in which the institution were located to generate tax revenue from the interest earned by the funds intended to support partner countries. It was also unclear whether donors desiring to withdraw could find a suitable trustee to take over their shares on a timely basis. After all, the success and credibility of such a financial institution would depend greatly on the parties who are shareholders or trustees.

Finally, it would be even more difficult to develop political acceptance for another financial institution that would inevitably compete with the EIB and EBRD. It would probably be difficult to assert a new institution against these "established brands" with their considerably larger portfolios. In addition, the cost of setting up and operating a new institution appeared to be relatively high.

For these reasons the development bank option was also rejected.

Creating an Independent Fund

Lastly, a third model was discussed that combines the numerous non-institutionalised funds and subfunds into a single regional fund in the form of a separate legal entity. This approach is superior to the other two by permitting a tailor-made, highly flexible governance structure that enables shares to be transferred to the partner countries in the near future while protecting the shareholders from misappropriation. By using the capital paid in by the donors as the first loss tranche – following the model of funds such as the Dexia BlueOrchard Micro-Credit Fund and the Global Microfinance Facility – additional capital can be obtained from financial intermediaries and social and/or commercial private investors who seek financial returns and/or social impact. If the fund will be set up in Luxembourg as planned, any interest earned is tax-free under Luxembourg law.

The only weak point in this alternative was that it entered in relatively unexplored territory. Existing funds with a comparable structure are much smaller. Many details had to be clarified in the process of incorporation. Nevertheless, the working group unanimously concluded that the advantages of a fund clearly outweigh the disadvantages, so it opted for this approach.

Although at this time some details were not yet clarified, a rough outline of the fund concept was assembled. Participating donors signed a joint memorandum of understanding on December 17, 2004. The basic framework is the subject of the following section.

A Basic Framework for an Independent Regional Fund

Legal Framework

The regional fund is to be established in Luxembourg under Luxembourg law (law of July 19, 1991) as a SICAV (Société d'Investissement à Capital Variable) exempt from income tax in Luxembourg.

The Luxembourg law requires a Promoter which should have an excellent reputation and good financial standing and should provide a considerable investment in the Fund. Therefore the donors decided that KfW takes the Promoter role and drives the effort to create the EFSE.

The fund's activities will be defined broadly in its articles of incorporation and in the "prospectus", which is similar to by-laws. The articles of incorporation define the main features of the fund's activities while the prospectus provides detailed regulations concerning the fund's policy. As a general rule, the articles of incorporation are modified only rarely, and the founders of the fund may prescribe qualified or super-majorities for this purpose. The prospectus may be changed more often to adjust the fund's activities to the development of the financial sector in the region.

An important element in the incorporation process is framing the development policy goal in the articles of incorporation, probably in the form of a mission statement, and requiring a high super-majority for any modifications to the mission statement. An artful balance has to be found between the issues regulated by the articles of incorporation and those defined in the prospectus. The fund should not be "gagged" by overloading the articles of incorporation and reducing its flexibility, nor should it be too easy to make changes to the general orientation and structure of the fund by modifying the prospectus.

Regional Framework

The fund is to serve mainly the partner countries and regions of Bosnia and Herzegovina, Montenegro, Serbia and Kosovo, but may extend its range to the remaining countries of the region: Macedonia, Albania, Romania and Bulgaria. A non-negotiable rule is that the funds used in the individual partner countries and committed to the partner governments cannot be retroactively regionalised: for instance, funds previously used in the credit lines for Serbia must be used exclusively for Serbia in the future. This requires that four country subfunds, corresponding to the previous country portfolios, will be placed under the umbrella of the regional fund. The only exception is the funds made available by the German federal government from the regional Apex Fund. These can be used flexibly across the region and as a basis for a regionally oriented fifth subfund that may receive additional donor resources. Several donors have already expressed an interest in participating.

The subfunds will operate independently and loans will be made directly from the five subfunds, not from the umbrella fund, which is a shell entity. Accordingly, while a complete pooling of donor funds will not be possible, this structure does combine the roughly thirty smaller funds into five larger funds under a uniform umbrella with synergistic advantages. Float or idle money will be reduced considerably, and administrative procedures will be greatly simplified because accounts and reports can be combined into a single document that reports the status of the five subfunds.

Graduated Risks – The Cascade Principle

By creating various risk categories, the fund can be an attractive investment for international and national financial intermediaries such as the World Bank, EIB, EBRD, KfW, FMO, IFC and private investors. In case of default the losses are borne solely from the first loss tranche. So far there has only been one case of default, and KfW as fund manager skilfully limited the damage. The first loss tranche would be formed from the donor capital utilised in the previous fund and by any further donor contributions to this risk category. Accordingly, the junior risk categories would not be affected by losses until the first loss tranche is completely exhausted. The shares acquired by the financial intermediaries mentioned above as investors would then be assigned to a mezzanine risk category. As a second loss tranche they would have second-rank liability for losses. Losses for commercial investors in the third risk category would not occur until the first and second loss tranches were already fully depleted, as in a cascade.

To ensure adequate safety for the third risk category, the statutes of the fund stipulates that the first and second risk categories must always cover a specified minimum percentage of the overall fund balance sheet. A similar proportion is specified for the ratio between the first and second risk category.

In this way the comparatively high country risk for the commercial investors posed by the Southeast European partners (ratings of single B or less) are considerably reduced: an investment will remain attractive even if interest earned is far below the rate that an investor acting without such safeguards would demand to cover country risks and Basel 2 regulatory requirements. Based on the experience of the Dexia und responsAbility funds mentioned above, it would be reasonable to infer that even if interest rates hovered around Euribor+1.25 % (plus any profit participation) it will be possible to attract sufficient private investors to the third risk category. Estimates suggest that the fund should grow to EUR 500 million within a few years, even without additional donor funds. In this way donor funds can produce a triple leverage effect through the graduation of risks.

A question is occasionally raised about the rationale of using development aid money to protect private investments. From the donors' point of view, the principal effect of graduated risks is that private investors increase the flow of funds into development activities. This effect will occur even if there are no material changes in the policy of the proposed fund with respect to its readiness to take risks and in its demands on the partner banks. This rationale should be clearly stated in the fund's founding documents, indicating that the ultimate effect is that more money is made available more quickly through the comfort provided to private investors by the donors' commitments. However, by no means should the loss risk cover high interest-bearing, speculative operations. Put differently, if the fund vehicle that has functioned practically without a loss retains its basic structure, it should continue to operate without defaults. The graduation of risks is merely a vehicle for structuring the balance-sheet side of the actual fund risk to financial intermediaries and strategic investors, which is far below the country risk.

KfW is willing to approach potential investors for the second and third risk category and to enlist them as partners. IFC, FMO and EBRD have indicated great interest in the second risk category and have joined the task force of donors, KfW and experts. This task force is operating throughout the formation stage and addressing details that remain to be clarified. In this phase it is important to have the potential shareholders in the second and third risk category participate in the discussions so that a model can be created that is congruent with their interests.

Distribution of Income – The Inverted Cascade Principle

A model for the distribution of income from the fund should take into account both the higher risk of the first and second risk category and the interests of the second and the third risk category in making a profit. Furthermore, whether and to what extent should reserves be accumulated out of the income to provide a cushion against a default? At this level the development and commercial interests diverge. The critical question is the extent to which the distribution of income can be reduced without jeopardising the appetites of the shareholders of the second and third risk category, which is thus the general design of the fund as a public-private partnership. Not all the questions in this area have been settled, but progress is underway.

There is agreement that the shareholders of the first risk category should only seek compensation equal to inflation. Because they do not have to generate much income, they can focus on attracting additional funds from private investors. The alternative is slower fund growth fuelled only from interest income on donor funds.

Furthermore, there is agreement that income distribution to the shareholders of the second risk category should be higher than to the more privileged shareholders of the third risk category.

Finally, there is consensus that income should be distributed in accordance with the inverted cascade principle. This means that the shareholders of the third risk category are to be satisfied first, followed by those of the second risk category, and those of the first risk category will be satisfied last. Any amounts then remaining can be used to replenish a loss reserve. If this loss reserve reaches its target volume, which is yet to be determined, any excess income could be divided among the shareholders of the second and third risk category as "profit participation".

Here again, the commercial investors will generally be satisfied before the international and national financial intermediaries, who will generally be satisfied before the donors. If performance is below the level on which the model is based, the donors would be the first to forgo interest income. Only the residual profit, after disbursement of all fixed distributions, would be divided evenly among intermediaries and commercial investors – and not according to the cascade principle.

Organisational Framework

The laws of Luxembourg prescribe three boards for a SICAV: the General Meeting of Shareholders, the Board of Directors and the fund manager.

General Meeting of Shareholders

The general meeting of shareholders is typically the organ that plots the general course the fund is to take. It appoints the board of managing directors, approves the annual accounts, determines the distribution of income, appoints the auditor and has the power to dissolve the fund. The general shareholders' meeting also decides on changes in the statutes of the fund, if necessary with a qualified or super-majority, as noted above.

Regarding the voting rights the principle of one share equals on vote shall be established. Subscriptions for shares will be accepted upon the creation of each subfund or upon new tranches with existing subfunds at the following initial offering prices:

- C Shares: 50,000 Euro per share

- B Shares: 25,000 Euro per share

- A Shares: 100,000 Euro per share

The result of these differences in the initial offering prices of each share class is that the European Fund for Southeast Europe is allowed to increase significantly the size of the A tranches while ensuring that the B and C investors maintain the development mission of the fund with a comparatively smaller portion of the EFSE.

This decision has far-reaching impacts. The rationale is not so much that those who take higher risks should therefore have more influence. The question is whether and how to ensure that the general meeting of shareholders – the only body that could change the developmental direction of the fund – contains a voting majority that is most likely to prevent mission drift. In particular, the shareholders of the third risk category must be prevented from directing the fund into speculative investments, misusing the developmental funds of the first risk category to hedge against such risks even though they hold the majority of shares. This is generally an argument in favour of greater weighting of the donors' shares in the first risk category.

However, the donors intend to withdraw gradually from the fund and transfer their shares to partner country representatives. Candidly, regardless of the region's political progress and the rapprochement between Southeast European governments (demonstrated by creating a common energy market and a free-trade zone), considerable ethnic and political resentment remains, and an impasse or breakdown in joint fund management by Southeast European government representatives cannot be ruled out. Awarding the majority of voting rights in the first risk category in the medium term would therefore not be very helpful in attracting investors to the second and third risk categories.

To safeguard the stability of the fund there are many arguments in favour of giving the shares of the second risk category, that is, the international and national development banks, a particularly heavy weight because these financial intermediaries can be expected to behave constructively and to protect the mission. The distribution of shares among the individual risk categories roughly reflects the safeguards described above. It is purely a mathematical exercise to determine the weights of the votes so that the distribution of shareholdings can achieve its fiduciary objective.

The Board of Managing Directors

The board of managing directors is appointed by and is subordinate to the general meeting of shareholders. It controls, for instance, the supervision of the fund manager and changes in the prospectus.

The members of the board of managing directors may be seconded from the institutions that are the fund's shareholders, but they may also be outside directors who are important figures in the financial sector. Donors may or may not be interested in taking a position on the board of managing directors. It is customary in Luxembourg but by no means obligatory that the promoter provides the majority or at least a large number of management board members. The appointment of management board members has to be approved by the Luxembourg regulatory authority, which may favour the appointment of managing directors who have experience with funds and their management.

Fund Manager

A professional fund manager will conduct the day-to-day management of fund operations. The manager will be a company selected by an evaluation committee and subject to Board approval. The details of fund management, particularly the obligations and rights of the fund manager, are defined in the Investment Management Agreement between the board of management and the fund manager. Typical obligations of the fund manager include the selection and review of partner banks, the allocation of fund resources, the definition of lending terms and conditions and the recruitment of new investors. The manager will provide periodic reports on the development of the fund. For efficiency and coherence, the fund manager will manage all subfunds. Management of the fund and reporting could be performed by the fund manager's head office, but each subfund should ideally be managed out of a local office in each of the respective partner states.

The fund manager will presumably be aided by a team of development policy experts (investment adviser). Transferring fund management to a team of investment and development experts selected through a transparent competitive process is clearly an objective of KfW, the present fund manager. KfW, as a development bank, plans to invest its own funds in the second risk category. Separating the functions of "investor" and "manager" is important for avoiding conflicts of interest.

Local Ownership

The current structure of the national non-institutionalised funds virtually excludes the partner states from having any influence on the design and operation of the fund. Although the establishment of the funds was discussed with and approved by the partner governments, representatives of the partner governments did not participate in the selection of the partner banks or in any decisions on lending terms and conditions or other details. A large portion of the funds made available by the donors has not been transferred to the partner states' ownership, remaining under the donors' control. However, the German funds have been transferred to the partners within a structure in which the German government has reserved the right to manage the funds in trust on behalf of the partners. Given the disastrous conditions in the partner countries' financial sectors when the individual funds were established, and considering that the partners had little market-based financial sector expertise, it is fair to say that donor-based fund management, at least in the early phase, was a factor that contributed to the successful results achieved.

But the situation has changed. Financial sector development in Southeast Europe has advanced considerably, relevant institutions have accumulated substantial professional expertise, and partners have developed managers who could be expected to play a fruitful role in the institutionalisation of the regional fund and its subsequent management. However, it is clear to the donors and potential investors of the second and third risk category that the regionalisation and continuing political tension between ethnic groups and states in the Balkans requires that the new fund cannot yet be solely or primarily managed by representatives of the partner states. The question therefore is how the target states can be more closely involved. Some donors are planning to transfer their shares to the partners in the near future, and it remains to be clarified how this can be done without complicating the management of the fund.

The distribution of voting rights discussed above will provide stability. The limited voting rights of the first risk category should prevent the Southeast European states from creating mission drift or paralysing the fund through internal strife after all donors have transferred their first risk shares. Every donor will be free to choose its own moment of exit, giving the partners a full mandate without jeopardising the purpose or operations of the fund or reducing its attractiveness for investors of the second and third risk categories.

Moreover, an advisory board will be created. This mechanism will enable the partner states to advise the board of managing directors and make recommendations on fund management during the transition phase leading up to the transfer of voting rights. The advisory capacity could continue after this transfer, bringing in expertise from volunteer advisers, for example.

Dissolution of the Fund or Exit by Shareholders

The fund can in principle be dissolved at any time. A decision by the general meeting of shareholders made by a qualified or super-majority and the approval of the Luxembourg regulator would be all that is required. However, the fund should maintain only small liquid balances: the greatest portion of its funds should always be committed in loans. If it is dissolved, the funds outstanding as loans could be disbursed to the shareholders as the loans are repaid, and within the relevant risk categories and in accordance with the shares they hold. If the German trusteeship were terminated and the portfolios or shares of the donors were already transferred to the partner states, the partner states could transfer the funds to their state budgets and use them at their discretion.

Individual shareholders could also withdraw from the fund. They can sell or give away their shares, or demand repayments out of the liquid assets of the fund or as repayments are returned to the fund. But the structure of the fund imposes some important limitations. The first risk category shareholders have a purely developmental objective and no commercial interest. Their contribution serves as first loss protection for other investors. For these reasons they are contractually bound not to sell or otherwise dispose of their shares prior to the dissolution of the fund, except by exercising the option of a one-time transfer of their shares as a donation to the partner states. (Germany has already transferred its shares and will merely surrender its trusteeship.) The structure of the fund and the primary liability of the first and second risk categories also limit the second risk category shareholders. Each third risk category share must be backed by shares of the first and second categories. A shareholder wishing to withdraw shares from the second risk category could do so only when the remaining number of shares in the second risk category exceeds the minimum guarantee volume for the third risk category, keeping a constant proportion among the three risk categories.

Final Step

The target date for the legal establishment of the fund is December 2005. All relevant steps have been taken, e. g. the validation of the EFSE by Luxembourg lawyers and auditors, reconciliation by current and potential stakeholders on the Term Sheet, Investment Guidelines and Management Contract, selection of Fund Manager, Administration Agent and Custodial Agent, appointing the management bodies and the advisory board; and concluding all agreements required for institutionalisation and transfer of funds. The EFSE has also been presented to the local authorities and the reactions in the region have been positive. The remaining step is the signing of all agreements and documents in December 2005.

Overall Developmental Overview

As already noted, the fund is not a development policy panacea for all problems associated with the financing of enterprises in Southeast Europe. Nonetheless, in many ways, this fund model is quite remarkable.

First, like its predecessors, the fund is a showcase example of donor coordination. Under the innovative and progressive leadership of KfW and participating experts, and with the committed and focused provision of funds – particularly by the EU and the German federal government – all the donors that are active in the Southeast European financial sector have agreed on a common approach. Right from the beginning, the development-focused parties acted in a spirit of cooperation and partnership. This high degree of collaboration has led to coherence and gives the donors special access and weight in the political dialogue with the partner governments that focuses on the financial sector. Even without institutionalisation, all the donors operating in the sector were able to benefit from the results of due diligence appraisals and from the experience in dealing with partner banks. The close coordination and frequent meetings among the donor representatives in the task force have enhanced these effects.

Second, the fund is also a showcase example of public-private partnership. Close cooperation with the private sector includes – besides IPC as the sponsor/promotor of these banks – Commerzbank's becoming a shareholder in some of the donor-founded microbanks that was selected as a payment agent on behalf of the fund. From discussions with potential investors, it appears that institutionalisation will enable about EUR 130 million of donor funds to mobilise an overall sum of around EUR 500 million. About 50 % of that amount will be sponsored by private commercial investors. The development aid funds will have dramatic leverage, creating greater benefits in a much shorter time.

Third and finally, the fund is a showcase example of sustainability. Even in their much less efficient non-institutionalised form, the size of the national funds grew slowly but steadily. Their revolving character and the absence of defaults increased disbursements. This structure was rated as "best practice" by independent experts. The introduction of further professional management and the resulting increases in efficiency will ensure even greater sustainability while also increasing the reinvestment rate.

Conclusion

The structure of the new fund appears to be a highly promising model. As the first fund of its size to use this model, close monitoring is important to ascertain whether the extremely positive predictions will materialise on a timely basis. If it operates according to plan, the model might be a blueprint for other regions facing similar issues. Having succeded in launching a pilot project in the International Year of Microcredit, that achieves a lasting improvement of living conditions for large numbers of households quickly, cost-efficiently and in a sustainable fashion where there is a great gap between human capital and investment capital gives this year an additional highlight. Against the backdrop of the Millennium Development Goals this effort might be among the desperately sought solutions for poverty reduction.

References

KfW Entwicklungsbank has sponsored two financial sector symposia that have included a focus on the banking sectors in Southeast Europe. Springer Verlag has published two books based on papers presented at these meetings.

Matthäus-Maier, Ingrid, and J.D. von Pischke, eds. (2004) *The Development of the Financial Sector in Southeast Europe: Innovative Approaches in Volatile Environments.* Heidelberg and New York: Springer Verlag.

Matthäus-Maier, Ingrid, and J.D. von Pischke, eds. (2005) *EU Accession – Financial Sector Opportunities and Challenges for Southeast Europe.* Heidelberg and New York: Springer Verlag.

Articles by KfW authors that relate to The European Fund for Southeast Europe and to structural issues facing partner banks are as follows:

Glaubitt, Klaus, and Haje Schütte (2004) "Providing Long-Term Funds to Local Financial Institutions – The European Refinancing Funds in Southeast Europe" in Ingrid Matthäus-Maier and J.D. von Pischke, eds., *The Development of the Financial Sector in Southeast Europe: Innovative Approaches in Volatile Environments.* Heidelberg and New York: Springer Verlag. pp. 61–77.

Glaubitt, Klaus, and Haje Schütte (2005) "Public-Private Partnership – Results in the Banking Sector in Southeast Europe" in Ingrid Matthäus-Maier and J.D. von Pischke, eds., *EU Accession – Financial Sector Opportunities and Challenges for Southast Europe.* Heidelberg and New York: Springer Verlag. pp. 303–321.

Hartmann, Klaus-Eckhard (2005) "Providing Long-Term Funds to Local Financial Institutions – The European Refinancing Funds in Southeast Europe" in Ingrid Matthäus-Maier and J.D. von Pischke, eds.,. *EU Accession – Financial Sector Opportunities and Challenges for Southeast Europe.* Heidelberg and New York: Springer Verlag. pp. 277–281.

Köhn, Doris, and Wolfram Erhardt (2004) "Competition and Complementarity: KfW's Approach to Financial Sector Development in Southeast Europe" in Ingrid Matthäus-Maier and J.D. von Pischke, eds., *The Development of the Financial Sector in Southeast Europe: Innovative Approaches in Volatile Environments*. Heidelberg and New York: Springer Verlag. pp. 51–59.

Closely related articles by other authors include:

Addai, Abenaa, and Kristine Nienborg (2004) "Enterprise Level Impacts of Financial Sector Projects in Southeast Europe" in Ingrid Matthäus-Maier and J.D. von Pischke, eds., *The Development of the Financial Sector in Southeast Europe: Innovative Approaches in Volatile Environments*. Heidelberg and New York: Springer Verlag. pp. 179–194.

Alexander, Helen (2005) "Sustainable Microfinance Banks – IMI as a Public-Private Partnership in Practice" in Ingrid Matthäus-Maier and J.D. von Pischke, eds., *EU Accession – Financial Sector Opportunities and Challenges for Southeast Europe*. Heidelberg and New York: Springer Verlag. pp. 289–296.

Baechle, Jan (2004) "Equity Participation in Microfinance banks in Southeast Europe and Georgia – A Strategic Option for a Large Private German Bank?" in Ingrid Matthäus-Maier and J.D. von Pischke, eds., *The Development of the Financial Sector in Southeast Europe: Innovative Approaches in Volatile Environments*. Heidelberg and New York: Springer Verlag. pp. 135–139.

Fischer, Per (2005) "Evolution of the Banking Sector in Southeast Europe – The Role and Business Strategies of Domestic Banks" in Ingrid Matthäus-Maier and J.D. von Pischke, eds., *EU Accession – Financial Sector Opportunities and Challenges for Southeast Europe*. Heidelberg and New York: Springer Verlag. pp. 163–167.

Gospodinov, Evgeny (2005) "The Business Strategies of Domestic Banks in the Long Run – SME Lending as an Attractive Market Segment" in Ingrid Matthäus-Maier and J.D. von Pischke, eds., *EU Accession – Financial Sector Opportunities and Challenges for Southeast Europe*. Heidelberg and New York: Springer Verlag. pp. 173–177.

Schmidt, Reinhard H., and Nina Moisa (2005) "Public-Private Partnerships for Financial Development in Southeast Europe" in Ingrid Matthäus-Maier and J.D. von Pischke, eds., *EU Accession – Financial Sector Opportunities and Challenges for Southeast Europe*. Heidelberg and New York: Springer Verlag. pp. 251–275.

Wisniwski, Sylvia (2004) "Impact of Financial Sector Projects in Southeast Europe – Effects on Financial Institutions and the Financial Sector" in *The Development of the Financial Sector in Southeast Europe: Innovative Approaches in Volatile Environments*. Heidelberg and New York: Springer Verlag. pp. 195–221.

Wisniwski, Sylvia (2005) "Bankers' Perspectives – Dynamic Banking in the Changing Market of Southeast Europe" in Ingrid Matthäus-Maier and J.D. von Pischke, eds., *EU Accession – Financial Sector Opportunities and Challenges for Southeast Europe.* Heidelberg and New York: Springer Verlag. pp. 131 – 162.

Witte, Alexander (2004) "Market Entry in Southeast Europe – Raiffeisenbank Belgrade" in Ingrid Matthäus-Maier and J.D. von Pischke, eds., *The Development of the Financial Sector in Southeast Europe: Innovative Approaches in Volatile Environments.* Heidelberg and New York: Springer Verlag. pp. 119 – 124.

Zeitinger, Claus-Peter (2004) "Sustainable Microfinance Banks – Problems and Perspectives" in Ingrid Matthäus-Maier and J.D. von Pischke, eds., *The Development of the Financial Sector in Southeast Europe: Innovative Approaches in Volatile Environments.* Heidelberg and New York: Springer Verlag. pp. 125 – 134.

CHAPTER 12:

Mainstreaming Microfinance –
Quo Vadis Microfinance Investments?

Klaus Glaubitt[1], Hanns Martin Hagen[2], and Haje Schütte[1]

[1] Vice Presidents, KfW Entwicklungsbank
[2] Principal Sector Economist, KfW Entwicklungsbank

Microfinance – Past and Present

Microfinance is a relatively new term. Its roots lie in the 1970s when tiny, subsidised loans were provided to low-income groups with a focus on the agricultural sector. With the failure of the donor-sponsored development banks that typically provided these services in developing countries through the 1980s (Gonzalez-Vega 2003), microfinance gained momentum and began to expand at break-neck speed. Donor-dependent microcredit programmes were implemented by non-governmental microcredit organisations (MCOs). These organisations successfully issued loans to poor households and microenterprises in the informal sector. The most important effect of these pivotal efforts was to demonstrate that the target groups (micro and small enterprises and poor households and individuals) were bankable even though they did not possess the usual marketable collateral. In spite of this important achievement, the overall developmental impact remained meagre, primarily for the following reasons:

- the range of microfinance services was restricted to credit,

- regional outreach was limited and

- the number of clients was small.

Moreover, these microcredit initiatives often lacked a systematic approach, leading to the prevalence of fragmented projects without a sound vision. And, they were heavily dependant on external grant funding.

The 1990's saw the emergence of microfinance programmes that sought gradual integration into the finance sector. Financial sustainability became a key concept and the objective of many microfinance practitioners and specialists. They viewed cost-covering operations as an imperative. This development was based on the realisation that only a financially viable institution could gain the trust of the target group that would be necessary to mobilise savings or to attract dual-objective private investors seeking development impact as well as meeting financial objectives. Consequently, there was a proliferation of microfinance models. These included, for example, the Grameen Bank, the scaling-up of MCOs into licensed microfinance banks championed by Acción International, or the establishment of greenfield specialised microfinance banks such as the ProCredit model, all of which aimed at integrating microfinance into the mainstream financial system.

By the end of the 1990s, an institutional framework was created that could increase outreach on a large scale and offer a variety of microfinance products. An example is the creation of networks of microfinance institutions (MFIs), such as the ProCredit Banks (discussed below) that enable these specialised microfinance banks to provide a broad range of retail financial services such as credit, savings products and money transfers for low income households on an unprecedented scale. By doing so, they empower economically weak sections of society by giving them the tools to improve their standard of living. The rapid growth of these institutions was made possible through funding provided from a group of public and private institutions, among them KfW Entwicklungsbank.[1]

The UN has designated 2005 as the Year of Microcredit (YOM), demonstrating that microfinance is now well established on the international development agenda. There is a widely acknowledged track record of successful MFIs. Their operations prove that banking the "unbankable" is commercially viable and that this target group of the working poor wants access to a broad range of services: credit, money transfers, savings and other financial products. Contrary to expectations, the solid portfolio quality of mainstream MFIs shows that uncollaterised loans are repaid. Even weaker MFIs in developing countries and transition economies often show a portfolio at risk (balances in accounts affected by a delay in loan repayment of greater than 30 days) of less than 5 %. Moreover, MFIs in urban areas have succeeded in implementing cost-covering delivery mechanisms, allowing them to operate in a sustainable manner. These experiences have convinced even the strongest sceptics that financial services can be extended to microenterprises and households in ways that benefit both the private financial sector and the rest of the economy. Successful microfinance projects provide an excellent example of a development process that does not by-pass the poor but that is driven by them.

---

[1] KfW Entwicklungsbank operations in microfinance go well beyond its leading role in supporting the network of ProCredit Banks. Overall, KfW Entwicklungsbank provides financial and technical support to 83 MFIs in 37 developing and transition countries. The total microfinance portfolio of KfW amounted to EUR 463 million at the end of 2004, making KfW Entwicklungsbank a leading financier of microfinance worldwide. Two-thirds of this support has been in the form of financial cooperation funds from the German government, while the remainder consists of funds provided by KfW Entwicklungsbank at its own risk.

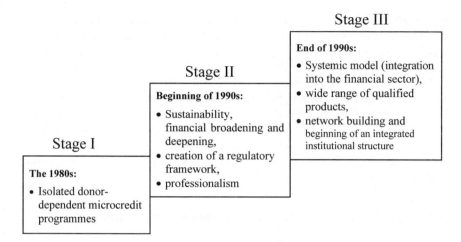

Figure 1. The Evolution of Microfinance

As a consequence, the meaning of "microfinance" has altered in the course of the two decades since the term was coined. Only a few years ago it meant, "...a credit methodology that employs effective collateral substitutes to deliver and recover short-term, working capital loans to microentrepreneurs" (CGAP 2003). Today the term encompasses a broad range of financial services, including microcredit, savings, insurance and money transfers.

There is a general consensus that 2005 marked yet another shift: microfinance services are no longer considered a niche market confined to the development community and carried out solely by specialised MFIs. Rather, it is apparent that for microfinance to achieve its full potential, it must be fully integrated into the financial systems of transition and developing countries. Full integration requires access to vast amounts of human, physical, and financial resources and management know-how (ADB 2005). To become fully integrated into the mainstream financial sector, microfinance must be driven by private commercial actors. This process will open increasing opportunities for new strategic partnerships between MFIs and the private sector that will help MFIs expand their range of products and services, and reach more low-income households in a sustainable manner. These partnerships provide MFIs not only with critical expertise and a point of entry into the mainstream, but also offer socially and financially rewarding opportunities for investors (KfW 2005).

Lessons Learnt – Mainstreaming Microfinance Is Key

Studies by the World Bank, the Consultative Group to Assist the Poor (CGAP), the Department for International Development (DFID) and others demonstrate the effectiveness of the promotion of financial sector development. Research has long confirmed that financial development boosts overall long-term economic growth.

Recent studies highlight the fact that development of financial intermediaries is pro-poor because it reduces income inequality, disproportionately boosting the income of the poor and reducing poverty (Beck et al 2004). These studies indicate that microfinance can contribute to the UN Millennium Development Goal (MDG) of halving world poverty by 2015 (Littlefield et al 2003). In this respect, MFIs are vehicles that reduce poverty. This research is supported by KfW's first-hand experience with the MFIs it has sponsored, such as ACLEDA Bank in Cambodia, SEWA Bank in India, Credit Mongol in Mongolia and ProCredit Bank Ukraine. This experience shows that microfinance services help poor people to diversify and increase their sources of income and empower women to confront systemic gender inequities.

A Comprehensive Strategy to Mainstream Microfinance

For many years KfW Entwicklungsbank has pursued a comprehensive strategy that has as its core objective increased access to microfinance services and to finance for small and medium-sized enterprises. A cornerstone of this strategy is the promotion of complementary approaches:

1. Greenfield approach (founding of new MFIs) and establishment of a microfinance network.

2. Down-scaling approach: restructuring local commercial banks that are willing to commit themselves to microfinance.

3. Up-grading approach: transformation of MCOs into microfinance banks.

4. Linking approach: connecting MFIs with the national or international banking market.

In the majority of transition economies and developing countries in which it operates, KfW implements these approaches simultaneously to foster competition and to contribute efficiently to the sound development of the finance sector.

KfW's strategy aims to integrate MFIs into the financial system. It also seeks to re-orient the business model of mainstream financial institutions by expanding their client focus and product range to include micro, small and medium-sized enterprises. The appropriateness of this comprehensive strategy has been confirmed by World Bank research that underlines the pro-poor impact of a strong mainstream financial system and the complementary and overlapping roles that microfinance and mainstream finance play in tackling poverty (Honohan 2004).

Greenfield Approach

The success of specialised microfinance banks is demonstrated by their strong growth record in providing financial services to the poor in a financially sustainable way. This performance is based on a clear vision and strategy that firmly positions MFIs as integrated players in mainstream finance. Outstanding examples include the ProCredit Banks[2] mentioned above, and the Microfinance Bank of Azerbaijan, which began operations with a full banking license and a strategy to provide its clients – micro and small enterprises as well as low-income households – with an entire range of financial services on a commercial basis.

The success of the ProCredit Banks led to the creation of Internationale Micro Investitionen AG (IMI AG) in 1998, and to its successor, ProCredit Holding AG, in 2005 as a specialised microfinance investment fund with equity participation in 19 ProCredit Banks. These banks do not ask for preferential treatment or continuing grants from donors, and they conform to banking law. In 2004, IMI's equity in the ProCredit Banks was increased to a majority holding by "swapping" the shares of the various owners for shares in ProCredit Holding AG. This makes it possible to manage the ProCredit banks strategically as a single business group consisting of a network of microfinance banks. Gains are created from efficiency and synergy in liquidity management, auditing, corporate culture, business polices, funding for lending activities, and other areas. Surplus liquidity of the ProCredit Bank in Kosovo for example, can be channelled to microfinance institutions in the network which require liquidity. ProCredit Bank Holding AG has vowed to maintain its target group orientation and to prevent "mission drift".

Up-grading Approach

As noted, MCOs have demonstrated their value as development instruments that reach the poor. While there have been a number of outstanding success stories of MCOs that have been transformed into licensed microfinance banks, such as BancoSol, ACLEDA or more recently Compartamos (Dugan 2005), many MCOs are severely constrained by their initial status as unlicensed institutions, often non-governmental organisations (NGOs) and sometimes even with no experience with target group finance. Usually endowed with start-up grant funding, they often lack the human, financial and physical resources as well as the management know-how to prosper as financial institutions. Experience shows that up-grading MCOs into licensed financial institutions and eventually into microfinance banks entails a complex transformation process that requires profound institutional changes which are time-consuming and costly.

For those that have the willingness and potential to commit to up-grading, it is crucial to establish an institutional environment which ensures their sustainability. First, it is necessary to end the strong dependence of these MFIs on the financial

---

[2] The ProCredit Banks in Eastern Europe were established by a like-minded group of institutions that included KfW Bankengruppe, International Finance Corporation (IFC), ProCredit Holding AG, Internationale Projekt Consult GmbH, the European Bank for Reconstruction and Development (EBRD) and FMO (the Netherlands Development Finance Company). Seven of these banks have attracted equity investment from Commerzbank AG, a private commercial bank.

support (grants) of donors and to encourage refinancing via local commercial banks. Second, MFIs have to professionalise in order to meet the regulatory demands of banking law that are required for formalisation and for their integration into the banking system.

Shortcomings of the up-grading approach are illustrated by MCOs in Bosnia and Herzegovina. These MCOs have a strong commitment to the target group, which are mostly micro and small enterprises. However, as the last major donor programmes which fund these MCOs' operations are being phased out, and due to their ambiguous ownership structure – as registered NGOs they are unable to attract private equity – their capacity to expand the outreach of their microfinance services is limited. These problems exemplify the institutional fragility of many MCOs. Moreover, they indicate that MFIs relying on a continuous flow of donor grants for operational purposes may eventually end up in a blind alley. While it is difficult to predict how long grants will be available to MFIs, the market is a reliable source for refinancing at all times for MFIs that are well-managed and profitable.[3]

Most MCOs therefore remain in an "institutional trap:" their initial mission did not include a vision and strategy to become part of the mainstream financial sector. While this may imply a waste of energy and resources, it has broader implications for the development of the microfinance industry at large. Recent surveys and research on the global scale of outreach and the financial depth of MFIs (or alternative financial institutions[4]) generally show that the few countries in which MFIs have comparatively high penetration ratios are characterised not by numerous MFIs but by a few large-scale operations (Christen et al 2004, Honohan 2004). Investing in the growth of a few high-performing MFIs therefore seems a wiser strategy than endowing numerous hopefuls.

---

[3] Subsidy in microfinance, such as grant funding, has been subject to long discussions. Many support the view that continuous refinancing through grants tends to erode or at least weaken an MFI's capability to stand on its own feet, and that "grants can be poisonous" (van Maanen 2004). Nevertheless, reality is complex and calls for a flexible response. Although in principle grants should not be used to subsidise microloans, donations can be justified when used to help MFIs shoulder the high initial costs of investment (start-up costs), in particular for the training of local staff and for creating the prerequisites, such as the costs of opening new branches, to increase outreach. Once microfinance services generate revenues that cover total costs, a newly established institution no longer needs operational subsidies. Against the conventional wisdom that sustainable MFIs need only three to five years to reach break-even, recent research shows that 30% to 50% of MFIs took longer than five years – some much longer (Gonzalez 2005). Profitability is absolutely essential if MCOs are to offer microfinance services in a sustainable manner and if they want to grow.

[4] CGAP recently introduced the expression "alternative financial institutions" (AFIs) as "institutions...which focus to some degree on extending financial services downward from the economic level of the traditional clients of commercial banks". These institutions have a "double bottom line": in addition to a financial objective, they also have a developmental or social objective. AFIs encompass specialised MFIs, commercial bank MFIs, financial cooperatives (including credit unions), low capital rural and/or local banks, state development and agricultural banks, postal savings banks and non-postal savings banks (Christen et al 2004).

Downscaling Approach

Evaluations indicate that the establishment of new microfinance banks has been more successful than the restructuring of local commercial banks committed to microfinance through the "downscaling approach" (Glaubitt, Schütte 2004).

One of the main criticisms of down-scaling is the limited outreach to the target group that these local commercial banks achieve in providing financial services to microenterprises. Their focus on small and medium-sized enterprises rather than microenterprises is often criticised as a lack of success. However, it would be detrimental to microfinance to concentrate only on the greenfield approach. KfW's experience is that local commercial banks often imitate the successful strategy and instruments of greenfield microfinance banks when confronted by their strong performance. This experience affirms the recent argument that greater competition in the financial sector is good for business (Claessens 2005). The latest research indicates also a strong correlation between the provision of financial services to small enterprises and economic growth. It seems that one of the main ways in which financial sector development accelerates economic growth is by removing growth constraints on small firms (Beck et al 2005).

The mixed results of classical down-scaling projects have led to their modification. The new approach stresses commercial banks' commitment of their own funds and co-investment in their institutional strengthening. Acción International has successfully established service and distribution agencies jointly with well-established mainstream finance institutions in Latin America that act as the retail link to the low-income costumer, while risk management and back office functions remain with the bank.

Thus the downscaling approach has a two-pronged focus: first, to increase the outreach of microfinance, and second, to alter the business model of the mainstream financial sector in ways that increase pro-poor impact (Beck et al 2004).

Developments in the increasingly competitive financial markets of Southeast Europe confirm the appropriateness of KfW's comprehensive strategy in financial sector deepening: Microfinance banks increasingly position themselves in the SME market to diversify risk, to cultivate new opportunities, and to accompany the growth of their most successful business clients. At the same time, particularly in the very competitive banking sectors such as in Bulgaria and Romania, commercial mainstream banks start tapping lower market segments as part of their corporate lending business or through their consumer lending windows (Winkler 2005). The latter is especially attractive for microenterprises seeking small loans (Wisniwski 2005).

Future Challenges

While significant progress has been made, the potential demand by low-income people for pro-poor financial services remains unfulfilled. CGAP estimates that about two billion people are "unbanked" globally, i. e., without access to financial services offered by commercial banks or alternative financial institutions, including MFIs (Christen et al 2004). Surveys and research consistently confirm the currently limited scale and penetration of microfinance (Honohan 2004) despite the successes in scaling up individual microfinance institutions (CGAP 2004). Hence, within the next decade, microfinance will have to confront the following key challenges if it wants to make a significant contribution towards reducing poverty[5].

Product Development

Whilst there has traditionally been an overemphasis on credit, deposit services are now recognised as being at least equally important in microfinance (SIRC 2005). Research has shown that clients value savings, which may also take the form of insurance or pension products. Savings also expand the basis for microfinance services and are vital for strengthening the liability side of microfinance banks. A study that included 3,000 alternative financial institutions in developing countries and transition economies found that deposit accounts outnumbered loan accounts by four to one (Christen et al 2004). Extensive evidence indicates an enormous unmet demand for deposit services for low income groups. The availability and quality of these services are highly uneven, not least due to the significant challenges posed by costs, control and culture that regulated financial institutions encounter when seeking to expand deposit services to include low income markets (SIRC 2005).

Furthermore, it is becoming clear that a wider range of products and services has to be offered to serve the complex economies of the working poor. MFIs offering loans, savings, insurance, pensions, money transfers and other facilities have to price their services effectively, offer them in a flexible format and deliver them in an unbureaucratic manner.

Introduction of the latest technologies may reduce transaction costs and repayment risks. There are promising examples of cases where branching strategies became redundant due to the deployment of smart cards (Prahalad 2005). Projects in India show that this approach has great potential for efficiency gains and cost reduction. A collector carries a pocket-sized smart card terminal on which all transactions such as clients' deposits in rural areas can be electronically recorded. Within its Financial Cooperation framework, KfW is currently supporting the establishment of a new money transfer and remittances system in Southeast Europe and the Caucasus, which allows clients to transfer money at rates which are up to 50 % below those of current suppliers.

Reductions in transaction costs translate into increased outreach by MFIs. Examples include the adoption of innovations in information technology such as

---

[5] The potential contribution of microfinance in reducing poverty leads to controversy. Microfinance devotees tend to propagate the myth that microfinance is a panacea for the problem of global poverty. Others warn against portraying microfinance as a "magic bullet".

ATMs (automated teller machines), PDAs (personal digital assistants) and biometric technology. Another interesting development in microfinance is credit scoring – determining repayment risks on the basis of repayment performance and the quantifiable data on loan applications. Seen by some as unfit to replace well-tested methods of determining repayment risks such as joint liability and the judgement of seasoned loan officers in their assessments of loan applicants' personal and financial situation, scoring is heralded by others as the next "breakthrough in microcredit". However, even the enthusiasts see scoring as appropriate only for those MFIs that have a solid lending technology, strong IT systems and a large database of historical loan information (Schreiner 2003, KfW 2003).

Innovations in product development and their delivery hold some promise for one of the biggest challenges – the deepening of rural financial markets. Their limited development reflects shortcomings in the physical and institutional infrastructure, and in human capital in rural areas in developing countries. Their absence increases transaction costs and accentuates information, incentive and enforcement problems that make financial transactions difficult. The recent successes by MFIs in providing financial services in rural areas are due to a more hospitable policy environment, innovations in financial technologies and improvement in the institutional design of financial institutions (Gonzalez-Vega 2003). While some progress has been made, the expansion of the frontier of rural finance remains a large challenge (von Pischke 2003)[6].

Institutional Issues

The expansion of existing MFIs and the creation of new ones will increase the pressure on capital which is already scarce. As public funds are limited, the private sector will be the source that will enable MFIs to finance and expand their operations. Investment funds for microfinance have begun offering new opportunities to dual-objective, private local and foreign investors. Experience indicates that these funds seem to be flexible and efficient instruments that can help to meet the present and future demand for capital in microfinance (Köhn, Jainzik, 2005) – a topic explored in other contributions to this book.

In addition, securitisation could help link local and international capital markets to microfinance. Offering private investors good microfinance portfolios that are segregated[7] from microfinance banks, may mobilise additional capital from the

---

[6] Von Pischke (2003) provides a succinct and highly informative account of "the Past," "the Continuing" and "the Present" situation of rural finance and outlines new institutional forms and responses – "the Open" – that could help more people through rural finance.

[7] Asset securitisation transforms (portions of) microfinance portfolios into fungible securities that are backed by claims and other assets. The microfinance portfolios are transferred to a special purpose vehicle (SPV) and thus legally segregated from the originator (an MFI, for example). This permits a separate rating of the securities, which is in general higher than the rating of the originator.

market. In fact, it is imperative that MFIs peer beyond the confines of the donor world and embrace the opportunities that the private sector can offer for the expansion of their business. In this respect, they should be ready to let professional institutions analyse the quality and efficiency of their work (rating) and compare important financial and non-financial indicators of different MFIs (benchmarking). The ProCredit group has demonstrated that measures to attract private capital can be successfully applied to microfinance. The maxims of transparency, openness and good governance are conducive to attracting new investors.

Policy and Legal Issues

Microfinance as a commercial venture can prosper only in countries that have a sound policy and legal framework. In view of high transaction costs, MFIs can survive only if they can charge cost-covering interest rates. An interest rate cap is detrimental to the development of the microfinance sector. A cap will limit the volume of loans that can be disbursed to poor people. Such limitation consolidates the position of commercial lenders in the informal sector, who often charge exorbitantly high interest rates on loans to the poor. Many countries have understood this lesson and have abolished or are about to abolish interest rate caps. Moreover, conventional collateral should not be required and unsecured lending should not be forbidden under the banking law. Other factors which hamper the growth of MFIs are complex reporting and loan documentation requirements.

These examples of enabling regulation undertaken by the national authorities responsible for regulation and supervision of financial institutions create framework conditions that foster the growth of MFIs. When MFIs take deposits and as microfinance grows to scale, MFIs should be prudentially regulated and supervised in order to protect the financial system as a whole and especially the safety of small deposits (Christen et al 2003).

At the same time, MFIs have to be committed to transparency[8] and build a reliable information infrastructure. Management information systems (MIS) and sound risk management procedures should be introduced, and external audits should become obligatory. Furthermore, a single standard rating system for MFIs and frequent benchmarking of MFI performance against financial and non-financial performance could be a useful tool to mobilise public and private capital for MFIs. Moreover, controls and monitoring can reduce fraud and the misuse of funds. The challenges surrounding these policy and legal issues lie less in insufficient know-how and expertise or the lack of consensus among those shaping microfinance systems, but rather in their sound and consistent application.

---

[8] For MFIs that are not prudentially licensed and therefore not regulated or supervised by government authorities, CGAP and the Small Enterprise Education and Promotion Network (SEEP) have developed disclosure guidelines for financial statements by MFIs (Rosenberg et al 2003).

Institutions and Investors

For microfinance to grow and reach the bulk of the economically weaker sections of the world, it will be essential to have more investors in microfinance. The integration of private investors, the "downstreaming" of mainstream financial institutions, and the participation of carefully selected alternative financial institutions are especially important in bringing low-income households and tiny businesses into the mainstream financial system.

To realise this objective, KfW considers collaboration with private investors to be absolutely indispensable. A pioneering way to do so is through "public private partnership" (PPP),[9] a concept that is becoming increasingly important in microfinance (Glaubitt and Schütte 2004). ProCredit Holding AG represents an outstanding example of a successful PPP. Internationale Projekt Consult GmbH (IPC GmbH), the Dutch DOEN Foundation (committed to development co-operation and human rights) and other dual objective investors hold about two-thirds of the capital of ProCredit Holding AG. The remaining shares are held by KfW, IFC, FMO and other public investors. The participation of public institutions serves as a catalyst that attracts private investors. Private investment not only enlarges the capital base for microfinance but also offers professional know-how for improving the range and quality of financial products (financial deepening) and expanding the outreach of financial services (financial broadening). This PPP approach helps the 19 ProCredit banks expand their microfinance portfolio, which currently grows by about EUR 400 million per annum and reaches 170,000 new clients each year. Another promising PPP project is the Global Microfinance Facility (GMF), which is supported by Cyrano, a private company, and has Crédit Coopératif as a further private investor. GMF offers medium-term loans to MFIs.

In order to realise the objective of providing sustainable and high quality financial services to as many lower income people as possible, the limited penetration of MFIs must be overcome. This requires a thorough assessment of the potential of financial institutions beyond the limits of traditional MFIs. Opportunities to include alternative financial institutions in microfinance initiatives should be assessed by donors, governments, social and private investors, and other stakeholders. The challenges of doing so should also be considered, keeping foremost in mind the criteria of financial sustainability, outreach to the poor, impact and transparency[10].

---

[9] Within the framework of Financial Cooperation "public private partnership" is defined as co-operation between the government and the private sector in programmes or projects. They are effective and efficient in meeting development objectives and are in the interest of private enterprises (German Ministry for Development, 2004).

[10] Von Pischke (2003) adds "transparency" to the microfinance triangle proposed by Manfred Ziller and Richard L. Meyer, eds., in *The Triangle of Microfinance: Financial Sustainability, Outreach and Impact*. Baltimore and London: The Johns Hopkins University Press, 2002.

Table 1. Synthesis of future challenges

Product Development	• Expansion of products and services: From credit to savings, insurance and pension products, transfers and payments • Technologies such as smart cards, ATMs, PDAs, biometrics technology, credit scoring • Cheaper and faster money transfer and payment systems • Deepening rural financial markets
Institutional Issues	• Institutional broadening • Raising capital to finance MFI growth by developing micro-finance investment funds (MFIFs) • Securitisation of MFIs' microcredit portfolios • Improvement of control and monitoring measures • Regular rating and auditing, establishment of management information systems (MIS)
Policy/Legal Issues	• Policy and legal framework: Allow unsecured lending, avoid interest rate caps and complex reporting and loan documentation requirements • Obligatory: Management information systems (MIS) and sound risk management procedures, external audits • Single standard grading system for MFIs and benchmarking
Institutions/Investors	• Assessing the potential of alternative financial institutions • PPP: Public institutions as catalysts for private investors • "Downstreaming" mainstream financial institutions

Finally, the "downstreaming" of mainstream financial institutions, making their business focus more pro-poor, holds much promise. Increased competition, a renewed focus on private retail banking, innovations in financial technology, advances in information technologies, as well as the success of microfinance banks seem to make the provision of financial services to lower income people an interesting business proposition for mainstream financial institutions. This development should be encouraged and promoted.

The Future Role of KfW Entwicklungsbank in Microfinance

KfW Entwicklungsbank will continue to promote microfinance as part of the mainstream financial sector. Our support for such integration will broaden access to financial services for micro and small enterprises as well as low-income households. As a development bank with a 60-year track record in promoting private sector growth, KfW is well positioned to leverage private sector interest and resources for development purposes.

For this purpose KfW will exert a catalytic role in mobilising funds for the refinancing of MFIs – fulfilling the objectives of its financial sector development mandate. KfW can facilitate access to private capital for MFIs that are committed to their clientele. KfW's professional know-how can demonstrate that securitisation in microfinance can work. In addition, KfW will continue to launch new equity and refinancing funds for microfinance activities.

There is still a large job to be done in helping MFIs bolster the target group's contribution to macroeconomic growth by providing a wide range of high quality financial services. This challenge will remain as long as there are large numbers of unbanked low-income households and businesses. The central stakeholder objective of KfW (within the framework of German Financial Cooperation) is to help private investors in microfinance fulfil their developmental role. By far the most important task is to ensure that microfinance banks maintain microfinance as a core business segment as they expand.

References

Asian Development Bank (2005): The Changing Face of the Microfinance Industry – Building Financial Systems for the Poor, in: ADB Annual Report 2004, Manila.

Beck, Thorsten, Demirgüç-Kunt, Aslı, and Levine, Ross (2004): Finance, Inequality and Poverty: Cross-Country Evidence, World Bank, Washington DC.

Beck, Thorsten, Demirgüç-Kunt, Aslı, (As above) Laeven, Luc and Levine, Ross (2005): Finance, Firm Size, and Growth, World Bank, Washington DC.

BMZ (2004): Financial Sector Concept, Bonn.

CGAP (2003): CGAP Phase III Strategy 2003–2008, Washington DC.

CGAP (2004): Scaling Up Poverty Reduction – Case Studies in Microfinance, Washington DC.

Christen, Robert Peck, Lyman, Timothy R., and Rosenberg, Richard (2003): Guiding Principles on Regulation and Supervision of Microfinance. CGAP Microfinance Consensus Guidelines, Washington DC.

Christen, Robert Peck, Rosenberg, Richard and Jayadeva, Veena (2004): Financial Institutions with a Double Bottom Line – Implications for Microfinance, CGAP Occasional Paper, Washington DC.

Claessens, Stijn, and Laeven, Luc (2005): Financial Dependence, Banking Sector Competition, and Economic Growth, World Bank, Washington DC.

Dugan, Maggie, and Goodwin-Groen, Ruth (2005): Donors Succeed in Making Themselves Obsolete – Compartamos Taps Financial Markets in Mexico, CGAP Case Study, Washington DC.

Glaubitt, Klaus, and Schütte, Haje (2005): Public-PrivatePartnership – Results in the Banking Sector in Southeast Europe, in: Matthäus-Maier, Ingrid, von Pischke, J.D., EU Accession – Financial Sector Opportunities and Challenges for Southeast Europe, Berlin/Heidelberg/New York: Springer.

Gonzalez, Adrian (2005): How Long Does it Take to Achieve Financial Sustainability? Glimmers from On-going Research, Microfinance Information exchange (Mix).

Gonzalez-Vega, Claudio (2003): Deepening Financial Rural Markets – Macroeconomic Policy and Political Dimensions (no location).

Honohan, Patrick (2004): Financial Sector Policy and the Poor – Selected Findings and Issues, World Bank, Washington DC.

Köhn, Doris and Jainzik, Michael (2005): Microfinance Investment Funds – An Innovative Form of PPP to Foster the Commercialisation of Microfinance, in Matthäus-Maier, Ingrid, and von Pischke, J.D., eds., EU Accession – Financial Sector Opportunities and Challenges for Southeast Europe, Berlin/Heidelberg/New York: Springer.

KfW (2005): 2005 Financial Sector Development Conference: New Partnerships for Innovation in Microfinance, Frankfurt am Main.

Littlefield, E., Morduch, J., and Mesbahuddin, S.H. (2003): Is Microfinance an Effective Strategy to Reach the Millennium Deveopment Goals? in: CGAP Focus Note, 01/2003, Washington DC.

Prahalad, C.H. (2005): The Fortune at the Bottom of the Pyramid – Eradicating Poverty through Profits, Wharton School Publishing.

Rosenberg, Richard, Mwangi, Patricia, Christen, Robert Peck, and Nasr, Mohammed (2003): Disclosure Guidelines for Financial Reporting by Microfinance Institutions. CGAP Microfinance Consensus Guidelines, Washington DC.

Schreiner, Mark (2003): Scoring – The Next Breakthrough in Microcredit? CGAP Occasional Paper, Washington DC.

SIRC (2005): CGAP Savings Information Resource Center. CGAP, Washington DC.

Van Maanen, Gert (2004): Microcredit, Sound Business or Development Instrument? Voorburg, The Netherlands.

Von Pischke, J.D. (2003): The Evolution of Institutional Issues in Rural Finance – Outreach, Risk Management and Sustainability. BASIS Collaborative Research Support Program, University of Wisconsin-Madison.

Winkler, Adalbert (2005): Financial Sectors in Transition Countries – Where Do We Stand? unpublished, European Central Bank, Frankfurt am Main.

Wisniwski, Sylvia (2003): European Fund for Southeast Europe – Market Study. Bankakademie International, Frankfurt am Main.

Ziller, Dominik (2005): The European Fund for Southeast Europe – An Innovative Instrument for Political and Economic Stabilisation, in this volume.

CHAPTER 13:

Commercial Investment in Microfinance: Fears and Fulfillment

Bob Pattillo

Founder and Partner, Gray Ghost Microfinance Fund

On the plane home from the KfW Symposium on microfinance investment funds, I thought about the facts, the ideas, and the feelings that we shared during those two days in November 2004. The feelings were especially important because they are what most motivate us, stir us to action or resign us to abstinence. One feeling I sensed several times was fear – the fear of private investment in microfinance. Are investors "short timers," getting in, making or losing a quick buck, and getting out? Will investors sitting on boards corrupt strategy, moving management towards consumer lending, away from the smaller borrowers and the rural markets? Will they load existing customers with more debt than they can handle? In response to such questions rooted in fear, and to explore another way of experiencing what lies ahead, I offer the view of one investor.

Can Microfinance Safely Attract Long-Term Investors?

A great debate in the microfinance industry centres on whether microfinance investment funds are long-term players or whether they are merely Trojan horses for commercial banks. Commercial banks bring scale, efficiency and the capacity to tap local savings. They also can bring credibility with regulators. But microfinance investment funds are as important as the commercial banks long-term for two reasons: 1) funds are where true innovation will occur, and 2) funds are the only mechanisms for private investors to enter this market, other than direct share ownership. The global microfinance market will become like the barbell financial market in the US. The Goliaths at one end are the huge banks that treat financial services delivery as a commodity. And at the other end, the risk takers and the relationship makers rule, creating innovative enterprises that find niches to survive and thrive.

One of the most powerful notions put forward at the Symposium is institution or enterprise building. It was the strongest point of agreement between two of the most respected people in the business, Maria Otero of ACCION and Claus-Peter

Zeitinger of IMI. An enterprise is a building block for the industry, whether an MFI, a bank, a network, or a fund. It is at the convergence of vision, strategy, and passion, making things work to attract the stakeholders that make things happen. The power of privatising microfinance is demonstrated by the fact that these stakeholders gather by choice. A compelling enterprise attracts employees, customers, and now, investors. Investors in time, experience, and financial resources are the owners, or at least those directly responsible in a way that leaves them clearly accountable.

There are now between 38 and 55 microfinance funds – depending on the reporting source. The growth in the number of microfinance investment funds is, as Damian von Staffenburg said, "one of the glories of microfinance." Each is putting forward its vision for a powerful enterprise and is just beginning to attract investors. The volume of private and commercial dollars that will flow into microfinance will be enormous. If the industry now has $ 500 million in private funds, $ 100 billion will surely accumulate before the growth trend levels off. There are three reasons for this expansion.

Why Private Investment in Microfinance Will Grow

First, microfinance is just beginning to tap its potential for profitability and growth. The relationship between the loan officer and the microentrepreneur is powerfully loyal, both ways. Do you remember who gave you your first loan? The opportunity to sell other very useful products and services such as life insurance or home loans through that existing distribution channel will add revenue at a low incremental cost, creating a profit for the bank. Competitive microfinance markets in Bolivia and Bangladesh demonstrate that MFIs can innovatively serve their customers at lower cost. These best practices will spread through the global industry, producing more profits in a healthy way for all stakeholders. Profits attract investors.

Growth potential in microfinance is well documented. Start with the current client base, expand that to some fraction of the 500 million potential customers, increase each loan by the potential growth of the microenterprise, then expand each client relationship with other services such as mortgages. The capital growth is enormous, far beyond the capacity of public money. The emergence and dominance of private capital is inevitable.

Second, private investors add value beyond the capital they provide. One unfounded fear is that private investors will charge too much, asking for higher returns that "squeeze blood out of a turnip." But, consider rates of return as part of a package. A privately capitalised microfinance fund can be innovative, efficient, agile and service-oriented. The cost of capital to the MFI is important, but of similar importance is the transaction cost of funds, which is low. Consider the flexibility of the capital provider, transparent strategy and decision making processes, timeliness, and smooth and quick approval and reporting processes. Funds can help attract additional sources of capital and can provide strategic advice. Even if private investors require higher returns, can they partner with the enterprise in a way that creates value, that expands the pie so that even after taking their slice, there is more for microentrepreneurs, management, employees? Broad experience says, yes, they can. The private investor is well equipped to manage risk and sense opportunity. In contrast, there is no place for the social investor in the commercial bank model.

Finally, consider why investors are attracted to microfinance. What are our motivations? Many ask "What can capitalism and market forces offer microfinance?" I also ask, "What can microfinance do for capitalism, for markets, for investors? In what ways will the lives of investors be more fulfilling, with more joy and hope through the experience of microfinance investing? In what ways does social investment connect people in a respectful, positive, uplifting way, folks across the globe, across cultures, language, religion, differences in resources? Should we care?"

Beyond Investment in Microfinance

Many fear concentration of wealth in the hands of a few. Given the history of some of the choices of the wealthy, a history of self-absorption, seeking happiness through consumption, using power to control governments and armies to protect narrow selfish interests, that is a reasonable fear. However, rather than curse the darkness, let's try lighting a candle.

Until now, wealthy persons who decided that their family had enough, that they would like to make their wealth available for the social good and began to look for an enterprise to make that happen, had only limited choices. They could give to their church, mosque or synagogue, pay taxes to the government, or start a foundation. These have their roles and do good. I've engaged in all three. But when it comes to really making a dent in world poverty in a powerful, sustainable way, none compare to the promise of the social investment fund. For starters, if you write a check to the first three, it is spent and gone. A fund recycles capital, well beyond a person's lifetime if that is their intention.

In addition, a fund has two built-in feedback loops to insure that it creates value on a continuing basis. First, the investor is co-invested with other like-minded investors. They have the ability to help keep the fund's mission sharp, and the power to shut it down or change management if it is not. Second, if the customers of the fund, the investees, do not see value in the product, they buy elsewhere. These loops have the power to keep the vision and strategy of the enterprise fresh, which is much more difficult to achieve in religious institutions, government, or foundations.

Will investors remain committed over time? The non-profit sector attracts tremendous numbers of extremely talented people who are willing to work for less money in a fulfilling job. These folks trade income potential for meaning. The fact that millions of people in the non-profit sector do this their entire lives suggests that there are many investors who, once they find a way, trade a little bit of future financial gain for a whole lot of fulfillment today. These investors are likely not only to never go back to pure financial investing, but also to expand the scope of their social investment, promote it among their friends, and teach it to their kids. They will learn that the balance between their physical wants and needs actually changes with time, many "needs" become merely "wants" or even disappear, and they free resources that they can invest for social benefit. This creates a feeling of connectedness and usefulness.

The last great hope I have for investors and their role in microfinance is that we care about the enterprises we invest in. Investment is not an event: it is a process. Caring does contribute to the bottom line because people thrive in and are much more loyal to an enterprise and in a relationship that contains a spirit of caring. They are more innovative, more willing to share their boldest dreams. But beyond the bottom line profit, people that have or control resources are hungry for ways to put them to good use, and in a way that has integrity. The investor would like to feel respected in the process, even cared for in return. These enterprises can teach us so much, offer us so much meaning, helping us grow.

If we look at the circles of life, the family circle, circles of friendship, volunteering, investment, civic engagement, career, we feel more at peace where these circles begin to converge. Our spiritual journey takes us towards the relationships that thrive in the places the circles overlap, to the hope that our role in life and our purpose for being become integrated and made whole. That oneness touches us deeply in our soul, our collective communal spirit. We can ask no more from life than this. And when we taste it, really savour it, we let go of so many things that we thought we needed but which hold us back, that get in the way, and relish the feelings of power, respect and care. This is our candle in the darkness.

"As we let our own spirits shine we invite others to do the same." (Marianne Williamson, author of *The Gift of Change*)

CHAPTER 14:

Microfinance Investment Funds: Looking Ahead

Ernst A. Brugger[1]

President, BHP – Brugger and Partners Ltd

Introduction: Thesis and Core Questions

In many developing countries, microfinance has clearly proved successful: the growth rate of microfinance institutions (MFIs) has been consistently high; loan volumes are becoming sizeable; and professionalism and governance have markedly improved. In addition to furthering social goals, the growth of microfinance suggests its potential as a sound investment opportunity for private investors and commercial institutions. MFIs have traditionally been funded by donor organisations that seek to provide financial services to low income households. However, the ability of donor organisations to support MFIs is often limited by their financial and technical capacity. As the market for MFI services grows and investment performance improves, private capital and know-how could play a critical role in bridging that gap.

Our main thesis is that, due to demand pressure in the huge informal markets of developing countries, the microfinance industry will grow rapidly and steadily. It will soon attract mainstream capital market institutions and institutional investors, boosting interest through the launching of additional products and innovations. Heightened interest is already creating a demand for investment vehicles that allow microfinance institutions to expand the range and quality of their services. We focus here on one vehicle: microfinance investment funds (MFIFs).

Microfinance investment funds are defined as funds that include microfinance institutions in their portfolios, and that provide a diversified, well-balanced, socially-minded investment opportunity to private and institutional investors, both locally and abroad. MFIFs come in many forms and cater to a variety of potential investors, and can thereby mobilise capital from sources otherwise hesitant to invest in microfinance.

The dynamic importance of MFIFs includes their potential to make microfinance markets more efficient, both for investors active in capital markets as well

---

[1] I would like to thank Bikram Duggal, Assistant Advisor, BHP – Brugger and Partners Ltd., for his contribution.

as for MFIs serving poor microentrepreneurs. Even more important, however, will be the fundamental changes in framework conditions that influence local savings, commercial law and property rights. These processes should be supported by donor organisations, which should shift their focus on microfinance away from direct support for MFIs and MFIFs that have become sustainable. Rather, they should promote innovation and support risk mitigation in ways that accelerate the flow of private capital to microfinance.

Given the central role envisaged for MFIFs, this paper focuses on two key questions:

- How will current market trends influence the future development of MFIFs?

- What factors favour MFIF success?

MFIFs: The Critical Demand-Supply Link

Since its inception, microfinance has struggled to raise capital to meet the demands of millions of economically active poor households across the world. This demand[2] cannot be fully met by donor agencies, making commercial investments therefore necessary. The industry has already made significant progress in linking up with the commercial finance mainstream by increasingly promoting the commercial viability of microfinance institutions, by generating awareness and by advocacy, thereby creating an interest among potential investors. MFIFs have emerged as vehicles for linking the microfinance and mainstream commercial markets.

MFIFs provide the essential missing piece in the microfinance jigsaw puzzle – positioned appropriately between the supply (the investors and the capital markets) and the demand (the MFIs). With the requisite skills and distribution capabilities, MFIFs can bridge the gap between sophisticated, resource-rich capital markets and the often remote and simple MFIs. The realisation of this inherent value appears to have favoured the mushrooming of many MFIFs around the world. As of October 2004, there were reportedly 55 MFIFs[3] in operation.

MFIFs also help to further the goals of the UN Year of Microcredit 2005, one of which is building inclusive financial systems. An important focus of inclusive financial systems must be the participation of the international capital markets in microfinance and, if possible, the participation of microfinance in capital markets. MFIFs, as the critical link between supply and demand, will be essential in achiev-

---

[2] It is estimated that there are nearly 500 million households (source BlueOrchard, CGAP) that could successfully use microfinancial services. Assuming a conservative loan amount of US$ 200 per such household, hypothetical worldwide demand for microcredit would be US$ 100 billion.

[3] Based on the survey conducted by CGAP. Please see Ivatury and Abrams in this volume.

ing this end: it is partially through the enabling work of the MFIFs that the aims of the UN International Year of Microcredit and the Millennium Development Goals, of halving poverty and empowering women, can be achieved.

In their role as the critical link, MFIFs connect the capital markets with micro-entrepreneurs across the world. In effect, they may be seen as linking the informal economy with the formal economy and as offering a formula for the sustained growth of the millions of low-income households currently operating in the informal economy.

The subsequent sections address the two core questions driving this paper and outline the complementary developments essential for microfinance to realise its true potential and satisfy its demand.

How Will Current Market Trends Influence the Development of MFIFs?

This section examines trends that are likely to influence significantly the development of MFIFs. The growth of the MFIFs is intrinsically linked to growth in demand for microfinance services, which drives the entry of new funds and investors. Hence, these trends should be viewed from both the supply and demand perspectives.

Supply-Side Trends: Entry of Mainstream Players

The supply-side is marked by a number of positive developments, especially the entry of mainstream commercial players, chiefly large commercial banks and institutional investors. Goodman in this volume provides an account of the growing involvement of traditional financial sector participants in microfinance including commercial banks, pension funds and traditional investment funds. Building further on his account, it is important to emphasise the potential of the two players whose involvement is the most critical for the future of MFIFs and microfinance: the large or high profile financial players and institutional investors. What are the associated trends on the horizon?

Large banks and financial institutions: These big players consist of local and international commercial banks and financial institutions. These parties can provide:

- Access to capital: The big banks and leading financial institutions can supply essential capital to microfinance. Banks with access to capital in the form of public or institutional deposits are amongst the largest reservoirs of financial resources. Effective linkages with banks can provide the microfinance industry the much-needed capital to meet its demands. The case of Indian banks, which have taken a keen interest in financing MFIs, is noteworthy here. The National Bank for Agriculture and Rural Development (NABARD), an arm of the central bank which encourages Indian banks to invest in microfinance, reports that during the year 2003–04 Indian banks lent an equivalent of US$ 412 million to microfinance self-help groups of poor women in rural areas.

- Access to capital markets: In addition to providing capital per se, banks can act as intermediaries in the funding chain by hosting MFIFs or otherwise channeling investments to MFIs. The Dexia Bank, which floated the Dexia Microcredit Fund, is a suitable example in this context. The Dexia fund, aided by professional fund management, has leveraged investments to provide loans of US$ 75 million (cumulatively) to 50 MFIs in over 20 countries since its inception in 1998.

A number of large, leading international banks are engaged in microfinance in various capacities, including the commercial and promotional along with soft funding. Dexia Bank, Deutsche Bank, Citibank and ABN AMRO Bank are notable examples. With increasing awareness and the realisation of the market opportunity presented by microfinance, it is likely that such banks would venture further, making far larger commercial investments in microfinance. Banks may envisage launching commercial microfinance funds, possibly in consortia with other banks with suitable structuring and guarantees – perhaps in partnership with development finance institutions – to attract a large number of investors.

Long-term funds, insurance and re-insurance companies: This category of investors consists of pension funds, traditional mutual and investment funds[4] and insurance and re-insurance companies. Pension funds in particular are suitable for microfinance investments. They are distinguished by their access to long-term "patient" capital. Microfinance offers opportunities for such investments with low defaults and stable returns. In addition, institutional investors have access to a substantial pool of capital. Pension funds in the US, for instance, reached a formidable size of US$ 4.8 trillion in 1995.[5] Estimates for the size of the same pension funds in 1999 were reported to be US$ 7 trillion.[6] Even if only 2–3 % of the investments of these funds could be allocated to microfinance, the industry would more than meet its demands. Pension funds in Peru invested in Mibanco's bonds – buying 82 % of a US$ 6 million issue.[7] A Swiss pension fund has also invested in the Dexia Microcredit Fund.

---

[4] See Goodman (2003) and in this volume for examples of traditional investment funds acting as investors in microfinance.

[5] Joint Economic Committee, Congress of the United States, "Economically Targeted Investments," June 1995. (http://www.house.gov/jec/cost-gov/regs/eti/solution.htm).

[6] "U.S. Pension Fund Chief, Labeled 'Darth Vader,' Gets a Chilly Reception in Paris", *The International Herald Tribune*, October 18, 1999. (http://www.iht.com/IHT/DIPLO/99/jf101899a.html).

[7] Conger, Lucy, "To Market, To Market," Microenterprise Americas, Inter-American Development Bank, 2003.

Demand-Side Trends: Factors Influencing Market Development

Microfinance institutions embody the demand for microfinance and are the clients of MFIFs. Growth of the MFIs will directly influence the market conditions and opportunities of the MFIFs. The factors or desirable trends that will create larger markets for MFIFs may be analysed as follows:

Making Local Currency Finance Available to MFIs: Availability of local currency indirectly influences the resources available to MFIs because such funding is largely insulated from country and currency risk. Financial support from international sources, including commercial investors, makes MFIs vulnerable to currency risks, which is a major challenge to promoting MFIF investment. Therefore, MFI viability may ultimately depend on the availability of local currency finance. Local currency finance could be mobilised through linkages with local commercial banks or via deposit mobilisation from clients. This will, of course, require building awareness in local markets and regulatory reforms to permit deposit mobilisation by MFIs – typically non-bank institutions. Developments in this regard are already noticeable: financial linkages on commercial terms are growing between banks and MFIs, and a number of developing country governments are involved in formulating microfinance policies.[8] Suggestions for fostering such developments, detailed later, stress the critical importance of enabling framework conditions.

Long-term Finance for MFIs: MFIs, like other financial institutions, must have a minimum amount of their own capital or equity. This capital is required for leveraging more capital and for reducing the risk of its lenders and depositors. International standards on banking (those set by the Basel Accord, for example) have specified a minimum risk-weighted level of capital adequacy for banks. Similar capital adequacy standards must also be applicable to MFIs. It is likely that commercial investors would demand these standards when entering the microfinance market.[9] The demand for equity investments in this context is significant. If MFIs meet international banking standards for capital adequacy, commercial investors will be more willing to invest in them. For instance, de Sousa-Shields[10] estimates that the capital requirements for equity investments in MFIs in Latin America exceed US$ 3.5 billion, based on the Basel recommendation of a ratio of 8 % equity to risk-weighted assets. This sum far exceeds the amount available from traditional development finance sources.

---

[8] Dr. Syed Hashemi of CGAP reported 62 MFI-bank linkages in 36 countries and that 50 countries were working on microfinance policies in his presentation at the ADB's Regional Workshop on Commercialisation of Microfinance in May 2004, in Bali, Indonesia.

[9] ICICI Bank required a minimum capital of 20 % when it agreed to invest in the equity of Bhartiya Samruddhi Finance Limited (BASIX) in India.

[10] Sousa-Shields, Marc de, "Financing Micro-finance Solutions to Poverty," Enterprise Solutions Global Consulting, 2001. Paper presented at the Inter-American Development Bank's IV Forum on Microenterprise, November 2001.

Structuring Complete Credit Packages for Clients along their Growth Track: MFIs must adapt their systems and lending criteria to match and augment the debt capacity of their clients. Most MFIs need to make intensive investments in promoting new and poor clients. Typically, these new clients – with low levels of economic activity – start with very small loans, which in turn implies high transaction costs for the MFI. With the growth of the economic activities of the clients, loan amounts can safely be increased. Most MFIs, however, restrict their product range to a maximum permissible loan size. As a result, clients who have successfully reached a higher economic level would either be restricted by taking loans that are smaller than optimum or would look for alternative credit sources. In the latter case, the MFI loses a valuable and less risky client who is also less costly to serve.

MFIs should attempt to develop strategies to accommodate the financial capacities of their clients as their activities grow and change, so that the MFIs continue to benefit from their initial investments in building clients' capacities. Such a strategy may be implemented by the MFI, with different internal divisions catering to different categories of clients, or in partnership with other local banks in a fee sharing arrangement.

Promotion of More Commercially Viable MFIs: Despite our claims of a strong MFI sector with vast outreach, only $250-500$[11] commercially viable MFIs exist. They cater to about 25 million microentrepreneurs.[12] To reach an estimated target market of 500 million microentrepreneurs,[13] a large number of commercially viable MFIs with the ability to interact with mainstream commercial markets would have to be promoted. This process would include promoting new MFIs in regions not yet reached by microfinance interventions, and building the capacities and skills of existing MFIs so that they could transact effectively in commercial markets.

Livelihood Promotion: Poor clients currently without the ability to make productive investments would require technical assistance. These services may take the form of training to build specific skills like marketing and financial management, and promotion of economic opportunities specifically suited to the local context. Investments may also be made in enhancing the productivity of local resources, which would impact the income earning capacities of the clients as well as nonclients in the area. Development of watersheds, irrigation facilities and market linkages are suitable examples. Such activities may not themselves constitute microfinance but would effectively work to create conditions for microfinance to flourish.

---

[11] Estimates of MFIFs such as BlueOrchard. Additionally, the survey by CGAP and The Mix revealed that 39 of the 55 MFIFs had invested in a total of only 439 MFIs, 150 of which had received investments from three investors.

[12] Assuming 50,000 active clients per MFI.

[13] Source BlueOrchard, CGAP.

New Technologies and Innovations: Microfinance is intrinsically transaction-cost-intensive and MFIs must constantly strive to develop more efficient solutions and methodologies through innovations. Solutions may lie in leveraging new technologies like smart cards, biometrics, point of sale (POS) terminals or automated teller machines (ATMs). Action research for the development of such innovations must be undertaken to reduce the costs and increase the profitability of microfinance operations.

Learning from the commercial retail finance industry may also be helpful for improving MFIs' efficiency. Credit scoring, for instance, is used by retail banks to determine the creditworthiness of retail borrowers based on the characteristics of these customers as reported in historical portfolio data. Many MFIs, especially the successful ones, have developed detailed information systems maintaining portfolio histories of all their clients over a number of years. These information systems can now be used to develop automated credit scoring systems that determine the creditworthiness of new clients, lowering the costs of credit appraisals. Of course, credit scoring systems would not replace existing microfinance methodologies but complement them by providing better evaluation of risks.

The last three factors – promotion of commercially viable MFIs, livelihood promotion and the development of innovations that include use of new technology – would require promotional investments that are ideally undertaken by the development finance sector. The role of development finance is discussed in a following section of this paper.

What Factors Favour MFIF Success?

The second question posed in the introductory part of this chapter asked "what factors favour MFIF success?" How will MFIFs be able to help leverage private capital? Answering this question requires an understanding of the key factors affecting the success of MFIFs, and the important risk factors affecting the industry. The risks faced by MFIFs include credit risk, country risk, currency risk, operational risk, risk to reputation and liquidity risks. Apart from these, a further risk should be highlighted: the risk associated with fast and dynamic growth. The microfinance market is currently growing at a very high rate (20–40% per year) with a large diversity of structures and frameworks around the world. Mistakes made at this stage could have severe repercussions for the future of the entire industry. This risk makes it vital for MFIFs to concentrate on the requirements for success.

In this section, we analyse two sets of success factors: those at the organisational level, i. e. the MFIF, and at the industry level.

Success Factors for MFIFs: The Institutional Level

A number of MFIFs have been started to serve MFIs. However, most MFIFs are fairly small and remain in the nascent stages of development. Achieving a minimum break-even size is essential for an MFIF to be viable and eventually successful. Positioned between MFIs and investors, MFIFs need to address several other issues as well in order to succeed.

Achieving a sustainable size: A break-even level of investments is required to make MFIFs commercially viable, which occurs when their transaction costs are fully recovered from interest and other income. Goodman's pioneering study (2003) analysed the size of MFIFs vis-à-vis the minimum sustainable size of typical commercial investment funds. He found that the minimum sustainable size of commercial funds is typically US$ 20 – 30 million. Most of the MFIFs are far below that size. An analysis of the 55 funds considered by Ivatury and Abrams (2005) reveals that only 22 of the 55 have an asset base of US$ 20 million or more. Some of these funds have invested in other markets as well. An even more dramatic picture is revealed by the microfinance assets of these funds – only 15 funds have reached a microfinance asset base of US$ 20 million or more. MFIFs need to address this issue. A possible route might be consolidations with funds of similar profiles and objectives.

The size of the funds is also critical for attracting investors. Pouliot (2004) illustrates the importance of fund size: the diversification policies of institutional investors (perhaps the most promising source for microfinance) would limit their holding to not more than 5 % of a fund. As most MFIFs are below the US$ 20 million threshold, institutional investors' stakes in them would typically not exceed US$ 1 million, which is small by industry standards. This small investment size would produce high total expense ratios (TER), a disincentive for investors.

Development of effective distribution capabilities: Distribution in the context of MFIFs has two perspectives: upward distribution to reach investors and enhance the size of the fund, and downward distribution to reach the MFIs.

Upward distribution to investors is influenced by the following factors:

- The nature of the agency hosting and offering the fund to investors: The offering agency must be credible, providing investors a sense of safety and comfort. While a variety of agencies can play this role, commercial banks of high credibility and an extensive outreach to potential investors might be ideal candidates for hosting such funds.

- Incentives for the offering agency, which are sufficient for it to continue to host the fund and attract investors.

- A clear message for investors, which has to include a clear risk-return profile of the investment product.

Downward distribution to MFIs: Given the geographical dispersion of MFIs, achieving cost-effective distribution is a daunting challenge. Keeping distribution costs low is essential: high costs directly affect the pricing of services to the MFIs. Highly priced services in turn affect the profitability of the MFI, ultimately leading to slower expansion of outreach. Lowering distribution costs may again favour the consolidation of funds. Specialist distribution agencies may be promoted, playing a role similar to asset managers who manage the distribution of a number of funds jointly, lowering the costs per fund. Better distribution and cost reduction may also be achieved by stronger networking among funds. Credit ratings and consortia of investors are common features in commercial corporate lending. Similar approaches could be adopted in microfinance as MFIFs join hands on specific deals to reduce assessment and monitoring costs.

Professionalism: The management of MFIFs must have a clear commercial orientation and a realistic sense of scalability for their fund and for microfinance as a whole. This will require a high degree of professionalism. The required professionalism entails:

- Developing appraisal systems for evaluation of potential investments (deal sourcing).

- Maintaining monitoring and management information systems (MIS).

- Networking with MFIs and others in the industry.

- Expanding knowledge of the local microfinance industry's capacities accompanied by world-class asset management skills.

- Innovation in products and services to enhance the industry's capacity.

- Building skills to raise capital from investors.

- Implementing asset liability management (ALM) in MFIFs.

These measures would lead MFIFs to design and implement an organisational structure that can accommodate professionals from the microfinance industry as well as from the traditional financial industry.

Governance: Governance is an important issue in the management of any business. In the case of the MFIF industry, which is still in its nascent stages, governance assumes even greater importance.[14] Governance in this context includes:

- Use of appropriate legal structures[15] and clear objectives of the MFIFs so that they can attract investments from a variety of investors and provide returns.

- Supervision and control of the management of the MFIFs, including performance incentives and disincentives for the management.

---

[14] See Pouliot in this volume for a detailed analysis of the importance of strong governance systems in MFIFs and the strategies for implementing them.

[15] Goodman in this volume illustrates the importance of appropriate legal structures using the example of Incofin, a co-operative company in Belgium which, to circumvent the legal restrictions of co-operation that make it difficult to attract investors, is changing its corporate status to become a Luxembourg investment fund.

- Influencing the governance of the investee MFIs, if required.

- Reviewing portfolio quality and composition (portfolio mix) on a regular basis to ensure compliance with the investment strategy.

- Maintaining high levels of transparency in the management and performance of the MFIF. Transparency provides current and potential investors an insight into the performance of the fund, which encourages more investments.

- Ensuring accountability and reporting to investors regarding the management of the fund. Given the nature of the industry and the social interests of many of the investors, reporting on social performance is necessary. Most MFIs do not yet have standardised systems in place to report on their social performance. The governance of MFIFs must ensure that such standardised systems are developed and implemented in order to maintain high standards of accountability in MFIFs.

Success Factors for MFIFs: The Industry Level

With the growth of MFIFs – keeping in mind important success factors and scope for leveraging trends that are likely to be positive on the supply-side – it is possible for MFIFs to make a substantial difference to the microfinance market. However, MFIFs will need to work on some important areas to be successful and attract investors:

Creation of Suitable Products: Leveraging Securitisation and Financial Structuring: Mobilising resources from institutional and private investors is essential, and appropriate instruments must be developed for this purpose. An instrument that has been successfully pioneered is the issue of bonds. Leading NGOs and MFIs such as the Bangladesh Rural Advancement Committee (BRAC); Compartamos in Mexico; Financiera América (Finamerica) in Colombia; Banco Sol in Bolivia and Mibanco in Peru have issued bonds in their domestic markets. Commercial banks with increasing interest in microfinance can also offer solutions. ICICI Bank, the largest private sector bank in India, undertook the world's first microfinance securitisation when it bought a portion of the portfolios of BASIX and Share Microfin Ltd. in 2003, which it then sold to another commercial bank. Such instruments have shown the way for facilitating investments. Further innovations along these lines should be fostered.

MFIFs with financial sophistication and in-depth understanding of the expectations of investors could serve as the ideal agents for carrying out such innovations that mobilise capital outside the existing route of raising direct investments from investors. Financial structuring and suitable partnerships can create a diversified range of products catering to different investor profiles. The world's first international microfinance securities issue by BlueOrchard is a case in point. This placement, on July 29, 2004, on the US market – undertaken by BlueOrchard in collaboration with the US government's Overseas Private Investment Corporation (OPIC), JP Morgan and Developing World Markets – managed to raise over US$ 40 million and provide long-term debt capital to nine MFIs in seven countries.

This issue illustrates the importance of both strategic partnerships and financial structuring. The issue brought together a number of different actors with an appropriate mix of roles: while BlueOrchard, with domain expertise in microfinance, launched a Special Purpose Vehicle (SPV) to issue the securities and provided the professional management and distribution capability; OPIC, a development finance institution, lent credibility to the effort by providing a guarantee[16] and JP Morgan Securities joined the effort to make distribution to institutional and private investors possible. The issue succeeded in attracting institutional, private and social investors.

Financial engineering, including using subordination tranches to attract commercial institutional investors to the Senior Notes, ensured that the investors were able to access a range of investments in the form of securities with varied risk-return profiles.[17] This issue in many ways shows the ideal future course that microfinance must chart to fulfil the demands of the millions of potential clients. Replication of issues and financial structuring of this type in different contexts and markets could raise capital from a wide range of investors.

MFIFs should also consider securitising the existing portfolios of MFIs. An SPV launched exclusively for this purpose could issue notes backed by loan portfolios of a number of MFIs that are selected for purposes of diversification across countries, regions and currencies. Here again, credit enhancements provided by development finance institutions could widen the appeal of such issues. In addition, securitisation would provide capital relief to the MFIs, which will be able to continue to increase their outreach without reducing their capital adequacy.

A related possibility is the securitisation of existing portfolios of MFIFs and banks. Many domestic banks – in India for instance – that have been active in microfinance could securitise their microfinance portfolios. Packaging these portfolios with credit enhancements would streamline distribution to institutional investors internationally, simultaneously attracting additional investments to microfinance.

In the years ahead, securitisation and further innovations in financial structuring will play a critical role in expanding the opportunities for MFIFs. Additionally, partnerships with a range of institutions such as guarantors, credit insurers and credit rating agencies will help MFIFs significantly expand their marketability. The importance of providing mechanisms that create conducive conditions for investors is discussed below.

---

[16] OPIC issued fully guaranteed Certificates of Participation (COPs) to institutional and private investors and invested the inflows from the COPs in the issue, in effect providing a guarantee to these new investors for their investments in microfinance.

[17] Goodman in this volume.

Creating Suitable Conditions: Enhancing Investor Confidence: Creation of favourable investment conditions will be an important factor in the success of MFIFs. Such conditions include risk mitigation for investors, enhanced credibility of MFIFs and their products, and transparent reporting systems. Possible mechanisms that could create such conditions include:

- Risk mitigation through guarantees: Provision of guarantees from large and credible institutions, including governments and development finance institutions, can mitigate investors' risks and attract new investors to the microfinance market.

- Credit insurance: Credit coverage is common in the commercial financial sector. Application of similar instruments in microfinance can create investor confidence. Credit insurance may be undertaken for an entire portfolio where, for instance, all losses beyond the first 15 – 20 % are insured. Insurance and re-insurance firms such as Swiss Re could provide such insurance. Coverage from such a firm would serve as a "quality seal," increasing the attractiveness of the investment product to large institutional investors who might not be familiar with the microfinance industry or the MFIF managing the investment product, but who are willing to consider investments with this quality seal.

   Credit insurance can also be used in combination with securitisation issues as a credit enhancement: the credit portfolio being securitised can also be insured.

- Credit Ratings: Commercial investors, especially banks and institutional investors, follow standard practices for credit appraisal, including rating of potential investments. Ratings from international agencies such as Standard & Poor's (S&P), Fitch or Moody's would enhance these investors' confidence. MFIFs – and perhaps MFIs too – must get themselves and their portfolios rated by credible and recognised rating agencies. Compartamos in Mexico, for instance, chose to get its US$ 15 million bond issue rated by S&P, which gave the issue a high rating in the Mexican market[18] and attracted both private and institutional investors.

Another effective means of enhancing investor confidence is making the investor community aware of the low risks of microfinance investments, including the low default risk and the low correlation with volatility in the larger financial markets. This strategy requires investor education, discussed below in the section on marketing and communication to promote microfinance investments.

Creating Fund of Funds Structures: Increasing Diversification: Greater portfolio diversification can be achieved through the creation of a fund of funds that assesses and invests in selected MFIFs and diversifies its risks over distributors and regions. The responsAbility Global Microfinance Fund and the Positive Invest-

---

[18] Conger (2003).

ment Fund are the first initiatives in this direction. Of course, the concept of fund of funds in microfinance – including these two funds – is still at a trial-and-error stage of development. Fruition of the concept may be years away, but its development could have significant implications for the evolution of the microfinance marketplace.

In the future, such funds could be promoted by banks themselves, leveraging their credibility and reputation to attract a large number of commercial investors seeking a high level of portfolio diversification. This would also enable a number of MFIFs to obtain capital.

It is also possible to develop similar structures of funds investing across industries. In this way, the existing market credibility of an established industry may be leveraged to attract investments in microfinance. For instance, a fund of funds focusing on sustainable investments may include an MFIF in its portfolio. As a result, the MFIF would be able to mobilise investments from investors who may not yet be interested in investing in microfinance directly or exclusively.

Creating Networks through Equity Participation: The strategy of creating networks of MFIs through equity participation could build successful MFIFs while creating a strong demand base of MFIs as well. This strategy would entail acquiring significant equity investments in selected MFIs and subsequently playing an active role in their governance – driving them towards sustainable growth and profitability. Such an approach implies a long-term commitment to the invested MFIs.

MFIFs with extensive knowledge and experience in promoting sustainable MFIs are well-suited to engage in network creation. Building on its knowledge and experience with its initial investments, an MFIF can go on to build a network of strong MFIs that are able to reach a larger clientele with the commercial funds they obtain.

ProCredit Holding AG (formerly Internationale Micro Investitionen Aktiengesellschaft "IMI AG") and the ACCIÓN Gateway Fund are notable examples of MFIFs adopting such an approach. ProCredit Holding has been able to build an asset base of €46 million with investments in 18 MFIs.[19] The average return on equity (RoE) of the invested MFIs was 13.5% in 2004. The network of these 18 MFIs (mostly registered as local banks) assembled a combined portfolio of €948.9 million.[20] ProCredit Holding has adopted a common name and corporate identity for its institutions (ProCredit Bank) so that they may benefit from the combined brand equity.

At the same time, the potential for gaining control or influence over an MFI through equity investments may be a temptation for existing fixed-income investment funds. Perhaps, it is this temptation that has led 26 of the MFIFs surveyed by CGAP to invest in both debt and equity. However, as Pouliot (2004) illustrates,

---

[19] As of June 2004. Source: IMI Website (http://www.imi-ag.com – now http://www.ProCredit-Holding.com).

[20] As of December 31, 2004.

this "twin capital approach" of providing debt and equity is a "potential minefield of conflicts of interests" and can have "dangerous" consequences. This is especially so as the two products – debt and equity – require specialists in the respective product operating in two different cultural approaches. Such a tendency must be avoided by MFIFs.

Creating Effective and Standardised Systems of Financial and Social Reporting: Pouliot (2004) has emphasised the importance of good governance, which requires high levels of transparency and accountability that in turn provide comfort to investors. The industry should standardise systems of reporting and the use of key performance ratios that will provide commercial investors greater comfort in their microfinance investments.[21]

Additionally, an essential aspect of transparency in microfinance is reporting on social returns. Microfinance is promoted as an investment with a double bottom line that includes economic and social returns. A large number of investors, especially private investors, who enter the microfinance market, do so with social objectives. However, no universally acceptable standards exist for reporting on the social performance of microfinance. Research to develop appropriate cost-effective and universally acceptable systems for tracking meaningful and significant social impact or social returns needs to be supported. The research results should provide a base for creating a consensus among the varied categories of investors and promoters of microfinance. Furthermore, reporting on social returns must be integrated with the financial rating of MFIFs to present a complete picture of their performance.

Effective Marketing and Communication: Effective marketing will stimulate the growth of MFIFs. Greater emphasis on marketing and communication is essential to attract investments. Communication can play a key role by building greater awareness about microfinance as an investment opportunity and the actually low risks associated with it.

An important issue that MFIFs need to address is the high perceived risk of microfinance investments. The risk perception arises from the unconventional form of this business and the country risks that often are superimposed on the industry. At the same time, returns are only moderate (200–300 basis points over LIBOR) creating a risk-return mismatch in the minds of potential investors. Marketing and communication campaigns must focus on generating awareness, highlighting the low default risk, the low correlation with volatility in financial markets and a certain level of independence from the commonly perceived country risks.

Marketing and communication efforts should target specific types of investors. Targeting institutional investors who may represent the most promising group of investors may be a good starting point.

---

[21] See Goodman in this volume for the importance of developing standardised industry-wide definitions of key performance ratios for MFIFs.

The Critical Importance of Enabling Framework Conditions

The success of MFIFs will necessarily require enabling framework conditions that govern the actors in the market. Framework conditions at the local level directly influence the growth of MFIs and their clients, which leads to the growth in the potential market available to MFIFs. In this section, we look at important areas requiring reforms.

Reforms in the Local Financial Sector and in Banking Law

Reforms in the local financial sector and banking law have direct implications for the development of the microfinance market. The removal of interest rate restrictions, elimination of subsidised and directed lending, and the creation of specially designed legal structures that recognise and include microfinance as part of the financial sector are notable examples of such reforms. Countries with progressive and liberal frameworks for microfinance will be able to develop stronger and larger microfinance markets that cater to millions of low-income households. Such vital regulatory reforms will need to be carefully conceived and properly implemented. A recent study by Loubière et al. (2004) that compares financial sector liberalisation and reforms in different countries shows that Bolivia, with progressive reforms and liberalisation, was able to create a larger microfinance market than Colombia, where the regulatory framework maintained features of a non-liberalised financial system, including interest rate controls and directed lending. The contrast between the countries is striking, especially when one considers that Colombia's population is five times that of Bolivia.

Reforms in the banking law can also help MFIs gain access to domestic capital through deposit mobilisation and linkages with local banks and financial institutions as discussed below.

Accessing Domestic Capital

Access to domestic capital is an important factor influencing the growth of MFIs. Domestic capital has the inherent advantage of having its sources in the immediate vicinity of the MFIs. This implies lower operational and monitoring costs for the suppliers and, importantly, no currency risk. Despite these advantages, most MFIs are unable to obtain domestic capital. Reforms to progress on this front include:

Enabling Deposit Mobilisation

Attempts to make MFIs viable financial institutions that play a role akin to local banks tend to overlook the importance of having regulatory provisions that permit MFIs to mobilise deposits from the local community. MFIs using deposits to finance microloans will be able to reduce their cost of funds and increase their profitability. In addition, savings are a very valuable financial service for clients, arguably even more important than credit in the case of the poorest clients. Providing access to saving services would benefit both the MFI and its clients.

However, most banking regulators do not permit non-bank MFIs to mobilise deposits from their clients. As a result, most MFIs are reduced to being purely microcredit providers fully dependent on debt from external institutions to finance their operations. Of course, the grounds for not allowing non-banks to collect deposits are not unfounded, but it is important to look specifically at the case of MFIs and make suitable exceptions. Deposit taking is a subject of much research[22] and debate, and further work on this important issue must be seriously considered. Meanwhile, simple solutions may be designed to allow MFIs in specific contexts to mobilise deposits in limited ways as follows:

- Institutions that have a limited and closely knit clientele may be permitted to accept deposits if their clients, being remote, have no other access to formal saving services or may be able to make deposits only in high risk or non-productive forms.

- Limited deposit taking may be allowed by MFIs subject to four conditions: a) deposits from individual borrowers do not exceed a specified fraction of their loan amount, b) a track record of high recovery rates, c) no defaults on their loan liabilities, and d) high capital requirements in order to provide greater security to depositors.

- More lenient standards may be set for issuing banking (and hence deposit taking) licenses to well-established MFIs with a history of high portfolio quality along with excellence in governance and management. Such concessions would allow successful MFIs to expand their outreach, lower costs and thus benefit many more clients. In effect, MFIs would be provided an incentive to maintain high levels of performance and governance.

Linkages with Local Banks and Financial Institutions

Savings from clients could contribute to the growth of MFIs, but an even greater contribution can come through linkages with banks and financial institutions in local commercial markets. Over and above reforms in the financial sector, local governments and central banks also have a vital role to play in this context by creating enabling framework conditions to encourage local banks and financial institutions to invest in the microfinance market. Encouragement may also come in the form of incentives for microfinance investments such as tax breaks, special rewards, recognition, and concessions.

---

[22] Robert Peck Christen, Timothy R. Lyman and Richard Rosenberg in their paper, "Guiding Principles on Regulation and Supervision of Microfinance," CGAP, July 2003 provide a detailed analysis of regulation and supervision issues with possible alternatives and policy recommendations.

But in order to invest in microfinance, the local banks must be able to attract deposits to enhance their own resources. This requires boosting public confidence in the local banking system. Stronger central banks with credible measures for safeguarding depositors' interests would have to be established in economies with low levels of savings that suggest a low level of confidence in the banking system.

Progress in Property Rights and Commercial Law to Facilitate Transactions

The task of building a sound and inclusive banking system would be incomplete if we stress only the reforms affecting banks. The overall policy and regulatory environment should be reviewed carefully to determine its capacity to facilitate commercial transactions. Can people transact effectively with the banking system and with each other? To do so, people must be able to leverage their assets as security for loans and for guaranteeing their obligations under contracts. In many countries this is not easily done. Property rights do not facilitate commercial contracts, retarding economic growth. Reforms in this area are a first priority in such countries.

The work of the *Instituto Libertad y Democracia* (ILD) in Peru is noteworthy in this context. ILD works to build inclusive property systems in which the businesses and assets of the poor may be recognised under the law and their records adequately standardised so that they are able to transact in the formal economic system. ILD's work has revealed eye-opening facts. For example, ILD's diagnosis in Egypt found that 90 % of the population held their assets outside the law and thus were not part of the formal economy. ILD suggested reforms that would help create an inclusive economy with the potential to offer growth for all. ILD also aims to make the processes of legalisation more pragmatic and effective.

The Complimentary Role of the Development Finance Sector

The continuing evolution of microfinance has led to an imperative, which is mainstreaming it, or aligning it with the mainstream financial markets. This process highlights the role that should be played by the development finance sector ("development finance") consisting of donor agencies and similar development finance institutions. Development finance has undeniably played a pivotal role in developing and promoting microfinance. The role of development finance will continue to be critical for microfinance, but its nature may have to be adapted to promote the growth of MFIFs.

Suggested Roles for Development Finance

Specific suggestions for the role of development finance in mainstreaming microfinance include:

Support Construction of Enabling Framework Conditions

As previously noted, creation of enabling framework conditions is critical for development. Development finance can influence the creation of enabling legal and regulatory frameworks by:

- Undertaking policy advocacy and lobbying with local governments and central banks.

- Working with central banks and local governments and supporting research to promote responsible deposit mobilisation by MFIs.

- Supporting reforms in property rights and commercial laws in specific countries.

Create a Conducive Investment Environment: Work Development Finance out of Its Job

The creation of a conducive investment environment has been identified as an important success factor for the MFIFs at the industry level. Development finance can play an important role in this process by:

- Exiting from the financing of sustainable MFIs: Development finance must cease financing commercially viable and sustainable MFIs, creating room for commercial players to enter. Donors and MFIs may in some cases use soft money to meet their respective targets, but this temptation must be controlled. Soft money with easy conditions may make MFIs dependent, weakening their ability to transact on commercial terms. Sousa-Shields (2001) provides an insight into the ill effects of using soft money: "…subsidies impose long-term structural limitations on the growth and development of the microfinance sector. In particular, the relative availability of inexpensive money discourages institutions from even bothering to tap private capital markets."

  Despite progress thus far, the number of MFIs with proven track records and established commercial viability is still small. Financing sustainable MFIs with soft money may crowd out and discourage the serious and potentially large commercial players from joining this niche market.[23]

- Risk mitigation by providing guarantees to encourage new investors: In an emerging scenario that includes securitisation and structured investment funds, development finance could serve as guarantors by co-investing as

---

[23] See CGAP Donor Brief No. 3, May 2002 which quotes the experience of a social investor who lost a deal with a promising MFI explaining, "…we were offering them a loan at 24-months maturity for a rate of Libor+4.5 %…. We were driven out by an international donor which was offering the same amount, at 15 years horizon, 5 years grace period, a nominal interest of 5 %, and an additional USD 100,000 gift for technical assistance."

junior note holders and as investors in subordinated tranches. The role of OPIC in the case of the BlueOrchard securities issue illustrates the role that development finance can play.

- Development finance agencies individually or perhaps in consortia may promote specialised guarantee funds to back securitisation deals, encouraging this important trend.
- Development finance can also explore public-private partnerships with private sector institutions such as insurance companies to launch microfinance guarantee funds.

- Promoting higher standards of governance and management: Development finance can provide technical assistance to MFIFs to promote higher standards of governance and management. This may be done through training programmes designed to raise managerial capacity and improve fiduciary practice.

- Promoting rating of MFIFs and MFIs by recognised rating agencies: Ratings would provide comfort to commercial investors regarding portfolio quality, governance and management of their investments. A continuous system of rating will promote transparency, which will in turn enable potential and existing investors to understand the microfinance market better. At the same time, the incentive to obtain high ratings in order to attract investors would promote higher standards of management and governance among MFIFs and MFIs.

  The unconventional nature of the microfinance market may prompt rating agencies to seek a special orientation to understand and develop systems for rating microfinance players. This is clearly a promotional role for development finance.

- Promoting systems of tracking and reporting on social returns: Efforts must also be made to provide social investors a better sense of their returns and to integrate reporting on social returns with the rating of MFIFs and MFIs. This combination will ensure that MFIFs and MFIs retain their focus on social objectives while pursuing commercial ends. An integrated rating method that combines financial and social performance may be an ideal means of discouraging mission drift – sacrificing the social for the financial or vice-versa.

- Marketing and communications to promote commercial investments: In its efforts to promote mainstreaming, development finance should focus on building awareness of microfinance as a new market opportunity among commercial players, including commercial banks, institutional and private investors. Focused international events and special fora targeting investors may be part of this awareness generation campaign.

Maintain a Promotional Role in Creating a Stronger MFI Demand Base

With the large potential for microfinancial services across the world and only a few strong, sustainable MFIs in existence, a lot of effort should be focused on developing the capacities of the market, primarily the MFIs and their clients. Many factors can contribute to the creation of a stronger microfinance demand base. Many of these involve capacity building and promotional roles, most appropriately undertaken by development finance and other donor agencies. Suitable strategies that development finance could use to promote a stronger demand base are summarised below, based on factors described earlier:

- Promotion of more commercially viable MFIs including new MFIs in yet unreached markets, and training and building capacities of existing MFIs to become sustainable.

- Promoting livelihoods of the poor, building the productive capacities of people and their resources.

- Promoting the use of new technologies such as smart cards, biometrics, POS terminals and ATMs targeted at poor clients and others in remote areas.

- Encouraging innovations in methodologies including the promotion of efficiency-enhancing measures such as credit scoring.

The Importance of Clear Delineation of Roles

Development finance must focus on developmental tasks including capacity building roles. These may consist of support for innovations, risk coverage, promotion of sustainable MFIs, livelihood promotion for the poor, and advocacy to support creation of suitable frameworks. However, development finance must discontinue its direct financing of sustainable MFIs while simultaneously creating conducive conditions for commercial actors to come into play. Development finance institutions – working in concert through consortia and fora – must engage in a dialogue with MFIFs and investors to devise standard guidelines for their respective complementary roles.

At the same time, several arguments have been raised regarding the potential role for development finance in a commercialised microfinance sector. These issues are open for debate; our views are as follows:

- Preventing mission drift: With increasing commercialisation and emphasis on profitability, it is possible that MFIFs and, in turn, MFIs may focus on bigger customers and go up-market, deserting the smallest and poorest borrowers. It is argued that development finance institutions can help to check such mission drift by continuing to be stakeholders in MFIFs and ensuring that investee MFIs adhere to their target markets. On the contrary, as recommended earlier, development finance should focus on promoting the development of rating systems for MFIFs and MFIs that measure social performance, including the poverty level of clients. This is important because commercial investors will eventually drive the industry ahead. Investor awareness of social performance will be critical.

- Providing stability: Another argument for development finance institutions' investment in MFIFs is that they can provide long-term and patient capital to protect the microfinance industry from market volatility and panic exits by private investors.

We believe that since the eventual goal is that markets drive microfinance ahead, positioning development finance agencies as providers of funds is not the best solution. In fact, investments from development finance are likely to dilute MFIFs' commercial motivation. However, the threat of panic exits by purely commercial investors cannot be ignored. Perhaps development finance institutions could perform a role similar to that which central banks perform to ensure the solvency of the commercial banking sector, maintaining reserves to bail out MFIFs and MFIs if a run or capital flight occurs.

References

BlueOrchard website (http://www.blueorchard.com)

CGAP, "Donor Brief No. 3: Water, Water Everywhere but Not a Drop to Drink", May 2002.

CGAP website (http://www.cgap.org).

Christen, Robert Peck, Timothy R. Lyman and Richard Rosenberg, "Guiding Principles on Regulation and Supervision of Micro-finance", CGAP, July 2003.

Conger, Lucy, "To Market, To Market", Microenterprise Americas, Inter-American Development Bank, 2003.

Dailey-Harris, Sam, "State of the Microcredit Summit Campaign Report 2003", Microcredit Summit Campaign, www.microcreditsummit.org, 2004.

de Sousa-Shields, Marc (see Sousa-Shields, Marc de)

Goodman, Patrick, "International Investment Funds: Mobilising Investors towards Micro-finance", Appui au Développement Autonome (ADA), Luxembourg, 2003.

Goodman, Patrick, "Microfinance Investment Funds: Players, Objectives, Potential", (this volume)

Hashemi, Syed (CGAP), "Presentation in ADB's Regional Workshop on Commercialisation of Micro-finance", Bali, Indonesia, May 2004.

IMI AG website (http://www.imi-ag.com) – see ProCredit Holding.

Ivatury, Gautam and Julie Abrams, "The Market for Microfinance Foreign Investment: Opportunities and Challenges", (this volume)

Ivatury, Gautam and Xavier Reille, "Foreign Investment in Micro-finance: Debt and Equity from Quasi-commercial Investors", Focus Note No. 25, CGAP, January 2004.

Joint Economic Committee, "Economically Targeted Investments", Congress of the United States, Issue June 1995 (http://www.house.gov/jec/cost-gov/regs/eti/solution.htm).

Loubière, J.T., P.L. Devaney, E. Rhyne, "Supervision & Regulation in Microfinance: Lessons from Bolivia, Colombia and Mexico", ACCION, August 2004.

Pouliot, Robert, "Governance, Transparency, and Accountability in the Microfinance Investment Fund Industry", (this volume)

ProCredit Holding website (http://www.ProCredit-Holding.com)

Microfinance Information eXchange (MIX Market) website (http://www.mixmarket.org).

MicroRate, Benchmark Table June 2003, MicroRate (www.microrate.com).

Sousa-Shields, Marc de, "Financing Micro-finance Solutions to Poverty", Enterprise Solutions Global Consulting, 2001. Paper presented at the Inter-American Development Bank's IV Forum on Microenterprise, November 2001.

"U.S. Pension Fund Chief, Labeled 'Darth Vader,' Gets a Chilly Reception in Paris", *The International Herald Tribune*, October 18, 1999 (http://www.iht.com/IHT/DIPLO/99/jf101899a.html)

CHAPTER 15:

A Donor-Investor's Vision for Enhancing the Future of Microfinance

Hanns-Peter Neuhoff

Senior Vice President, KfW Entwicklungsbank

Finding ways to engage private capital in microfinance requires use of the most valuable capital available in the fight to alleviate poverty: the human capacities of compassion, ingenuity, and resolve. Applying capital through microfinance investment funds (MFIFs) for poverty reduction in turn requires the evaluation and forecasting of trends in socially responsible investment and in microfinance.

Key Issues in Play

As more questions are answered, more are unearthed:

- Private capital is starting to flow into microfinance, but will this cause a shift away from micro-clients in efforts to reduce costs? What happens when margins decline as a result of increased competition, which is – on the other hand – indispensable to the sustainable development of the real sector?

- Investment funds can provide capital, but how can microfinance be linked to the capital market most effectively?

- New investors are being attracted to microfinance investment funds, but will management resources be sufficient to guide these funds fruitfully?

- There is a proliferation of MFIFs. Will their influence focus MFIs on only the same business segments, or will they broaden the frontier of microfinance to reach poorer households and rural areas?

- Sound governance structures are essential. How will they be created and sustained? What innovative structures are required?

Asking new questions is a measure of learning, and the lessons that evolve must be applied in order for financial cooperation to be effective. At KfW we learned in the 1990s that business-oriented microfinance banks have vast potential to fight poverty. Now these banks contribute to achieving the Millennium Development Goals. As early as 1994 we helped establish micro banking in Albania, and later we were instrumental in setting up a network of microfinance institutions (MFIs). We have now reached a new level of cooperation as we contribute to the consolidation and strengthening of those networks through the creation of holding companies such as IMI AG (now ProCredit Holding AG) and AIM.

Our present challenge is to develop MFIFs as a standard, core instrument that will strengthen the entire commercial microfinance industry. We already have relationships with MFIFs that have a broader investment perspective, such as LA-CIF, and through the Global Microfinance Facility, for example. But to meet this challenge effectively we must innovate.

Funding for the Future

What is the appeal of microfinance investment funds; what purposes do they serve? The answer is that microfinance has the potential to contribute massively to the fulfilment of the Millennium Development Goals. But this is possible only with substantial amounts of refinancing. Our outreach is limited: tremendous volumes of financial resources are likely to be mobilised only through MFIFs. These funds offer the opportunity to manage risks and transaction costs in such an efficient manner that private capital will be attracted to microfinance.

The difficult government budget situation around the world means that private capital has to play a pivotal role. Some argue that the only successful way to engage sufficient private capital is through private funds that are purely commercial and credibly rated. In my view, at least for the next decade donor funds will continue to be a major source, which means that development banks like KfW will still play a decisive promotional role. Donors' support in establishing well-functioning MFIs is not being phased out – to the contrary.

But what should and shall be our role in building well-functioning MFIFs and mobilising private capital? In this regard, and taking KfW as an illustration, the following functions are increasingly important as microfinance evolves:

- *Public-private cooperation:* KfW is an institution that integrates public and private institutional strengths. It is therefore well-positioned to serve as a platform for the creation of innovative financial tools and products that involve a range of actors in both the government and private sectors.

- *Leverage:* Applying public development aid to the financial structuring of microfinance investment funds leverages the flow of private capital. KfW's participation in a MFIF signifies a certain quality assurance and builds confidence for private investors, especially the institutional investors who will take the lead. KfW can also provide comfort for the ethically-motivated investor who is willing to accept an adjusted return in deference to development objectives, while accepting a certain level of risk. To do this, KfW can use public funding to insure the first loss of a structured fund or to provide emergency loans to manage country risks.

- *Promotion and support:* Other important functions include intensifying our promotional activities in assistance to new MFIs while improving their management and governance via public-private partnerships. This in turn creates attractive opportunities for investment by MFIFs.

- *Facilitation:* The tremendous task of delivering know-how, technical assistance and refinancing requires innovation and some donor seed capital: public funds will have an enormous influence in attracting and raising private capital. Public development banks will also perform the indispensable function of convincing central banks and regulatory institutions in their partner countries to create the framework conditions that are essential for microfinance.

To summarise, KfW and other development institutions have an important role to play, especially in bringing microfinance to the poor who remain beyond our frontiers.

New Initiatives for Donors

We at KfW are convinced that the German government and BMZ in particular will continue to provide generous support as in the past. But we have an innovative vision that takes us even further: a broad MFIF that would pool funds from our government, from KfW and from the private sector. This fund would of course be open to other donors, and could even be launched as a joint initiative of several donors. (I have a special interest in Africa because of the challenges of that region, and because I am convinced that microfinance is an excellent recipe for Africa, I have – successfully – proposed such a fund to my government.)

Microfinance funds are essential, but they are not the only tool that addresses the refinancing of MFIs. Securitisation is another option, offering a huge potential to enhance and expand the spectrum of possibilities. KfW is not only willing and ready to support our partners in that regard; we have already initiated the first project of this kind in Southeast Europe.

New methods of refinancing are just one direction in which the industry will move. The establishment of promising new products and services such as micro-insurance, money transfers and remittances, local currency funding, mortgage loans, and agricultural finance are others.

Synergistic Partnerships

The microfinance industry can grow and become more successful only if we develop and nurture partnership. Partnership allows us to combine experiences, strengths and resources. And we seek all kind of partnerships: with donors, public sector institutions and the private sector. It is clear from our Berlin Symposia that public-private partnerships (PPP) are complex and sensitive structures, and that open discussion helps to make PPPs efficient. I am confident that the seeds of this interaction will bear fruit in the coming years.

The United Nations' Year of Microcredit offers opportunity for partnership and a unique opening for a microfinance public relations campaign. Product innovation has never been greater.

In June 2005, KfW, CGAP, AfD, FMO and DFID hosted an European event dedicated to creating partnerships in microfinance. It featured an original in-depth academic and professional assessment of questions surrounding new partnerships. Organised to build upon and contribute to the Year of Microcredit, this event in Frankfurt served as a high-level forum, similar to the financial sector symposium series inaugurated in Berlin in 2002, but on a larger scale.[1] Experts and decision-makers explored opportunities for new and innovative partnerships to take microfinance to greater levels of client outreach based on new and improved products and services.

Special events of this type create bridges between microfinance players (such as microfinance institutions and investment funds) and the commercial mainstream (such as investors), as well as between microfinance and governments that seek to create a facilitating environment for microfinance.

Conclusions

In summary, microfinance entered a critical phase of consolidation in 2005. It will no longer be sufficient for the majority of MFIFs to continue simply as fundraising and investment institutions. A more pioneering role is in order. The "frontier of microfinance" has not yet reached a point at which it is widely regarded by private investors as a credible and efficient financial product. It has not yet sufficiently penetrated the poorest and most difficult countries, and the agricultural sector. The private sector is not in a position to take the lead in deepening microfinance so that it can address these challenges. This means that the role and fundamental duty of KfW Entwicklungsbank remains that of the promotional investor, stimulating the private sector in close co-operation with our like-minded friends. We face interesting challenges at the new frontier of microfinance.

---

[1] For further details on the 2005 Microfinance Conference please refer to KfW's website: http://www.kfw-entwicklungsbank.de/EN/Fachinformationen/FinancialS15/Events29/FinancialS3/Inhalt.jsp.

A Glossary of Fiduciary Practice, Conventions and Concepts

Recommendations and Best Practice for Microfinance Investments and Investors

Robert Pouliot

Chief Analyst, RCP and Partners, Geneva

This annex consists of definitions, conventions and concepts used in investment management, with explanations of their application to, or potential uses by, microfinance investment funds. Terms and concepts are listed in alphabetical order. Asterisks (*) are used to denote cross-references.

The glossary includes the following terms:

- *arbitrage, asset liability management, attribution analysis,*
- *benchmark,*
- *corporate governance, counterparty rating, credit risk,*
- *diversification, duration,*
- *efficient market theory, entrepreneurial finance, exit,*
- *fiduciary audit, fiduciary governance, fiduciary organisation, fiduciary rating, fiduciary risk, fiduciary systems, financial strength rating,*
- *going concern risk, governance (including corporate governance and fiduciary governance),*
- *interest rate risk, investor risk,*
- *liquidity risk,*
- *market risk, moral hazard,*
- *operational risk,*
- *private equity, probability of default,*
- *rating (including credit rating and fiduciary rating), risk patterns,*

- *settlement risk, social hazard, solvency, sovereign ceiling, specific risk, support rating,*

- *total expense ratio, transaction cost analysis, transfer risk, transparency,*

- *value at risk, volatility,*

- *yield curve management.*

Abbreviations used include:

- *GAAP – generally accepted accounting principles*

- *GARFP – generally accepted and recognised fiduciary practice*

- *LIBOR – London inter-bank offered rate*

- *LLP – limited liability partnership*

- *MFI – microfinance institution*

- *MFIF – microfinance investment fund*

- *MFIM – microfinance investment management*

- *NGO – non-government organisation*

- *RAROC – risk adjusted return on capital*

- *TER – total expense ratio*

- *USD – US dollars*

Arbitrage: The way capital can be allocated between various investments. In pure financial terms, arbitrage means buying a security cheaply on one market and selling it dearly on another. If the reverse were done (buying high and selling low), it would uncover a huge opportunity cost. More generically, to arbitrage means to render a judgment with a clear notion of opportunity cost. It is a decision process to ensure that the choice made is the best and does not hide an opportunity (thus a cost) that an alternative choice would offer, all other things being equal. A good example under fiduciary risk would be for an investment manager to pay a lot of attention to the corporate governance of a microfinance institution (by say, assessing its credit risk and sustainability) while ignoring the fiduciary governance duties the manager owes to his own investors. Another illustration is the critical role of arbitrage that members of a board must exert constantly on behalf of shareholders. (see Fiduciary Risk, Governance, Fiduciary Governance)

Asset Liability Management (Alm): To ensure full accountability for risk and return, an investment institution's board of directors or trustees specifies the annual risk and return investors should expect, based on investors' status and objectives. For example, these may include small retail investors, high net worth investors, socially driven investors or institutional investors. This exercise specifies the risk tolerance and return appetite of investors. Establishing these benchmarks* makes it easier for the board of directors or trustees to ensure a constant alignment of the assets, the investment portfolio and the liabilities (expectations) and to compare risk/return attribution* with management goals. (Note: a somewhat different definition is used in commercial banking.)

Attribution Analysis: Risk/return attribution breaks down portfolio performance to determine what was achieved and at what cost or risk. Its purpose is to assess the real value a fund management firm creates and to judge whether the value generated justifies the management fees. The process of attribution compares an investment fund's risk/return with specific benchmarks.* All numbers should be calculated gross, before expenses, in order to compare apples with apples.

On the return side, attribution analysis generally includes:

a) The composite return of the aggregate specific risks (interest income and capital gains earned from the investment). What if the investor was rewarded only for his or her investment in MFIs, with no return for other risks?

b) The composite return from the aggregate country risks. What if the investment had instead been made in prime local government bonds?

c) The return/losses from currency fluctuations (if the fund is subject to currency risk). What would have been the interest rate return if the investment had been placed in a prime bank in the currency used by the MFI?

d) The return from strategic allocation and geographic diversification. What if the portfolio had replicated a representative sample of the global universe of MFIs (say 40% Latin America, 35% Eastern/Central Europe, 15% Asia and 10% Africa)?

e) Any unaccounted-for residual performance that cannot be attributed to any meaningful driver or management factor.

On the risk side, a risk-weighted composite should generally include:

a) The aggregate of specific risks, expressed in a credit or fiduciary risk rating, which is the average risk represented only by MFIs, regardless of country or currency risk.

b) The aggregate of country risks, expressed in a credit risk rating, which is the average risk of country or regional markets, regardless of the MFI risk.

c) The aggregate currency risks, expressed in terms of volatility and convertibility, which arise from the volatility* of the currency in which the investment is made, which equals its value-at-risk* (VaR).

Benchmark: Benchmarks are used to measure the performance of an investment vehicle against one or several alternative vehicles or references, such as a market index or peer group vehicles handling comparable investments. The purpose of a benchmark is to assess the value created by the investment manager or to evaluate the opportunity cost of the investor. A benchmark may also be used to define the goal of a fund. The best-known benchmarks are market indices such as Morgan Stanley Capital International (MSCI/Barra), Standard & Poor's (S&P500), Dow Jones Industrial Index, and The Financial Times *(Footsie index)*. But a benchmark can be any statistic that represents the options actually available to investors. For example, several funds use the 6-month London Inter-Bank Offered Rate (LIBOR) as a basis for calculating the return investors should expect in the micro-finance industry. However, this benchmark, which may be useful as a basis for setting the price at which MFIs might borrow, clearly does not reflect the real opportunity cost of investors exposed to emerging markets. The Emerging Market Bond Index (EMBI) handled by JP Morgan is probably the most representative indicator of what investors could earn from emerging market debt instruments. Lehman Brothers, another investment bank, as well as Citibank have also generated their own emerging market debt instrument market.

Benchmarks are generally used for three purposes:

a) To set the overall expected return in the form of a strategic benchmark for a specific portfolio and to determine the kind of asset profile it should have. At one extreme, a benchmark index could simply be copied and applied to a fund. Under these circumstances, management is passive, reacting only to keep the portfolio in conformity with the index. At the other extreme, the goal set by the board or the valuation committee will specify that the expected return should beat the benchmark by 1 %, 2 % or more because of the edge of the asset manager's process and active management.

b) To measure risks spread across the market and select those which best fit the requirements of a particular portfolio strategy.

c) To set reference points for attribution analysis.* These benchmarks can be selected to set currency values, to determine risk by using published ratings, and to specify cash levels to meet redemption or other liquidity demands, etc.

Corporate Governance: (see Governance)

Counterparty Rating (see Specific Risk) refers to the credit rating of an organisation rather than a specific debt issue. "Since 1998, Moody's has published issuer ratings that assess the creditworthiness of a firm, even if the company has no outstanding public debt. These issuer ratings* reflect Moody's opinions on an entity's ability to meet its senior (unsecured) financial obligations. Moody's issuer ratings appear to be a slight adaptation of the agency's previous 'counterparty rating' product, which was already in use for nearly 900 issuers, and was more explicitly focussed, at least in name, on default risk in bilateral financial contracts. Similarly, issuer credit ratings can be used as measures of a company's repayment ability under a variety of financial contracts, including swaps, forwards, options under a variety of financial contracts, including swaps, forwards, options and letters of credit. Indeed, the ratings' applications beyond the public debt markets include the extension of credit lines, the provision of information to potential suppliers or customers, and the marketing of derivative products and various other counterparty transactions." (Quoted from *Global Credit Analysis* and from *Moody's Investors Services* various sources.)

BankWatch (acquired by Fitch in 2001) was the first to issue counterparty ratings when it started rating banks in the early 1970s. Most MFI credit ratings, as well as the more generalist rating agencies such as the local associates of Fitch and S&P, also include counterparty ratings on MFIs. MicroRate seems to be moving in this direction. However, ratings by M-Cril in India and Microfinanza in Italy more closely resemble bank loan ratings.*

Credit Risk (or creditworthiness – see Going Concern Risk) is the risk that a party to a financial transaction will default, that is, to fail to perform as contractually agreed because of bankruptcy or other reasons, causing the asset holder to suffer a financial loss. The main distinction between credit and fiduciary risk is that default on a credit obligation has to be reflected on the lender's books as an asset under potential litigation. By contrast, assets managed by fiduciaries, and hence subject to fiduciary risk, do not belong to the fiduciary and never appear on its books. (See fiduciary organisation*.) Banks are now taking a more proactive approach to credit risk assessment using decision support technology. New risk measurement techniques now permit banks to price loans and fees based on mathematical models. For example, Barclays' risk tendency measurement system calculates the average probability of default on each loan. Such tools enable banks to make before-the-fact provisions.

Diversification: Risk diversification in fiduciary practice consists of avoiding the creation of concentrations of similar investees in terms of size, risk profile or geography. (Investees are the parties receiving funds from investors, including MFIFs.) Across the MFIM industry, rules of asset concentration and portfolio mix are not yet very precise. There is little appreciation of how diversification should actually be managed at the MFI or specific risk* level and at the systematic country risk level. (Systemic or systematic? Systematic risk refers to the overall risk of a group of investments, such as an entire market or a sector or region. Systemic risk refers to a sequence of events that occur simultaneously or that are part of a domino effect, one risk triggering another, as a result of a single tripping point such as a bank failure.)

Duration: Duration is the average life of a debt instrument as measured by its discounted cash flow. It is defined as the weighted average of the periods that terminate at the time payments are made, with weights proportional to the present value of the payment. Duration is a fundamental concept in fixed-income asset management: first, because it is a simple statistical indicator of the effective average maturity of a portfolio; second, because it is an essential tool in immunising portfolios from interest rate risk* by matching the duration of assets with the duration of liabilities; and third, because duration is a measure of the interest rate sensitivity of a portfolio. Price sensitivity tends to increase with time to maturity, with virtually no sensitivity for a 1-year money market instrument to very high sensitivity for a 20-year bond. In the MFIF industry, maturities are usually less than three years, so that duration is relatively short and therefore often not calculated.

Efficient Market Theory posits that in liquid securities markets prices quickly and accurately reflect all relevant information, which is provided by thousands of investment analysts and the trades that result. Liquidity and information make it extremely difficult for individual investors to beat the market. Indeed, only about 20% of managers beat the market year after year, and the mix of winning managers changes from year to year. This suggests that beating a market index becomes easier as an investor moves away from mature markets towards emerging markets. The least efficient asset class is venture capital in emerging markets, which is the home of the microcredit asset class, both equity and debt. Credit markets in emerging countries can be very inefficient as a result of poor liquidity, disequilibrium in the form of unbalanced supply and demand, discretionary government manipulation and weak access to foreign exchange, money and capital markets. Although the London Inter-Bank Offered Rate US dollar market may appear efficient on a global basis, LIBOR-based pricing remains a floating rate indicator that has nothing to do with the underlying local currency markets of MFIs, and may therefore be inefficient.

Entrepreneurial Finance (see Social Hazard) consists of venture capital and private equity funding involving an entrepreneur who holds a high proportion of the equity of his or her enterprise. This contrasts sharply with classic investment or corporate finance and also with the main features[1] of the private equity class of MFIs. The main characteristic of NGOs or what is known as "social entrepreneurship" lies in ownership of the "mission" as opposed to "capital," which creates a clash over the issue of fiduciary governance.* Mission is the exclusive privy of shareholders (or an equivalent "principal") and cannot be set by any other stakeholder. In the NGO world, the social entrepreneur tends to abandon his "financial rights" for his "mission rights," creating confusion of his role as agent (which he is) with the role of principal (which he is not). As a result, financial viability may at worst be threatened and at best be weak.

---

[1] *Entrepreneurial Finance* by Janet Kiholm Smith and Richard L. Smith, John Wiley & Sons, 2000. The authors state: "Just as corporate finance is concerned with financial decision making by managers of public corporations, entrepreneurial finance is concerned with financial decision making by entrepreneurs who are undertaking new ventures." (Note that public corporations in this context refers to joint stock companies that are widely held by the public, that is, private investors.) The author of this glossary has added comments and outlined aspects of the 8 features of entrepreneurial finance in items a) through h) to elaborate the importance of entrepreneurial finance.

Entrepreneurial finance has eight features that are important in microfinance investment:

a) The separability of investment decisions from financing decisions (especially for equity), is particularly important in the MFIM industry in the numerous cases in which managers act as creditors as well as investors in unsecured paper to fulfil their fiduciary obligations. Put differently, investment funds are not disguises for banks lending to MFIs. Their role is to make a profit for investors.

b) Diversification of risk is an important determinant of investment value.

c) The extent of managerial involvement by outside investors introduces complexities. In the case of NGO MFIs, the issue of mission must be treated carefully because the role and expectations of investors are not always very clear.

d) Information problems are important determinants of the management firm's ability to undertake a project successfully.

e) The role of contracting to resolve incentive problems and the alignment of interests of top management has hardly been treated by any rating agency.

f) Options can be used as critical determinants of project value and of transactions. (Some investment funds use put options to cover the risks of eleventh-hour defaults.)

g) Harvesting or exit* is an important aspect of valuation and of the investment decision, especially for equity funds that want to exit to recapture liquidity.

h) The relationship between maximising value for the entrepreneur, as distinct from maximising value for shareholders, requires clear definition (see e) above).

Exit is the most critical stage of any venture capital or private equity* investment, even though it attracts the least amount of managers' time and resources: rarely more than 20 % of the general partnership's time, more often 10 % according to an RCP & Partners' survey of best fiduciary practice in private equity and venture capital. Three major exit routes are available to MFI equity investors:

a) Set initial goals and options for sales to a commercial bank, another local financial institution or a foreign MFI network.

b) Prepare management or leveraged buy-out (MBO-LBO) options, closely involving the management in the governance* and financial ownership of the MFIs.

c) With some markets growing rapidly, initial public offerings (IPOs) will become realistic exit options before 2010, offering scope for innovative investment techniques.

Fiduciary Audit refers to professional examination and verification of documents and data regarding services and operations on behalf of investors. The purpose of a fiduciary audit is to render an opinion on the fairness, integrity, consistency, completeness and conformity of fiduciary practice, data and relationships in an organisation. Fiduciary audit is sought or conducted by investment management firms wishing to bid for investment mandates (that is, to assume fiduciary powers) from institutional investors or to respond to regulators' new risk control requirements (such as Basel capital adequacy requirements for non-credit operations in Singapore, Ireland, Luxembourg, UK and elsewhere). Investment management companies have to provide third-party evidence of services, track record and performance for their submissions to prospective clients. Some banking supervisors also require "reliability audits" by audit firms that review a bank's management or practice in the area of money laundering or risk controls (SAS 70 or FRAG 21 reports) or overall regulatory compliance. Fiduciary audit is especially useful for emerging or early stage MFIs having little track record. Ratings* by PlanetRating, Microfinanza and MicroRate are in effect fiduciary audits.

Fiduciary Governance: (see Governance)

Fiduciary Organisation consists of the entire set of conditions required to manage a third party's money in a way that preserves capital through custody and back office systems and enhances it through an investment system, based on clearly defined contractual expectations. Documentation of the whole value chain – from deal flow and money intake to management, intermediation, administration, custody and distribution practices – is critical in order to provide evidence of adequate fiduciary governance and fiduciary systems, and, by extension, fiduciary institutions.

The financial world is divided into two core families of institutions: credit and trust. The former are commercial banks, leasing, finance and factoring companies, which put client money on their books. By contrast, trust finance or fiduciary institutions do not put client money on their own books, or do so only partially, as do life insurers. Trust finance has three functions: asset management, asset protection and asset intermediation. The behaviour, regulation, compliance rules, agency status, risk control environment, extent of fiduciary responsibility, exposure to systemic risk and reaction to changes in market conditions are very different between these two types of financial institutions.

Fiduciary Rating: (see Rating) Generally accepted and recognised fiduciary practice (GARFP) for asset management organisations is beginning to emerge in the US market, and some European industry associations are looking into such standards to increase confidence in their members' clients. Fiduciary rating evaluation is centred on two major activities of asset management organisations: fiduciary governance* (defining structural risk) and fiduciary systems* (defining process risk), generating two independent though complementary sets of risk measurement. Fiduciary governance is a function of management quality, the overall managerial and trusteeship capability of an investment house. Fiduciary systems* determine investment quality, the performance of advisory capacity in selecting securities and providing sustainable performance.

This twin rating perspective is critical and very practical. An asset manager must earn an institutional grade rating to act as a portfolio manager for a major trustee organisation such as a pension fund, mutual fund, a university endowment, or a life insurance company. Where fiduciary systems are weak, measurement generally provides corrective incentives that will raise them to the institutional grade level. However, weak governance could ultimately lead to a breakdown of fiduciary systems, and may also prevent a firm from managing a portfolio even if its fiduciary systems are more dependable than the firm's organisation. This frequently occurs in emerging market start-up investment firms when a star manager leaves a well-reputed organisation to set up a shop independently. The start-up generally focuses on systems before organisation, neglecting the environment in which fiduciary systems operate. As a result, the start-up is unfit to act as an investment manager but can still act as an advisor in selecting stocks.

Fiduciary Risk (or risk of trustworthiness) is the potential financial impact of failure to meet investors or shareholders' contractual expectations. Contractual expectations are targets and conditions of execution determined by investors and the fiduciary in establishing a mandate for a segregated portfolio or for a collective investment scheme. A fiduciary charged with such a mandate may be a broker, an investment management firm, a custodian, an administrator, a pension fund or any other intermediary which does not own the assets. The failure can arise from defective governance* due to structural risk, or an investment process risk arising from operating systems, processes and organisation. Assessment of fiduciary risk includes corporate governance, especially in the case of a listed corporation, since governance could have a strong effect on the way investors are treated.

Fiduciary risk is also called ϕ (phi) risk to distinguish it from the α (alpha) risk represented by the borrowing MFI or investee company, and the β (beta) country risk. Fiduciary risk includes structural risk and process risk. Structural risk is inherent in representing the organisation and its governance, marketing or fund raising, risk control, compliance, back office, administration and portfolio valuation. Process risk includes the investment system and activities from research to asset allocation (both strategic and tactical), investment selection, portfolio mix, entry/exit* strategies, and performance (volatility, style consistency, etc.).

While coherence is the paramount goal with respect to structural risk, consistency is the ultimate objective of process risk. The combination of both will provide performance stability and sustainability over time. Fiduciary risk and governance are not yet accorded much importance by regulators, and the authorities with the most experience and long track records, the American SEC and the British FSA, are only beginning to refer to fiduciary risk and practice. The British approach, based on the notion of fairness, may appear appropriate in dealing with main street retail investors, but remains far too vague to be useful in applying the notion of trustworthiness, which is what fiduciary risk is all about. Fairness does not imply trustworthiness. Fairness is about equity and arbitrage,* whereas trustworthiness is about reliability – regardless of the conditions under which a judgment must be made. The bottom line is that accountability is what investors are really looking for from their money managers.

In the private equity* business, advisory boards play a critical role in ensuring full fiduciary compliance, although the powers of such boards remain rather weak compared to a trustee's responsibilities for mutual funds and pension funds. Yet, the current regulatory framework in the US, UK and Australia is not at all clear about whether independent directors can truly add any significant value to fiduciary governance. The accountability of these trustees still remains far too confusing and untested to satisfy investors. Sheldon Jacobs, editor of the "No-Load Fund Investor" newsletter in the US thinks regulators should consider moving in a radically different direction: scrapping fund boards entirely because they are not very effective watchdogs over fund management companies. But then, who ensures full compliance of fiduciary governance other than the regulator?

Financial Strength Rating was introduced by Fitch in the early 1980s, followed by Moody's in 1995. These ratings* give an opinion on a bank's "intrinsic safety and soundness," excluding external credit risks and credit support elements that are addressed by traditional debt and deposit ratings. Financial strength ratings measure the likelihood that a bank will require assistance from third parties, such as its owners, an industry group, or official institutions. Unlike traditional bond ratings, financial strength ratings do not measure the risk that principal and interest payments will not be made to investors (depositors) on a timely basis. In countries with strong explicit or implicit government safety nets protecting investors in bank securities, banks' bond ratings should be higher and exhibit less variation than they would in the absence of government support. Investors may demand financial strength ratings for at least two reasons. One is that they may disagree with the agency's opinion on independent financial strength. A second is that they may simply want to avoid exposure to a "bad name" even if the risk of actual credit loss is minimal.

Fitch issues a similar rating for banks, which they call individual ratings. These reflect an opinion on the hypothetical creditworthiness of a bank as if it were entirely independent, which can be thought of as the likelihood that the bank will run into difficulties that would require external support. In both cases, the symbols used to rank quality differ substantially from those applied to long-term debt obligations. Individual ratings are expressed on a five-notch scale: A, B, C, D and E with modifiers of + (B+, C+, D+). Financial strength rating could be applied to mature MFIs having a definite going concern* status. A complementary support rating* would be more appropriate for MFIs at earlier stages.

Fiduciary Systems are the functions of fiduciary governance* that enhance capital. Fiduciary systems have two major components: the overall investment system and each process supporting the system. The overall system is often called "investment strategy" or "investment policy."

Going Concern Risk occurs when:

a) a business enterprise is in operation,

b) could reasonably be expected to continue its operations for at least 12 months,

c) is generally profitable or financially sustainable,

d) with a positive cash-flow

e) but without necessarily being profitable.

The going concern risk is the difference at the date of valuation between going concern value and tangible asset backing. The going concern value is the present value of all future earnings expected to occur from ownership. The alternative to going concern value is the liquidation value of its tangible assets. This risk is that of not being able to remain a going concern. The accounts of a non-going concern will generally be qualified by its auditors. Most MFIs require some time to become going concerns.

Governance, Corporate Governance and Fiduciary Governance:

Governance refers to the decision-making progress in an organisation. Governance is a generic term that describes the ways that rights and responsibilities are distributed to and exercised by participants, who are stakeholders.

One element of governance applies to principals, the equity investors or shareholders whose capital is completely unsecured. This activity is based on high levels of trust and is designated as "fiduciary governance," formally called "shareholder value." Another element involves the management of a corporation where most stakeholders are bond-holders, suppliers, employees, retirees, public and community services, clients, etc. who are mainly credit sensitive with predetermined relationships in the form of salaries, pension funds, credit from suppliers, tax liabilities, etc. This form of activity has different types of risks that are not entirely unsecured, but based on creditworthiness, and is usually known as "corporate governance." These considerations are especially important in dealing with investment management organisations exposed to investments in privately-held microfinance institutions. Indeed, the arbitrage* between fiduciary and corporate governance could make a significant difference between success and failure of a microfinance investment firm.

Corporate Governance refers to how a private, formal organisation coordinates the performance of its activities and resources, whether human, financial, tangible or intangible. "Corporate governance is the interaction of a company's management, its board of directors, and its shareholders to direct and control the firm, and to ensure that all financial stakeholders (shareholders and creditors) receive their fair share of the company's earnings and assets" (by George Dallas, Managing director and Global Practice Leader for S&P Governance Service Group). The combination and interaction of fiduciary and corporate governance change according to the nature of the organisation and the weight of its overall fiduciary responsibility. For example, a private equity* firm has key fiduciary responsibilities upstream to its own investment clients, and strong corporate or decision-making responsibilities in dealing with the management of investees in which it has injected capital.

Fiduciary Governance refers to how an organisation deals with its shareholders. Its purpose is to ensure that expectations about risk and return are adequately reflected in an organisation's mission, strategy and resource management. Fiduciary governance is supplemented by systems and processes that form the backbone of corporate practice. A wide range of standards such as SAS 70, FRAG 21, GIPS (Global Investment Performance Standards) in the fiduciary world or ISO 9000 and 14000 for corporations help to assert the reliability of these practices.

Fiduciary governance is focused on shareholders, as opposed to bondholders (who have benefited from credit ratings for well over a century). Fiduciary risk and rating for the investment management industry appeared less than 10 years ago. The methodology is still not fully developed for listed corporations. A very comprehensive review is required in order to determine a corporation's fiduciary risk.* This is required simply because a corporation generates its own revenue, and its mission must be adequately implemented based on its strategy and resources. This is especially true of a listed corporation where the arbitrage* role of the board of directors is of critical importance.

Compared to other jurisdictions, US shareholders have relatively few rights, effectively deferring many ownership rights to the company's directors – who, in turn act in a fiduciary capacity on behalf of the company and its shareholders. Because of the wide range of shareholders, investors may find it difficult to ensure the full alignment of interest of management with their own. This parallels the case of mutual fund investors who cannot control managers and related trustees because each unit holder is simply too small to exercise a meaningful influence. In Europe, block-holders or *actionnaires de référence* are more important and generally have more influence on the governance of listed corporations.

For privately-held corporations, equity may be less important than the debt held by banks, leasing companies and bondholders: corporate governance trumps fiduciary governance by far in this case.

In the case of an investment management service (mutual fund, segregated portfolio, LLP, pension fund, trust agreement), fiduciary governance should be at the centre of all considerations because the business depends essentially on meeting client investors' expectations. In other words, corporate governance plays a very minor role where most activities are of a fiduciary nature. In the case of a fund of funds, such as the Positive Fund, fiduciary governance is important both upstream towards the Fund's own clients and downstream towards the underlying funds in which the Positive Fund has its own exposure.

In the same way that standard certifications have improved practice and sustainability, fiduciary governance has helped investment management firms enhance their practice and raise the consistency of their performance. Rating* upgrades have exceeded the number of downgrades in over 100 fiduciary ratings issued so far in Europe by various organisations, reflecting the European trend towards enhanced fiduciary governance. Fiduciary governance is supplemented by systems and processes, which form the backbone of any good corporate practice. Furthermore, when an organisation's core business is fiduciary (such as an asset management firm), it considerably diminishes the corporate governance* mission of its management in favour of its fiduciary responsibility.

Interest Rate Risk (see Volatility) is the risk of loss due to the sensitivity of earnings to future movements in interest rates. The higher the volatility,* the greater the probability that an investor may have to redeem his or her holding at a loss when markets are down. Interest rate risk includes income risk, which is the risk of loss arising when movements in borrowing costs and returns from lending are not perfectly synchronised, that is, when asset and liability positions are mismatched (see Duration). Interest rate risk also includes investment risk, which is the risk that the market value of financial instruments – such as a bond – will decline over time as a result of changes in exchange rates or interest rates.

In the microfinance investment industry, interest rate risk appears through cash flow from interest payments. The investment or sensitivity risk expressed by marking all investments to their market price – "marked-to-market." (Marking securities to market means that their prices must always reflect what the market would pay if they were liquidated immediately. Marking to market means that securities must constantly be revalued; any difference between cost and market must be made up by cash adjustments.) Interest rate risk is diminished in microfinance because maturities tend to be short (less than 18 months), and does not appear clearly as there is no secondary market that would permit opportunity cost comparisons. But maturities in microfinance investment are lengthening to nearly 18-24 months and new vehicles offer maturities of 5 and even up to 7 years.

MFIs and MFIFs perceive interest rate risk differently. MFIs view it as part of overall asset-liability management* that focuses particularly on interest rate and maturity gaps as well as foreign exchange risks. Interest rate risk applies increasingly to emerging markets when maturities lengthen significantly, beginning in the sovereign borrowings of the State and on down to prime corporations. The Asian crisis of 1997-99 revealed that many corporations borrowed short abroad and invested long at home, creating a severe mismatch that resulted in catastrophic losses when collateral was called. For MFIs, the maturity mismatch becomes obvious if long term funding is not subsidised and interest rates on the loan portfolio decline.

Investor Risk: Aside from the default of one or several debtors (specific or alpha risk) and fraud, the greatest risk faced by an investor is under-performance caused by the failure of the investment firm to meet the expected return. Such underperformance, measured by the difference between an agreed benchmark* and the effective net return, can result from high total expense ratios* and costly transactions, which are very common in the microfinance industry because of due diligence requirements and legal costs. Other factors include absence of investment policy, lack of discipline and a structured process, weak diversification and poor strategic allocation, unreliable valuation, etc.

The risk of misvaluation occurs through mispricing or charging interest rates below those that the risk should normally command. This risk does not yet apply to microfinance debt instruments because there is no market and hence no trades, or because there is not enough information. The only indication that some mispricing may occur is the gap between rates paid by MFIs to various investment funds for equivalent maturities. However, that information that an open market would readily provide is not generally available across the microfinance market. Most microfinance fixed income funds are flow-through credit vehicles with virtually no recourse to liquidity through a secondary market. Portfolios are valued at cost, and promissory notes or certificates of deposit are treated as loans instead of tradable debt securities. This treatment is the main reason why volatility* of returns is so low: the net asset value of these types of funds varies only on the basis of the interest cash flow and not on the value of the principal.

What should the investor earn on the microcredit market? This is the critical issue: For example, LA-CIF's average yield is 9.8 %. Imagine a fund lending at LIBOR (=2 %) plus 6 % for country risk. If its total expense ratio is 3 %, the usual case, only 5 % is left for the investor (2 %+6 %=8 %-3 %=5 %). Assuming safer sovereign treasury bills earn 2.5 %, a risk adjusted return on capital (RAROC) to an MFIF investor would earn only 2.5 % net. If an MFI risk premium ranges between 2 % and 4 % (confirming its low specific risk), the cost of reaching that single MFI in a risky emerging market country is a net deficit of around 6 %. The investor gets nothing for bearing country risk under current conditions and hardly gets 2 % over LIBOR for lending to the MFI.

Liquidity Risk arises from the possibility that a party will not have sufficient funds to meet its obligations. Because of the size and spread of its resources, a bank is able to borrow short and lend long, taking advantage of the interest rates on different maturities along the yield curve.* MFIs are generally in the opposite situation, lending short while borrowing long at a low interest rate. Commercial banks use all sorts of instruments to manage risk: stand-by facilities, revolving underwriting facilities (RUFs) and note issuance facilities, as well as guarantee and documentary credits, although provisions for advances in this case are generally "subject to the availability of funds." These instruments are only beginning to be useful for MFIs.

In the case of investment, liquidity is the investors or investment manager's ability to enter or exit* a market freely. Liquidity risk and foreign exchange risk are the most important factors determining the future development of the MFIM industry. The recent CDO (collateralised debt obligation) entity created with some USD40 million of microfinance credits paves the way for a new model – with a 12x (12:1) leverage. A useful further development that could help local commercial banks lending to MFIs to liquefy their credits would be bridge vehicles to local or international funds that have a strong appetite for short term/high yield exposure.

Market Risk (or beta risk or systematic risk) arises from the market or from exogenous factors and is likely to affect the behaviour or performance of specific risk.* There are two definitions of market risk. The more common one applies to commercial and investment banking when securities are subject to market price movements from systematic risk. Those movements are not directly related to the specific risk of a single security: "systematic" suggests that it applies to all securities, regardless of their individual intrinsic value or quality. For example, in a recession, shares of automobile manufacturers tend to decline in value regardless of the performance of the car manufacturers. The market perception is that consumers will not spend money on new cars.

Aside from CDs (certificates of deposit) or other short-term deposits, MFIs rarely hold tradable securities that are liable to fluctuate in value. The most significant risks to MFIs are over-indebtedness and high-pressure competition. The better known systemic risk or domino effect that causes banks failures has little bearing on MFIs because they rarely borrow from banks. But as MFIs continue to grow and seek formal status, systemic risks will become more important. Formal status occurs through transformation into a bank, or into a non-bank that is not permitted to accept deposits from the public but that can borrow from banks and other domestic and possibly foreign sources.

Are MFIs vulnerable to economic cycles? Some argue that the main characteristics of MFIs insulate them from the economic booms and busts to which commercial banks are so vulnerable. In contrast to commercial banks, MFIs serve widespread pools of micro-debtors, have very little debt concentration, do little borrowing from banks, and serve an economy that is at a survival level, The Triodos-Doen Foundation, a Dutch fund managed by the Triodos Bank, reported in its 1999 annual report that "during times of economic crisis, micro-businesses continue to repay their loans, often in contrast to bigger companies. In countries such as Russia, Indonesia and Colombia, the quality of the portfolio of microcredit institutions remains good despite (or, perhaps sometimes, thanks to) the crisis."

Moral Hazard arises from any protection that provides an incentive for the protected party to change its behaviour in a manner that increases the probability that a risk might occur. For example, protection in the form of insurance may offer comfort that leads to complacency, lack of diligence, or negligence. (Insurers use deductibles or other loss-sharing arrangements to diminish moral hazard.) Excessive protection under a social umbrella could lead MFI executives to become reckless. MFIM professionals may believe that MFIs are "too nice to fail" and therefore may not be sufficiently cautious in portfolio selection. The history of development assistance suggested for many years that "there is always another donor."

Operational Risk: (See Fiduciary Risk to understand how the latter includes the former but should not be treated as synonymous.) Operational risk is the risk of random failure of systems, processes and technology that could have an impact on the day-to-day functioning of an organisation. Operational risk is generally very high for MFIs that are not fully mature. This risk applies to credit and fiduciary environments. But, it should not be confused with the generic concept used by the Basel accords that define as residual all risks beyond the frontier of credit risk. The danger of considering operational risk as a residual is that it can be used to shield those in charge of operations from all forms of responsibility and accountability.

Private Equity: Any equity subscribed to a company which is unlisted or is not traded on any stock market, whether regulated formally as an exchange or quasi-regulated or not regulated at all on an informal over-the-counter market. Most microfinance institutions are good examples of private equity: they are not listed anywhere and there is virtually no trading of their shares. (The certificates of deposit, promissory notes, commercial paper, bonds or debentures they may issue could be traded over-the-counter. However, these forms of debt have nothing to do with equity.)

Probability of Default: Although many rating* agencies use "probability of default" (PD) to explain what they measure, very few actually calculate this probability explicitly for the issuer or a specific issue. Instead, the rating ranks the likelihood of default. The Bank for International Settlements' Special Report on Rating Agencies notes that, "Only two agencies, Moody's KMV Corporation (US) and AB (Sweden) undertake the calculation/derivation of an explicit PD. The rest of the agencies base their ratings on the relative likelihood of default, pointing out that they are not in the business of assigning absolute probabilities of default to the issuer/issue, but rather they seek to construct an ordinal, relative ranking of the ability to service debt. No specialised MFI rating agencies calculate or provide a PD scale. A related aspect is the 'total expected loss approach,' which Moody's KMV calculates as an automatic complement to the "assessment of likelihood that the issuer will default (i. e. miss payments) on a security." A relative likelihood of PD should be enough for MFIs, although some suggest that a liquidation value should be added to alert management to the prudence with which they should deploy their resources.

Rating: A rating measures the probability of default* on obligations. It should not be confused with an audit or evaluation. Two basic financial risks – credit risks* and fiduciary risks* – create a market for ratings:

Credit Rating measures the creditworthiness of an organisation. This is the most common and best-known form of rating; measuring the likelihood that a debtor may fail to meet its financial obligations. The rating process goes beyond ratio analysis. The starting point for analysis is an examination of the environment in which an organisation operates. As such, the country's financial system is a major consideration. Ratings express a clearly defined evaluation of the level of risk on a widely accepted and meaningful scale. Ratings are based on audited data, generally for a five-year period but in the MFI world, commonly for three years. Analysis of audited financial statements begins by reviewing the auditor's opinion and the summary of accounting principles. This opinion can be qualified, finding basic faults, or unqualified or "clean" with no negative findings.

The rating process is generally top-down, looking first at the market environment, the regulatory context and the competitive setting in which an institution operates. Then the ownership is examined and the legal status of the rated entity is verified before a full review of operations is carried out.

Fiduciary Rating measures the trustworthiness of an organisation and the probability that it may breach investors' trust by failing to take all steps necessary to fulfil its mission in accordance with generally accepted ethical practices and in response to business conditions. It evaluates an organisation's:

a) Stability based on its corporate, economic and social governance.

b) Ability to sustain investment performance through its processes and compliance.

The probability of fiduciary breach is measured against best practice. Where past performance is unlikely to predict future performance, the past and current practice of an investment manager can suggest whether current performance is sustainable. This form of rating is designed to provide comfort and protection to investors and other stakeholders.

A company may be creditworthy but not trustworthy, as demonstrated by recent corporate scandals in OECD countries. The best illustration is the collapse of Arthur Andersen when it suddenly lost major corporate clients around the world due to its dealings with Enron. Conversely, a trustworthy company, such as a start-up or a very early stage entity, may not be recognised as a "going concern"* or creditworthy, but its shareholders or management's track records or determination to succeed makes them credible without necessarily being creditworthy.

Risk Patterns consist of different causes or scenarios leading to a breach of contract, a breakdown of operations or a transaction freeze that prevents the satisfactory completion of an operation. For example, poor checks and balances leading to a lack of compliance produced the failure of FinanSol in Colombia. Over-funding in poor countries can lead to a temporary surge in liquidity and cause over-indebtedness.

In turn, an over-indebted market can seriously imperil the quality of credit portfolios of healthy MFIs. This happened in the Philippines in the mini-taxi market and may occur in Nicaragua if donors continue to pour millions of dollars of soft aid to MFIs. Unseasoned credit officers may not be able to implement a sound credit valuation process efficiently. Weak market monitoring may lead an MFI to an excess liquidity niche activity and contaminate the rest of its healthy loan portfolio. Many causes can lead to a materialisation of risk. Risk patterns should not, however, be confused with risks themselves.

Settlement Risk arises when a bank or broker pays out funds before it receives reimbursement from a counterparty. For instance, when A settles the obligation (say USD1 million) on behalf of client B (who purchased goods in the US but has only local currency) to foreign counterparty C in foreign currency but does not get reimbursed by B in time and thus cannot continue operating. The collapse of Bankhaus Herstatt in 1974 was a classic case of bank failure affecting others through settlement risk. The Bundesbank closed Herstatt, freezing its New York accounts, before New York banks received dollar settlements on outstanding foreign exchange transactions involving Herstatt. The New York counterparty banks were exposed to the full value of the Deutschmark deliveries. It was also a good illustration of systemic or domino risk, which prompted establishment of a special committee in Basel at the headquarters of the Bank for International Settlements. (BIS). That committee eventually drew up the Basel I and II capital adequacy rules for banks. Jawad & Haidar Abulhassan & Company, a leading exchange house in Kuwait, temporarily defaulted on its obligations in 1985. After rescuing the firm, the Central Bank of Kuwait agreed to fully reimburse banks that had suffered from settlement risk.

Social Hazard is created by non-financial biases likely to affect the rational functioning of a market. The microcredit industry is subjected to a wide rage of social hazards due to the social dimension of its activities and the impact it can have on a community or a country. The classic example is an NGO that gives more importance to its mission than to its effectiveness. NGOs typically make a trade-off between social fulfilment and financial benefit, with the former overtaking the latter. This tends to create ambiguity about how the mission of the investors or funders should be implemented. In most NGOs, "social entrepreneurs" set the mission of the organisation with no clear fiduciary responsibility towards funders. In microfinance the five most critical social hazards are:

a) **Lack of regulatory supervision** – Because few MFIs are deposit-takers, they usually are not included in safety nets provided by local financial authorities. But also, they are not generally exposed to systemic risks and bank runs, which are authorities' major concerns in emerging markets. An MFI's not being subject to regulations, or its lack of recourse to a lender of last resort in the event it encounters problems, constitutes a social hazard.

b) **Concessional funding** – Most MFIs have access to concessional or "soft lending conditions" and benefit from various "social supports" sponsored by bi- and multilateral institutions, large non-profit organisations, etc. Such funding is generally provided at below market prices: "After all, how can we help the poor if we charge too much?" Subsidy distorts the true financial condition and sustainability of an MFI, which at some point will have to adjust to market prices.

c) **Excess funding** – Too much money chasing too few MFIs can create a social hazard leading to moral hazard* or greater leniency in setting performance targets: "If so much money is available, why do we need to improve performance?"

d) **Alignment of interest** (see Fiduciary Systems) – It is difficult for a funder to align his or her interest with that of the senior executives of an NGO MFI driven by social considerations. The financial incentives that would apply under normal business conditions that would induce MFI management to reach and even exceed their goals may not work properly in this situation.

e) **Mission ownership** is the very strong sense of ownership of MFI managers who, like most other non-profit organisation executives, have a tremendously high level of resilience and determination with a medium to long term perspective, unlike non-shareholding executives of many small to medium size enterprises. This "ownership culture," expressed by shaping the mission and its execution, is the most critical counter-balance to poor systems and governance by board directors or trustees, ambiguous legal structure and weak or missing financial incentives. This constitutes social hazard because the determination of the owner is not financially driven in a way that a "settlement price" could be set. It is cause-driven and the social purpose of the owner is complex and not subject to dealing with in an objective way.

Solvency denotes an excess of assets over liabilities, that is, a positive net worth on the balance sheet. Country risk is generally the central concern of an MFI risk analysis exercise, and solvency should be the second most important consideration for an MFI or for an investment management firm that invests in MFIs. Bank runs are a major concern of bank regulators in emerging markets, but local regulators are generally too weak to prevent major failures that, in the absence of safety nets, are liable to rock the whole banking industry[2]. Few MFIs are deposit-takers, making them less exposed to local market risks* than banks, but without safety nets, solvency risk requires attention.

Sovereign Ceiling: Rating* agencies usually will not assign to corporate entities, such as banks and MFIs, ratings that are higher than the rating for the country in which the entity is based. The country rating is therefore the sovereign ceiling. Rating agencies apply the sovereign ceiling principle with some flexibility. The sovereign ceiling rating usually coincides with the foreign currency bond rating assigned to the national government. Rating agencies usually assign a sovereign ceiling even when there is no foreign currency sovereign debt to be rated.

The major exception to the sovereign ceiling occurs when an international corporate borrower structures an offshore collateral arrangement in which funds never enter the country where the firm is domiciled. S&P and Fitch are willing to relax the sovereign ceiling by a few notches for high quality corporate issuers domiciled in low-rated countries with dollarised economies, such as Argentina.

A typical case is CAF, a multilateral development bank in the Andean region, which earns a better rating than the country in which it is headquartered. Others

---

[2] Most exceptions are in Latin America, where regulators such as in Peru have developed fairly advanced and thorough processes.

are Citibank in the Philippines in the late 1980s and ABN-AMRO in Pakistan in 1999. Both banks belong to global organisations with ready access to foreign currency, but were caught under very strict host country foreign exchange controls that made them unable to meet their foreign currency obligations. Sovereign ceilings are the upper limit of any rating, and ratings for MFIs would in most cases be below the ceiling because of various risks.

Specific Risk (or alpha risk) is the "risk of risk." It refers to a specific institution such as an MFI, and excludes market risk* or external risk. Specific risk covers a wide range of endogenous operational factors that contribute to credit and fiduciary risks.* Examples include problems in attracting and keeping qualified personnel, and failure to educate and train staff sufficiently. A lender or investor may attempt to evaluate these risks based on its knowledge and experience in the sector.

Support Rating: (also see financial strength rating) "Fitch also issues ratings specifically on the support available to the bank in the event of financial distress, called 'support ratings.' The individual rating and the support rating of banks are then combined to arrive at its traditional long-term and short-term entity, and senior debt ratings."[3] In 1998 Capital Intelligence, using the same approach, started to issue support ratings and ratings of "domestic strength," similar to Moody's financial strength or Fitch's individual rating. As with Fitch, they combine both to compile their long-term debt ratings. A support rating could be quite useful for MFIs as a complement to fiduciary risk rating during the period before the organisation attains going concern* status. This type of rating would create a greater sense of responsibility and ownership on the part of funders or financial backers.

Total Expense Ratio (TER) compares all expenditures made to achieve an investment return divided by the assets under management, calculated on an annual basis. These expenditures are the numerator of this widely-used ratio, and are important in analysing how performance was achieved. The TER is often compared to benchmarks,* which incur no expenditures, and are calculated on both a gross basis and on an after-expenses or net basis. These expenses generally include:

a) Asset management contractual fees, normally in the 2.5-3 % range.

b) All non-management expenses of transactions, including the costs of making contracts, due diligence and monitoring costs not invoiced to the MFI or absorbed in asset management fees, etc. Under conventional management, a €500,000 to €1 million transaction would incur a transaction cost in the form of brokerage fees of about 15 basis points (0.15%) or €7500 to €15,000. Some managers calculate their transaction costs on the basis of their overall relationship with an MFI. It would be more meaningful, for performance measurement attribution, to calculate such cost on a transac-

---

[3] "Credit ratings and complementary sources of credit quality information," Basel Committee on Banking Supervision Working Papers, No. 3 – August 2000, pp. 97-99.

tion per transaction basis. Some MFIM firms charge fees of between several hundred to a few thousand USD per loan to the MFI to cover the cost of transactions and risk monitoring.

c) All other administrative expenses such as custodial services, accounting and fund administration.

Total expenses (including management fees) should then be measured against average total assets under management during the year.

Transaction Cost Analysis shows the fiduciary risk* that investors were exposed to through portfolio management, highlighting the risk (or gap) between the goal (or benchmark*) and the actual results. This analysis explains why the portfolio out-performed or under-performed independently set benchmarks, in terms of risk and return including the expected target return set at the beginning of the year by the board of directors or trustees on behalf of investors.

Transfer Risk is the risk that in a particular country all or most economic agents including the state will become unable to fulfil international financial obligations. Brazil provides a good example of high transfer risk. Its domestic economy appeared quite healthy in early 1982 when its foreign debt was estimated at USD60 billion. Brazil rescheduled its international debts, which by year-end were close to USD100 billion. Another example is the freezing of the offshore assets of Kuwaiti banks by foreign governments when Iraq invaded Kuwait. The international freeze prevented Iraq from gaining control of offshore Kuwaiti assets, but it also prevented Kuwaiti banks from honouring foreign currency obligations, creating a transfer risk.

Transparency is of prime importance in six key areas of investment management: fiduciary systems and processes, alignment of interests, expected return targets, net asset value (NAV) disclosure and frequency, portfolio content and market exposure, and complying with best industry practice in NAV calculation. Each is described below:

a) **Fiduciary systems* and processes** are the heart of a fiduciary organisation's operations. Systems and processes constitute the minimum threshold of transparency requiring explanation to institutional investors. Systems and processes include the following aspects of investment operations:

- The system is determined by a goal, expressed as a policy or course of action, often defined as the "investment strategy," which is an algorithm of integrated processes or segments of activities. Investors are generally reluctant to invest in a "black box" or a strategy that cannot be properly grasped. Therefore, from the outset, the system must be clear and easily understandable by potential investors. Three features of a good system are: clarity, discipline and flexibility. The system must have a discernible edge explaining how the manager can protect and enhance the investor's capital.

- The processes are components of the system. Once assembled, they form a continuous chain to ensure consistency and complementary. The chain starts with research on the target investees or countries, regions and MFI universes, and analysis by an investment committee. The responsibility of the investment committee is to define the strategic allocation in the construction of the portfolio ("portfolio mix") to meet target risk/return objectives set by the board on behalf of investors. Tactical guidelines generally accompany the allocation rules that are intended to produce the expected return.

The next step is to execute the transactions that close the investment deal. This is followed by active management with clear tactical guidelines for tradable securities and position management, which refers to the relationship with each investee through the final liquidation of the investment. Each quarter, the board should review portfolio mix to ensure that the actions of the investment committee fully comply with the mandate and corresponding risk and control policies.

Professional investment organisations are unlikely to be able to develop relationships with serious institutional investors without full disclosure. Yet, very few organisations handling investments in microfinance have documented their process to ensure the stability and consistency of their performance, transfer of know-how and continuing improvement. Most have an intuitive approach to their process and few, if any, have analysed ex-post their process against their performance. Performance accountability remains low.

b) **Alignment of interests** is a typical social hazard* in microcredit, reflecting the chronic agency problem in trust finance. The agency problem arises when the incentives of principals and agents are not fully aligned. In investment, principals are investors or shareholders and agents are investment managers. Alignment problems arise because the agent has no obligation to produce a result, but rather only an obligation to follow certain instructions and procedures. Investors face this alignment problem in dealing with their investment managers, which in turn face the same problem in dealing with the MFIs in which they invest.

The agency problem is acute in microfinance. Alignment of interest is currently blurred by the aid that supports microfinance institutions. Subsidy obscures the true level of risk, distorting information required by a rational arm's-length investor. It also lowers expected returns and weakens investment practice because there is no appropriate benchmark.* The two large microfinance funds, Oikocredit and Triodos, and the largest investment guarantee funds sponsored by Rafad, show continuing annual losses or poor returns – certainly not very good examples for arm's-length institutional investors. A majority of institutions supported by MFIM firms have these characteristics, especially NGOs and quasi-charitable organisations. The "concessional mindset" entertained among investors and by a new generation of funds goes directly against the requirement for greater professionalism in the investment management business.

c) **Expected return targets** – The absence of generally accepted benchmarks that would serve as reference points for the evaluation of the performance of collective investment schemes (CIS) in microfinance also have an impact on the pricing of MFIFs. Multiplication of local guarantee funds and the entry of many commercial banks lending to MFIs since 2001 has created far more competition among funders. This places international investment funds in the awkward role of "swing funders:" as marginal but nonetheless virtual lenders of last resort. In a period of spectacular MFI growth,[4] investment managers play an increasing role in price setting. But if they fail to evaluate risk accurately, pricing could become increasingly wrong. Several managers fail to take advantage of their "first lender" position towards emerging MFIs, charging them an "entry premium," but one that is quite below a rational economic price. Or, they apparently fail to recognise that some markets with high country risks, such as Eastern Europe or Africa, deserve to pay more for funding.

d) **Net asset value (NAV) disclosure and its frequency** – Very few MFIM firms disclose their results publicly. Most funds are assessed quarterly or annually while some provide monthly return data. Best practice suggests a general rule that no investment manager should raise funds on the open market unless its track record is transparent, with a clear explanation on how returns are calculated. The reporting frequency should be at least monthly to meet the minimum risk control compliance rules of institutional investors and recognise that the average maturity of most debt instruments is less than 18 months, producing a portfolio turnover that is 6.5 times more rapid than most venture capital funds or 3 times more than that of most private equity buy-out funds. Reaction time is important: an MFI default can happen very quickly, within three to six months. Quarterly reporting is far too slow and risky for investors in microfinance. Disclosure is not only about performance but also about the underlying portfolio and MFI[5] investees. Basic data on the capital base, ownership, assets/liabilities, growth and management

---

[4] Current MFI growth rates of 35 to 40 % per annum make it difficult for local commercial banks, growing at a much slower pace, to lend increasing amounts to MFIs. This means that the marginal price set by investment funds could have a decisive impact on the funding pattern of many MFIs. And if price-setting is wrong or grossly underestimated, it will affect the local MFIs' pricing and cause significant over-capacity at a time when size factors could start to have systemic effects on the market.

[5] In the private equity asset class, the most critical debate is actually on the disclosure of investee financials and general conditions. Competition and risk of transparency have led several leading venture capitalists to refrain from disclosing any meaningful information about their investees because of the consequence it may have on future merger and acquisition deals involving these same investees. The MFIM industry has not reached that stage yet and thus disclosure should be far more extensive than it is in the more conventional venture capital world.

features, as well as medium term expected return, provided in quarterly or annual reports are insufficient to justify the level of resources at risk or to demonstrate the results of the fund manager's strategic allocation process.

e) **Portfolio content and market exposure** – Beyond a description of the portfolio, it is imperative for any fund manager to describe how and by what criteria the investment process led to the selection of "X" MFIs and "Y" countries. The portfolio mix should be explained along with risk control specifications, such as not too many loans to the highest risk markets but not too many on the lowest segment either to avoid portfolio concentration, maintaining risk diversification* among a wide range of MFIs. In addition, the strategy used to optimise the yield curve* requires testing.

f) **Complying with best industry practice in NAV calculation** – The MFI investment management industry has idiosyncrasies that probably require specific performance evaluation. These include:

- The valuation process of loans and their related cash-inflow is very important because interest revenue remains the only source of volatility* (aside from a sudden default) in the absence of a secondary market. A net present value (NPV) approach based on fair market value might be advisable, as recommended by most GAAP accounting rules.

- Short to medium-term fixed-income assets with maturities of less than 36 months do not require complex evaluation. However, maturities tend to lengthen as more and more MFIs grow and adopt modern asset-liability management. A cost base reference, minus potential hair cut (loss) provisions depending on credit quality, should be appropriate to calculate the NPV.

- The various capital structures of MFIM firms should lead investment managers to provide two lines of reporting: one for each asset class, according to their risk grade (equity, subordinated, senior and junior debt) or currency of reference, and another structured as a composite to include all capital resources employed by the fund (a sort of weighted average capital cost – WACC). These indicators would allow investors to compare their own risk/return against that of all investors treated as a pool. This approach is particularly useful because of growing pressure on MFIFs to provide cash cushions in their portfolios to meet redemption requirements and take advantage of investment opportunities. This is usually done through gearing (leverage).

Value at Risk (Var) is the portion of a portfolio most likely to vary significantly and trigger potential losses, similar to the weakest point in a body. A chain is as strong as its weakest link. That weakest link could put the whole portfolio at risk if it breaks. The probability that this link may break has to be accepted if you use the chain. According to Philippe Jorion, editor-in-chief of the *Journal of Risk*, VaR "is a method that measures the worst expected loss over a given horizon under normal market conditions at a given confidence level. For instance, a bank might say that the daily VaR of its trading portfolio is USD35 million at the 99% confidence level. In other words, there is only one chance in a hundred, under normal market conditions, for a loss greater than USD35 million to occur." (*Value at Risk*, McGraw-Hill, 2001). Each month, a microfinance investment manager must assess the value at risk of her portfolio under normal market conditions, although when a crisis occurs, market conditions are never really normal.

Volatility (see Interest Rate Risk) is the propensity for the market price of an asset to fluctuate around its mean, or the variability of the return of an investment. In the case of MFIs, volatility depends essentially on the cash flow of interest income. Volatility is illustrated statistically by the variance or standard deviation of the return calculated on a periodic basis. Three major factors increase volatility in microfinance investment management: new accounting rules such as marking to market, longer duration* and increased leverage. These features are gaining importance, but marking to market is seldom done.

Yield Curve Management: A yield curve shows the evolution of interest rates over time based on maturities of different lengths, or according to risk. As a general rule: the longer the maturity, the riskier the debt instrument. But even if maturities were all identical, the yield curve correlating risk and rate can show significant inconsistencies. Very few fund management houses seem to be aware of the potential for yield curve management in risk diversification and reduction, and for greater returns. The purpose of yield management is to maximise return at lower risk or with fewer resources. As the culture of the microfinance industry remains dominated by credit with few benchmark* optimisers available to improve the yield curve, yield curve management is virtually non-existent. However, it prevails across the entire spectrum of conventional fixed-income management.

Index

KfW Bankengruppe. Brands for the Future

KfW Bankengruppe (KfW banking group) gives impetus to economic, political and social development worldwide. As bankers we strive to work efficiently every day. As promoters we stand for the meaning and sustainability of our actions. The proceeds from our work flow back into our promotional activities and help to secure our promotional potential in the long term. As a creative bank we not only encourage innovations, but we ourselves also develop new financing instruments for our customers and partners. Our competence and experience are combined into five strong brand names.

KfW Förderbank (KfW promotional bank): It is the right address for all measures in the product areas construction, infrastructure, education, social services and the environment. Through low-interest loans we help many citizens realize their dream of owning their own home, just as we promote interest in environmentally friendly modernization measures. As KfW Förderbank we also provide support to companies investing in environmental and climate protection, municipal infrastructure measures as well as training and advanced training.

KfW Mittelstandsbank (KfW SME bank): The name tells all. Here we have combined all of our promotional activities for business founders and small and medium-sized enterprises. These include, on the one hand, classic long-term loans and, on the other, innovative programmes aiming to strengthen the companies' equity base. Both are offered to our customers through their regular bank. Target-oriented advice is naturally also part of our business.

KfW IPEX-Bank: Our export and project finance has become the KfW IPEX Bank, which does business under the umbrella of KfW Bankengruppe. It is customer-oriented and competitive, operating at standard market conditions. For companies with international operations it is a reliable partner for the long term who can offer them customized financing. The financing solutions that the KfW IPEX Bank offers to its customers include structured finance, project finance, corporate loans and traditional export finance. The success of KfW IPEX Bank is due above all to many years of experience all over the world in the most important markets and industry sectors.

KfW Entwicklungsbank (KfW development bank): On behalf of the German Federal Government it finances investments and advisory services in developing countries. It typically works together with governmental institutions in the corresponding countries. Its aim is to build up and expand a social and economic infrastructure and to create efficient financial institutions while protecting resources and ensuring a healthy environment.

DEG: As a partner of the private sector DEG supports companies wanting to invest in developing and reforming countries. It provides financing for profitable, environmentally friendly and developmentally effective projects in all economic sectors. In this way it sets the foundation for sustainable economic growth – and better quality of life for the people in these countries.

KfW Bankengruppe has also become a strategic partner of the economy and politics. As an advisor to the Federal Republic we offer our expertise in the privatization of federally owned companies. On behalf of the government we also handle business for the Federal Agency for Special Tasks associated with Unification (Bundesanstalt für vereinigungsbedingte Sonderaufgaben, BvS) and the Compensatory Fund of Securities Trading Companies (Entschädigungseinrichtung der Wertpapierhandelsunternehmen).